The Terror of Our Days

The Terror of Our Days

Four American Poets Respond to the Holocaust

Harriet L. Parmet

Lehigh
University
Press

Bethlehem: Lehigh University Press
London: Associated University Presses

Associated University Presses
440 Forsgate Drive
Cranbury, NJ 08512

Associated University Presses
16 Barter Street
London WC1A 2AH, England

Associated University Presses
P.O. Box 338, Port Credit
Mississauga, Ontario
Canada L5G 4L8

The paper used in this publication meets the requirements of the American National Standard for Permanence of Paper for Printed Library Materials Z39.48-1984.

Library of Congress Cataloging-in-Publication Data

Parmet, Harriet L.
  The terror of our days : four American poets respond to the Holocaust / Harriet L. Parmet.
    p. cm.
  Based on the author's doctoral dissertation (Lehigh University).
  Includes bibliographical references and index.
  ISBN 0-934223-63-7 (alk. paper)
  1. American poetry—20th century—History and criticism.
2. Holocaust, Jewish (1939–1945), in literature. 3. Plath, Sylvia—
Criticism and interpretation. 4. Heyen, William, 1940-—Criticism and
interpretation. 5. Stern, Gerald, 1925-—Criticism and interpretation.
6. Rothenberg, Jerome, 1931-—Criticism and interpretation.
7. Literature and society—United States—History—20th century.
8. World War, 1939–1945—United States—Literature and the war.
9. Jews in literature. I. Title.

PS310.H64 P37 2001
811'.5409358—dc21

                                                              00-061244

To the honor of my beloved husband, Sidney Parmet,
For his steadfast loving support

For my children, Jonathan Parmet and Howard Parmet

And my grandchildren, Andrew, Daniel, and Tamar Belle—

May they live in a world of beauty and loving-kindness

A world in which the prophet Isaiah's words will be realized

"Nation shall not lift up sword against nation
Neither shall they learn war any more"

Contents

Special Thanks

Thank you to the following publishers and holders of copyrights for their permission to reprint all or part of the poems included in this volume.

Brodsky, Daniel. Time Being Books
  Falling from Heaven: The Holocaust Poems of a Gentile and a Jew: "Lover's Last Evening in the Warsaw Ghetto," "For the Time Being"

Heyen, William. Time Being Books
  Erika: "Legacy," "The Uncertainty Principle," "The Baron's Tour," "The Spire," "The Car," "Kotov," "Blue," "Simple Truths," "The Children," "A Snapshot of My Father," "Three Fragments from Dreams," "Riddle," "Darkness," "Three Relations," "Letter to Hansjorg Greiner," "For Wilhelm Heyen"
  The Swastika Poems: "The Trains," "This Night," "Two Walks"
  Falling from Heaven: The Holocaust Poems of a Gentile and a Jew: "Canada," "A New Bible," "Coin," "Men in History"

Moss, Thylias. University Press of Virginia
  Pyramid of Bone: "There Will Be Animals"

Plath, Sylvia. Albert A. Knopf
  The Collossus and Other Poems: "The Thin People"

Plath, Sylvia. Harper Collins Publishers
  Ariel: "Mary's Song," "Daddy," "Little Fugue," "Lady Lazarus," "Getting There," "Munich Mannequins"
  Winter Trees: "Brasilia"

Rothenberg, Jerome. Hawks Well Press (No longer publishing)
  White Sun, Black Sun: "Seeing Leni Riefenstahl's *Triumph of the Will*"

Rothenberg, Jerome. New Directions Publishing Company
  Khurbn: "In the Dark Word Khurbn," "Passing Chelmo on the Main Road Driving Past It," "Dos Oysleydikn," "Dib-

bukim," "Di Magilas fun Auschvitz," "Hidden in Woods Bagged," "Dos Geshray," "The Domain of the Total Closes Around Them," "Those Who Are Beautiful and Those Who Are Not," "Nokh Auschvitz," "Di Toyte Kloles," "Der Vidershtand," "Peroration for a Lost Town"

Rothenberg, Jerome. New Directions Publishing Company
Poems for the Millenium: "A Poem for the Sefirot as Wheel of Light," translation of a Hebrew poem by Naftali Bacharach.

Rothenberg, Jerome. New Directions Publishing Company
Poland/1931: "The Wedding," "The Student's Testimony," "The Connoisseur of the Jews," "Poland/1931," "The Fish," "The Mothers," "The Fathers," "Aleph Poem," "The Bride"

Rothenberg, Jerome. New Directions Publishing Company
Seedings: "14 Stations"

Rothenberg, Jerome. New Directions Publishing Company
Vienna Blood & Other Poems: "Abulafia's Circles," "The Danube Waltz," "Vienna Blood"

Stern, Gerald. Harper Collins
Bread without Sugar: "Bread without Sugar"

Stern, Gerald. W. W. Norton Company
Leaving Another Kingdom: "The Rose Warehouse," "Grapefruit," "Romania Romania ," "The Same Moon above Us," "Kovalchik's Garden," "Sycamore," "Magritte Dancing," "Knowledge Forwards and Backwards," "Soap," "The Expulsion," "The Dancing," "Blue Skies, White Breasts, Green Trees," "The Shirt Poem," "Adler," "Burying an Animal on the Way to New York," "Behaving Like a Jew."

Stern, Gerald. Harper Collins
Lovesick: "My First Kinglet," "It Was in Houston," "Tashlikh"
Odd Mercy: "Hot Dog," "The Jew and the Rooster Are One "

Stern, Gerald. Metro Books
Rejoicings: "Burst of Wind between Broadway and the River"

Stern, Gerald. Personal permission
Lucky Life: "Four Sad Poems on the Delaware"

Acknowledgments

I AM MOST GRATEFUL TO GOD, WHOSE BLESSINGS AND GLORY ARE daily made manifest in our world. For the divine gift of health and vigor that has enabled me to bring this difficult and draining project to fruition, I humbly offer my sincere gratitude.

What compelled me to select this somber topic for exploration in the poetic genre? Three very large shadows hovered over my childhood, adolescence, and womanhood—the Depression, the decimation of six million Jews, and the ensuing struggle to create and build a homeland for the Jewish people. One is able to rise above financial deprivations, and triumph is often taken for granted. But the unwarranted destruction of the Six Million has never left me consciously or unconsciously. Every family has known what it means to be a mourner without cause and mine was no exception. All we are left with are faceless names and limited personal histories. And so over the many years of teaching and studying I have searched to find a way, however presumptuous it might seem, to offer a kaddish for those for whom mourning is past.

An age is known by the books it produces as well as by those it labors to preserve and pass on to succeeding generations. Holocaust poetry on both counts—that of original creation as well as that of vital cultural transmission—must be counted among the most compelling writings of our day. In addition to the history their poetry tells, their writing becomes a moral obligation as commemoration, catharsis, atonement, appeal to and insistence on human sensitivities, resistence to brutalization, indifference, and flight from consequences.

To write this book, which had a prior life as my doctoral dissertation, I have called upon and received unstinting help from colleagues, friends, family, students, and institutions. Thus my appreciation is extended to my dissertation committee, Professors Addison C. Bross, Elizabeth Fifer, Barbara

11

Traister of Lehigh University's English Department and Roger Simon, technical historian, for their close reading of this manuscript and above all for their encouragement. Professor Rosemary Mundhenk, chairperson of the Graduate Program in English, was instrumental in my course selection, ever mindful of the fact that I carried a full teaching load. For technical know-how and forbearance in the light of my mechanical ineptitude my gratitude goes to Johanna Brams and her staff of the IMRC and to Mary Ann Haller, Coordinator of the Graduate Program of the College of Arts and Sciences. A sympathetic ear was always tendered by Lehigh's director of graduate studies, Ingrid Parson. Heartfelt thanks are owed to Professor Judith Lasker and Erica Nastasi, of the Department of Anthropology and Sociology, for giving me a home in Price Hall at Lehigh University.

Libraries and their staffs have been indispensable in my search for research materials. Of special assistance has been Kathleen Morrow, one of Lehigh University's reference librarians, whose cheerful detective work in ferreting out esoteric sources is amazing. The Interlibrary Loan staff, especially Pat Ward, has been essential in locating articles and books (hardly household references) for me. The Tuttleman Library of Gratz College had especially rich resources and was most generous in making them available to me.

Philip A. Metzger, director of the Lehigh University Press and Judith Mayer, able administrator, have favored me with sound counsel concerning procedure and protocol. When difficulties arose they were invaluable aids in problem resolution.

Deep appreciation to Pamela Ween Brumberg, program officer for the Lucius N. Littauer Foundation, for the award of funds to defray permission costs for reproduction of all or part of the poems by my selected authors whose works are analyzed in this book.

How fortuitous it was for me to meet with Gerald Stern on several occasions to discuss his sensitivity to the Holocaust and its impact on his life and writings. He signaled those poems that articulated this feeling. And Jerome Rothenberg answered my many questions, assuaged my anxieties, and sent me unpublished lectures, which amplified his thinking on the effect of the *Khurbn* (destruction of six million Jews) on his life.

Through the dean's office, Lehigh University has supported my attendance and presentation of papers on the Holocaust at Yad Va Shem in Jerusalem.

I find Dianne P. Levine's artistic rendition of her response to the Holocaust, in which the menorah—eternal symbol of the Jewish people—engulfed in blood and smoke, to be awesome in its power. Dianne, dear friend and relative, spent many months thinking about how best to do this, and I could not be more pleased with the outcome.

As to the early life of this manuscript as well as its present reincarnation, there are not enough words of praise and reverence for my advisor, mentor, and beloved friend, Professor Addison C. Bross, who extended himself above and beyond any job description. And those exhilarating conversations will remain with me for many years to come. His patience, guidance, and understanding were unfailing. He gently but firmly prodded me into refining my thinking. He was with me every word of the way with illuminating criticism and questions that penetrated to the heart of the matter. Differences of opinion surfaced in the area of written expression, never in its content. There were humorous moments, too, as grammatically the professor preferred the infinitive as opposed to my love of the gerund. Professor Bross, at all times, was respectful of and never compromised my intellectual integrity. And I who have spent the major portion of my life in Jewish studies have constantly been astounded by Dr. Bross's encyclopedic knowledge of material I thought I had owned.

In fact his was the faith that *The Terror of Our Days* should find a wider readership, another home in book form. Professor Bross never wavered in that faith and urged me to submit this manuscript for publication. And here we are.

Additionally, Professor Bross, an internationally recognized Conrad scholar aware of my Polish ancestry, motivated me to do research and write articles and to present papers (on topics relating to the Jewish Presence in Poland) on this subject at sessions of the mid-Atlantic Slavic conferences. My proposal to study and to work in the Jewish archives in Warsaw, to interview survivors, and to visit the sites of Treblinka and Auschwitz, with the professor's recommendation, was funded by the Gipson Institute for Eighteenth-Century Studies and Lehigh's graduate research office.

Ethics of the Fathers admonishes us to "provide yourself [with] a teacher, thereby acquiring a friend." Happily I have heeded this dictum and my life has been enriched immeasurably by this special relationship.

I am forever in debt to my life's companion of more than fifty years, Sidney, whose unconditional love and support have sustained me throughout this challenging and arduous process. My son Jonathan and his wife, Dena, have been a reservoir of strength, understanding and fortification. Lastly, I wish to acknowledge the birth of my grandchildren Daniel and Tamar Belle during this time of study and of writing, whose joyous arrival has helped me keep my perspective at all times.

Work on this project has often seemed alienating, lonely, and long. The persons cited on these pages have assured me that despite the grimness of my chosen subject, whenever I looked up from this work, I would find a sturdy, bountiful, and beautiful world. For this I give thanks.

The Terror of Our Days

1

Introduction: Key Critical and Literary Approaches to Holocaust Literature

WHAT WAS THE HOLOCAUST? A HISTORICAL PHENOMENON, THE story of what happened to the Jews of Europe between 1933 and 1945? A psychological phenomenon, a study of how cruel people could be to one another if the restraints of ordinary civilization were removed? A political phenomenon, an example of a sick leader unifying most of his society by using others as scapegoats? A theological phenomenon, a series of events that forces us to examine the role of the Divine in human affairs? Or since the bombing of Hiroshima and Nagasaki, has the Nazi decimation of the children of Abraham become a metaphor for universal rather than particular tragedy? However we think of it, the Holocaust remains incomprehensible to the world at large and without a strong claim on most people's lives. The implication of the horror and the darkness of such diabolic motives are beyond the human capacity to comprehend. Given the complexities of quotidian living people tend to avoid additional trauma.

The term Holocaust is rooted in the Hebrew word *olah,* the sacrifice that had been offered on the altar of the Temple in Jerusalem up until its destruction in C.E. 70. Not to be eaten as food, the *olah* was totally consumed by fire. While Elie Wiesel may not have actually coined the phrase, he was prominent in popularizing *Holocaust* as the term of choice to designate the Nazi assault against the Jews. In this usage, *Holocaust* is intended as a term to point specifically to the sufferings and intended genocide of European Jewry. More recently, the language of Holocaust has been appropriated by those who want to draw public attention to the crimes, abuses, and assorted sufferings that mar the quality of social

17

life in today's America. In the passionate debates presently under way about abortion, one frequently encounters terms like "the abortion Holocaust," the "killing centers," where a genocide is being directed against baby "victims," and so on. In effect, the term is being transformed from a proper noun to a common noun, a semantic switch signifying an important conceptual and ideological transformation as well. Language that hitherto had been employed to refer essentially to the Nazi crimes against the Jews is now frequently applied to social life and human pain, barbarisms, disasters, and diverse cruelties. Indeed, the Israeli historian Yehudah Bauer argues that in the process of becoming Americanized, the Holocaust is in danger of becoming de-Judaized: "In the public mind the term 'Holocaust' has become flattened," so that "any evil that befalls anyone anywhere becomes a Holocaust." The semantic extension of the term brings with it in turn a cognitive shift, resulting in what he fears will be a "total misunderstanding" of the historical event that the term was originally meant to designate (Rosenfeld 1995, quoting Bauer, 8). The term, for all of its inadequacy, has come to occupy a central place in Jewish vocabulary and is kept current in American letters, theater, and film. At no time, however, will the victims be treated as an offering to the Lord of history. This would be unworthy of God—and of us.

The title *Shoah,* which means desolation, wastedness, and by extension, annihilation in Hebrew, is the term for the Holocaust used in Israel and increasingly by scholars in the United States. While other peoples suffered under the Nazis, the Shoah was directed specifically at Jews, a unique tragedy in world history. With the universalizing of the Holocaust, the enormity of the evil perpetrated against the Jews has been minimized. This study utilizes Holocaust as the major term of description, since it is the word by which most of the world names the event. *Shoah,* however, is designated by scholars in selected quotations throughout the text, its meaning being quite clear.

A dominant theme in postmodern literature, the Holocaust has been written about extensively by European survivors of the death camps. And in recent American literature, this dark time in human history has been the subject of learned works in history, philosophy, literary studies, social sciences, and psychology, as well as of poetry, drama, and the novel. There are tens of thousands of such works, a number moreover that has increased even more rapidly in the past decade (Lang 1988, 1), and there is no reason to believe that this increase has yet peaked. For Jewish writers, Norma Rosen holds that the Holocaust must be recognized as a cataclysmic event or it is nothing:

> The Holocaust is the central occurrence of the twentieth century. It is the central human occurrence. It cannot therefore be more so for Jews and Jewish writers. But it ought, at least, to be that. (Alexander 1979, quoting Rosen, 124)

And for Alvin H. Rosenfeld (1980), this event profoundly alters the meaning of such Jewish concepts as sacrifice and indeed of death itself. He identifies two forms of resistance to the Holocaust: physical combat and poetry.

> "Holocaust" implies not just death, but total destruction; not murder, which carries with it some still-lingering if dreaded sense of personal violation, but annihilation on so massive and indiscriminate a scale as to render death void of all personal characteristics, and hence virtually anonymous or absurd. "Holocaust" suggests not only a brutally imposed death but an even more brutally imposed life of humiliation, deprivation, and degradation before the time of dying. The earlier Greek and Biblical connotations of sacrificial offerings are submerged by the dominant political, racial, ideological, and technological strains of Nazism, which not only accompanied but seem to have dictated the systematically planned annihilation of the Jewish people. The resistance to that genocide, both physical and spiritual, also looks to find expression in "Holocaust,"as to the poetically elegiac and commemorative strains of remembrance itself. (3, 4)

An age is known by the books it produces as well as by those it labors to preserve and pass on to succeeding generations. On both counts Holocaust Poetry—as original creation and as vital cultural transmission—must figure among the most compelling writings of our day. It brings new poetic conventions to the thematic treatment of the Holocaust.

The impact of the Holocaust itself and the types of images and structures it inspires demand a thorough discussion.

Whether this subject can be treated as literature at all is a crucial question. To clarify this issue, I will summarize several critical approaches to Holocaust literature, discuss important works that typify treatments of the Holocaust in fiction, poetry, and drama, review the history of American Holocaust poetry since the end of World War II, and finally introduce the four selected poets and their works. Criteria for selecting literary texts discussed embody their treatment of the Holocaust, whether it be imaginative or historical, plus the fact that their work is representative of multiple genres, and the authors' prominence in American literature. Furthermore the criticism of the various genres has defined the standard criteria for Holocaust literature. To cover this subject in all literatures would be a mammoth undertaking, and thus I have chosen to examine American poets who are crucial to this endeavor because the United States contains the largest survivor community outside of Israel. American response to the heinousness of the Holocaust was often disbelief, and many American Jews felt a sense of guilt related to the security and comfort of their life in the United States. Attached to the guilt was the gnawing realization that more could have been done to save Jews.

What then informs the poets' work? Can historical memory in a nation obsessed by popular culture be determined at all by an "unpopular" form of representation? For these poets, who must accommodate what they cannot ignore or deny, writing is commemoration, catharsis, atonement, history, an insistence on human sensitivities. They choose to do battle with brutalization, indifference, and flight from consequences. William Heyen, Sylvia Plath, Gerald Stern, and Jerome Rothenberg are contemporary poets, all removed from direct experience of the devastating destruction of European Jewry and therefore denied a survivor's truth—his direct pain and suffering, a personal mandate to tell the story. Nevertheless, they feel constrained to remember as a Jew remembers slavery in ancient Egypt, when recounted in tranquility (in the comfort and ease of their Jewish homes), to morally instruct, and to protect future generations. With the critic Sidra Dekoven Ezrahi (1980) they recognize

a basic tension within the artistic enterprise between the in-
stinctive revulsion against allowing the monstrous creatures to
emerge and the basic sounds to be heard—as if by exposing them
to the light of day the artist were somehow affirming or legitimat-
ing the deformities of man's nature—and the equally compelling
instinct against repressing reality against the amnesia that comes
with concealment. (2)

These writers nevertheless believe that objectivity is possible
and that poetry has the power to interpret humankind's
earthly existence. Furthermore, for Plath, Heyen, Stern, and
Rothenberg, writing about the Holocaust became a search to
define themselves as well as to articulate their poetic conception and form their representation of evil.

The critics grapple with multiple issues in varied and distinctive ways. The disparate views encompass the following
thinking. The enormity of the Holocaust belies the possibility
of any literary treatment as an appropriate medium because it
only glorifies the Nazi program of annihilation, and robs the
victims of their dignity. Or survivors have trouble dealing with
the Holocaust imaginatively. Or there is no appropriate language for expressing this world without values. Or, since literature is irrational, it alone can handle the irrational Holocaust. All the argument and commentary notwithstanding,
the presence of the Holocaust in literature is enormous.

A classic position on the matter was articulated by Theodor
W. Adorno (1965), Frankfurt philosopher, who eschewed faith
in the redemptive potential of art. He holds that the very act of
reconstructing intolerable reality somehow contaminates the
writer, and hence the writing of poetry after Auschwitz is
in fact a barbaric act (125). Adorno of course overlooks the
classic understanding of tragedy: that out of human suffering
art may come. His argument, that giving Nazi policies a place
in a work of art grants them meaning and order, confuses the
order and harmony of the work of art with the work's subject,
which remains no less chaotic and horrific even when embodied in a carefully ordered work of art. For Adorno, then,
the artistic autonomy of Pablo Picasso's *Guernica* works to
obliterate   not to represent—the calamity upon which it is

based, making a superbly integrated whole out of the shambles of a massacre.

Adorno's position also fails to recognize the success of the literature of the absurd in rendering artistically some aspects of the degrading and dehumanizing experience of our century. This movement ineradicably absurd, a product of Europe that emerged in France, revolted against essential beliefs and values of both traditional culture and traditional literature. Jean-Paul Sartre and Albert Camus wrote of the isolated and alienated individual adrift in a universe possessing no inherent truth, value, or meaning. Human life, as they represented it, is anguished and absurd as it moves from the nothingness whence it came toward the nothingness where it must end.

Contra Adorno, who claimed that after the Holocaust language itself was corrupt and should not be used as an artistic medium, the absurdists managed to produce plays that responded precisely to the collapse of language in contemporary civilization. Eugene Ionesco challenges the power of language to communicate anything at all. *Rhinoceros* is covertly a response to Nazism and fascism with totalitarianism depicted as a disease that turns human beings into savage rhinoceroses. Beringer, a simple everyman, remains steadfast in his loyalty to humankind, alone and alienated from the mob, his former peers. Thus Ionesco, in perverting language, manages to combine a nightmare of alienation with grotesque yet whimsical humor that beckon the reader.

Samuel Beckett's post-Holocaust world likewise is devouring, unknowable, incoherent, and frightening. With grotesque linguistic distortions and troubling silences, his highly crafted plays show us what horror is, yet remain objects of art. In *Waiting for Godot,* two derelicts converse in repetitive, strangely fragmented dialogue that possesses an illusory, haunting effect while they await Godot, a vague, never-defined being who will bring them some word about—what? Salvation? Death? A reason for living? Direction to their lives? No one knows. The tramps are umbilically attached: for all that they bicker and for all that they have exhausted conversation—their mutual loneliness and weakness binds them to one another in mystical interdependence. But there is no communication. For Beckett, indeed the point is that modern society has witnessed the total collapse of communication. And the accumulative effect is a devastating commentary on the failure of language in the twentieth century. Language in his work expresses the longing for meaning even as it is simultaneously a cover up for its absence—silence, the bare stage, the dialogic gaps.

Thus whereas for Adorno no language can explicate anything after Auschwitz; for European absurdists, only a language of metaphorical farce—itself a sort of insanity—can (however perversely) symbolize the pain and chaos of a post-Holocaust universe. But the Holocaust did not happen in America. Hence, the instigating factor of European absurdism was absent from American experience and thus remains missing in American absurdist drama.

Standing in strong contrast both to Adorno's position on the Holocaust and to the absurdist's rendering of a dehumanized world is the response to suffering and annihilation found in the Judaic tradition. David G. Roskies (1988) writes in his work *The Literature of Destruction: Jewish Responses to Catastrophe* that "no matter how long the list of martyrs grew to be and no matter how many disasters crowd the memorial calendar, they ultimately confirmed the covenantal relationship between the Jews and the God of History" (4). The Hebrew Bible can serve as the model for the literature of despair, and in modern times the chronicling of destruction has become the means for combating a sense of abandonment and desolation. For Roskies, in contrast to Adorno, the dissemination of this literature is a sacred task: "Sacred, because the destruction of European Jewry was so total. Sacred, because the literature of the Holocaust will soon be our only link to that terrible ending. Sacred because of its insistence on the knowability of destruction. Sacred, because in the reading of it, one discovers the ultimate value of life" (9).

Jewish responses abound and a decade after Roskies, Sara R. Horowitz (1997) has probed yet another literary way of looking at the horror of the Holocaust. She shows that muteness not only expresses the difficulty and almost impossibility of saying anything meaningful about the Holocaust; it also represents something essential about the nature of the event itself. As the Holocaust ruptures the fabric of history and memory, emptying both narrative and life of meaning, so at the heart of Holocaust fiction there lies a tension between the silence that speaks the rupture and the narrative forces that attempt to bridge it. Muteness then is the central trope functioning as an index of the trauma that both compels and disables testimony as the mute witness of Holocaust fiction stands both in and out of language.

Jerzy Kosinski, Primo Levi, and others also utilize muteness as a narrative strategy to explore the struggle of the survivor/ writer to devise a vocabulary that conveys the atrocity. And thus fictional characters cease speaking as they negotiate crises in memory and credibility.

In *The Painted Bird* (1981), Jerzy Kosinski creates a mute unnamed boy to depict the experience of a self undone by atrocity, told from the perspective of the undone self. The boy's speechlessness defines a topography different from the muteness of the perpetrators. In limning the boy's speechlessness, Kosinski works toward a "poetics of atrocity," to use Wiesel's term. *The Painted Bird* traces the desperate wanderings from village to village of a six-year-old Eastern European boy during World War II. He seeks shelter from the harsh elements and refuge from SS roundups, experiencing horror after horror, only finally to lose the power of speech. This loss of speech forms the structural and symbolic heart of the novel, and witness to the conditions that imposed it on its deeply scarred survivor.

Even as the boy struggles to interpret and to find meaning in his muteness, the narrator suggests that the foreclosure of speech also forecloses the possibility of finding meaning and interpretation. His muteness facilitates his function as scapegoat, blamed for society's repressed passions, ritually slaughtered to purge the guilty and restore them to innocence. It strengthens his associations with other nameless victims of Nazi atrocity destroyed to preserve the racial "purity" of Germany.

Moreover, the restoration of speech and the moment of healing with which the novel closes do not neutralize the rupture symbolized by muteness, do not offer a promise of wholeness. The boy's sounds call upon the reader to pit himself against the absence of words to really try to approximate the boy's truth, and to imagine its frightening implications. One is at once reminded of a saying current during the Nazi era: Lieber Gott, Mach mich stumm, dass ich nicht nach Dachau kumm [Dear God, make me mute so I don't go to Dachau].

In his poem "The Survivor" (1976), Tadeusz Różewicz searches for "a teacher and master" to instruct him in piecing together a fractured world:

> let him restore to me sight hearing and speech
> let him once again name things and speech and concepts
> let him separate light from dark.
>
> (23–25)

He yearns for the restoration of order and values—a restoration both demanded and blocked by the experience of survival that opens and closes the poem:

> I am twenty-four
> led to slaughter
> I survived.
> (1–3)

Graphically and simply, Różewicz speaks for his peers, his "I" the voice of his generation. And his wartime experiences in the Polish underground move from apparent triumph to ironic despair as antitheses repose in one body:

> Virtue and vice have equal worth
> I've seen
> a man who was both
> vicious and virtuous.
> (18–21)

The poem's survivor cannot dismiss what he has witnessed, yet he cannot absorb it. The poem focuses not on atrocity itself but on the moral chaos left in its wake. The "hacked up bodies" call all beliefs into question. Witness to events so searing that they blind him, Różewicz's survivor is gripped by hysterical blindness and muteness psychologically deterring him from sight and speech. Yes, he recalls words—"man," "beast," "Virtue," "crime," "truth," "falsehood,"—but not their meanings. Is humankind invariably a beast? The blending of "light and dark" evokes the primeval void of Genesis, *tohu-vavohu* (unformed and void), before the "beginning," before the "Word."

Like Kosinski's protagonist, Różewics's survivor no longer believes in the efficacy of words, though he cannot abandon them. His orderly universe has been shattered. Since neither humanly nor divinely sanctioned values exist, he negates the value-laden language of abstract moral concepts. Still he wants the moral and ethical guides—a clear distinction between good and evil. He wants something beyond the human, someone godlike to differentiate between light and darkness, to give meaning to words to return order to the chaos. But ultimately, Różewicz implies, this task may prove beyond mortal ability. The poem concludes as it begins, with the fact of survival—but a survival burdened with a devastating knowledge, a knowledge that undoes all other knowing (Horowitz 1997, 110).

Others have posed different questions of the literature of the Holocaust. Writers and critics such as George Steiner, Alfred L. Alvarez, Alvin Rosenfeld, Edward Alexander, Sidra Dekoven Ezrahi, Czeslaw Milosz, and Susan Sontag have described the literature of the survivors and evaluated the nonautobiographical and nondocumentary materials by American writers in terms of their validity as renderings of the Holocaust. Countering Adorno's position, all of them, with the exception of Steiner argue that the Holocaust was unique in human history and charge writers with the task of representing it, for all the inherent difficulties. Consequently, they judge individual literary efforts by how well they convey the subject and by how valid their interpretive voice is. But scant attention is devoted to structure, language, and diction.

Only George Steiner, one of the early critics of Holocaust literature, complains of the failure of art to civilize in what was perhaps the most civilized country in Europe "When barbarism came to twentieth-century Europe, the arts faculties in more than one university offered very little moral resistance, and this is not a trivial or local accident. In a disturbing number of cases the literary imagination gave servile or ecstatic welcome to political bestiality" (1967, 61).

For him this is the definitive conclusion possible after Auschwitz. "We are post-Auschwitz homo sapiens because the evidence, the photographs of the sea of bones and gold fillings, of children's shoes and hands leaving a black claw mark on oven walls, have altered our sense of possible enactments. Hearing whisperings out of hell again we would know how to interpret the code, the skin of our hopes has grown thinner" (158, 159).

Steiner's personal history explains his position. His parents left Vienna in 1924, five years before he was born, and lived in Paris in 1940: "So I happened not to be there when the names were called out" (1967, 140). Though he has spent most of his life in America, Steiner regards his way of being in the world, like his way of being a Jew, as indissolubly tied to "the black mystery of what happened in Europe" (140) at those terminals of modern culture known as Auschwitz and Dachau. Applying this to all language is an obvious non sequitur: "Since language was used by the Nazis in planning and performing these atrocities, every language is thereby a hopelessly corrupted medium" (1987, 157, 166). This must be recognized strictly as Steiner's own personal, highly emotional "reason" for his belief that language *in itself* is tainted.

The reality of the Holocaust, Steiner holds, addresses the contemporary mind most effectively with the authority of silence: "The world of Auschwitz lies outside of speech as it lies outside reason" (1987, 123). Under Nazism, "words were committed to saying things no human mouth should ever have said and no paper made by man should ever have been inscribed with." The German language, used to dehumanize man for twelve years, had been pushed beyond the breaking point, its resiliency and usefulness for art exhausted. According to Steiner, "Everything forgets. But not a language" (99).

Language, however, is only a tool of the wordsmith, without independent memory, perception, or conscience. And when writers were prepared to employ it once again in the name of imaginative truth, the German language proved as adequate to the challenge as any other national idiom, limited only by the talents of the writer. But Steiner persisted in his linguistic claims into the 1980s, extending his views to all languages·

"The languages we speak on this polluted and suicidal planet are 'post-human,' they are serving creatures less than man" (1987, 156). Yet taking a contradictory stand, he locates the theological-metaphysical levels of language, of metaphor, of symbolism as the foundation for Paul Celan, who takes us to the "unspeakable center of the Holocaust experience," placing the "sense of the experience within the definition of man, history, and human speech" (1981, 166). Thus Paul Celan escapes, in Steiner's view, the indictment against language. Luckily, Steiner often fails to take his own dictum seriously, for he knows that the poet who falls silent simply ceases to be a poet.

Though scholars have taken Steiner's strange position seriously, few have readily accepted his totalist condemnation of language per se as a human phenomenon. Czeslaw Milosz, for example, did indeed recognize that a powerful faction in German society in the 1930s had taken over the mass media and appropriated the meaning of words for their own heinous ends. Milosz never followed Steiner in condemning language itself. The individual is exposed to a double attack. On the one hand, he must think of himself as the product of social, economic, and psychological determinants. On the other hand, his loss of autonomy is confirmed by the totalitarian nature of political power. Such circumstances make every pronouncement on human affairs uncertain (Milosz 1983, 94). Steiner could not drop pre-Holocaust assumptions, that is, prewar literary and cultural principles, in his discussion of contemporary writers. Though faulting the principles as well as the writers, he sensitively observes that "ideas of cultural development, of inherent rationality held since ancient Greece . . . are still intensely valid in the utopian historicism of Marx and stoic authoritarianism of Freud [both of them outriders of Greco-Roman civilization] can no longer be asserted with such confidence" (Steiner 1967, ix). For exactly this reason, much of the Holocaust literature is compelling. A new world view is reflected in new poetic forms, in a new concept of the role of the poet, and in new personae in poetry. Steiner formulated these postulates between the late 1950s and the middle 1960s, before much of the later fiction and nonfiction on the Holocaust had appeared. However, the idea that the Holocaust is beyond the capacities of literature has been accepted by many later critics.

As for those directly involved in the Holocaust, Steiner argued that they have trouble dealing with it imaginatively. With this Milosz concurs (1983, 81), with specific reference to Holocaust poetry: "People thrown into the middle of events that tear cries of pain from their mouths have difficulty in finding the distance necessary to transform this material artistically." One might say that Steiner is critical of Holocaust literature because it does not do what, in effect, he considers it impossible to do. Although few critics have challenged him on this directly, it has been a starting place for many essays on the subject.

At the very least, Steiner's insistence that language is affected by its use and that the writer thus has a special responsibility is shared by many critics: Alvarez, Adorno, Rosenfeld, Alexander, and Ezrahi. Alvarez (1969, 26) speaks of the difficulty for the writing of language to express this "world without values, with its meticulously controlled lunacy and bureaucracy of suffering." A strange pronouncement, indeed, for writers long before the Holocaust have written about the behavior of persons who have or observe no moral values. Oscar Wilde's *The Picture of Dorian Gray* and Budd Schulberg's *What Makes Sammy Run* immediately come to mind. Nevertheless, Alvarez insists that the task of art is to make us face the violence. For only art can restore the moral values that can make further totalitarian atrocities impossible (1969, 23). But time and distance do not make it easier to write fiction about Auschwitz. Because of ominous political developments and a nuclear military buildup since the Second World War, the "camps" have taken on new meaning as the symbol of a world where everyone, like the camp inmates, sits at death's border, a bomb's throw from destruction. Thus is the artist thrust into a system of symbols defined by the Nazis—symbols, as Alvarez indicates, that carry "an existential meaning beyond politics or shock or pity. They have become symbols of our interned nihilism" (1969, 28).

Writing about Plath, however, Alvarez does not join in Steiner's objection to her poetry on the Holocaust on the ground that she did not experience the event. In fact, he finds the use of outside events for expressing personal trauma a strength in her poetry. Referring to "Lady Lazarus," which employs a number of vivid images from the camps, he finds remarkable "the objectivity with which she handles such personal suffering. Instead, it is the very closeness of her pain which gives it a general meaning; through it she assumes the suffering of all modern victims" (1963, 53).

Lawrence Langer (1975, 1978) uses the term "literature of atrocity" for his own works dealing with the literary responses to the Holocaust. In the earlier work, *The Holocaust and the Literary Imagination* (1975), he counters Steiner and Adorno: the critic's job is not to judge the appropriateness of the artist presenting atrocity, (the atrocity is already a *fait accompli*); it is rather to evaluate the presentation, judging its effectiveness, analyzing its implications for literature and society (1975, 24). With others, he too doubts that someone who has not experienced the Holocaust can successfully convey it in literature, but he nonetheless rejects Adorno and Steiner. And he argues that works of the imagination can in fact "establish an order of reality," "in which the unimaginable becomes imaginatively acceptable." Art therefore is a proper medium for treating the Holocaust (1975, 43).

In his study of Solzhenitsyn, Delbo, Mann, and Camus, Langer (1978) aims to examine the form atrocity takes in literature and to determine the image of man in the frightful world of his creation. Langer traces a "gradual erosion of the human image" (xii) in the work of these four authors. He assumes that the artist's work is influenced more by the general flow of history than by the work of previous writers and literary conventions. So, for Langer, the concept of art for art's sake holds little interest.

He therefore embraces the artistic enterprise of writing about the Holocaust, but at the same time he has very high social expectations of the literature of atrocity. One may "seek sustenance for the 'inner imagery' which permits the individual to endure" (1978, 16), but, he continues, "Can art indeed conjure a reality that itself must remain forever unredeemable?" In a world of absurdity, says Wiesel, "we must invent reason; we must create beauty out of nothingness" (Halperin quoting Wiesel in *Jewish Heritage*, 41). To create beauty out of nothingness, this is the dark challenge facing the human spirits who sought expression, if not renewal, by translating the agony of annihilation into the painful harmonies—and discords—of an art of atrocity. Langer views art as the last frontier against death.

Since the late 1970s, Rosenfeld and Ezrahi have used the criteria of truth and accuracy to evaluate literary presentations of the Holocaust. They, too, are concerned with the corruption of language after the Holocaust and return to the earlier position of Adorno and Steiner, who had done most of their own work when there was a much smaller corpus of substantive material on this subject. Rosenfeld and Ezrahi agree that writing on the Holocaust presents technical problems for the author and they discuss shortcomings of particular pieces.

Like Langer, Rosenfeld expects the literature of the Holocaust to articulate a religious or moral point of view, as he comments in an essay:

> Holocaust literature at its heart of hearts is revelatory in some new way, although of what we do not yet know. We must acknowledge, however, that it returns us to biblical revelation in newly compelling and urgently critical ways, which forces us to rethink all received truths about God and man and world under the pressure of history's worst crime. (Rosenfeld and Greenberg 1978, 23)

Unlike Langer, Rosenfeld suggests that the fiction on the Holocaust is weaker than the nonfiction. After surveying various novels and plays, he writes that "imaginative literature on this subject does not carry sufficient authority in its own right and needs support from without" (1978, 79). He concedes nonetheless that fiction is a more effective medium than nonfiction, and therefore cautions novelists especially to represent the Holocaust accurately. Of course such a heavy reliance on the facts can limit a novel's possibilities. Rosenfeld applies the same standards of clarity to all genres and therefore prefers Wiesel's essays over his novels because they are clearer and less shrouded in mystery.

For Rosenfeld any writing on the Holocaust that fails to accurately document the frightful fate of Hitler's victims not only has little value, but worse, distorts reality. The Holocaust,

Rosenfeld argues, is beyond metaphor. Writing on the subject must serve to clarify, or it is not a valid exercise. To do anything but explore the meaning of the Holocaust directly, he contends, is "to exploit atrocity by misappropriating it for private or political ends. All such efforts at 'adapting' the Holocaust are bound to fail artistically, for reasons of conceptual distortion, and morally, for misusing the sufferings of the other" (Rosenfeld 1980, 154). Artistry in this view is inseparable from the moral issue, and the former cannot be judged apart from the latter, a connection drawn by many other critics on this subject.

Further, Rosenfeld rejects all universalizing of the Holocaust, and not surprisingly finds William Styron's treatment of the subject in *Sophie's Choice* exploitative and distorting. "To generalize the victims of the Holocaust"— Styron's chief victim is a Polish Catholic woman mistreated by a Jew—"is not only to profane their memories but to exonerate their executioners" (Rosenfeld 1980, 160). But this position seems rigid and narrow. It could be argued that Styron's universalizing in fact strengthens his condemnation of these atrocities, for if the Holocaust were identified as wholly unique, most readers could not respond to its meaning. The irony that the victim is a Catholic who is later oppressed by a schizophrenic Jew forces the reader to confront a pervasive madness. The narrator's guilt about his civilized, slave-owning grandparents suggests a link between slavery in the United States and the camps in Europe. Rosenfeld's objection to sexuality in the novel can likewise be challenged, for Styron's portrayal of sexual perversity in the death camps and in the sadomasochistic relationship between Sophie and Nathan may be a valid insight into the psychological underpinnings of fascism.

Rosenfeld also objects to Sylvia Plath's Holocaust victims' private use of suffering in such poems as "Daddy" and "Lady Lazarus," and contends that this weakens her poetry because the images outweigh their subject. Rosenfeld dismisses the possibility that theme and metaphor may merge in Plath's poetry, that her own suffering and the suffering outside of herself become one. It is remarkable that this poet, an American non-Jew, wholly uninvolved in the Holocaust, chose these images. Her work demonstrates both the extent of the Holocaust's impact on our age and the transformation of historical events into personal poetry.

Ezrahi identifies as the main problem for writers the fact that the Holocaust lies "beyond the realm of anything that has happened before" (1980, 3). According to her painful, brooding book, all literary expression is dwarfed by the enormity of the Nazi atrocities. The Holocaust has so drastically distorted the image of man such that the artist "cannot draw upon the timeless archetypes of human experience and behavior" in order "to render" unlived events familiar through the medium of the imagination. Realism and metaphoric expression are inadequate: "Even the most vivid representation of concrete detail . . . is blunted by the fact that there is no analogue in human experience. The imagination loses credibility and resources where reality exceeds even the darkest fantasies of the human mind." Metaphor and fantasy, Ezrahi concludes, are often an escape from reality (1980, 2, 3).

The major problem with her position then is that no form of literary expression can adequately convey reality. It is a goal beyond any and all writing—and a position that most creative writers would dismiss. They would reject first the assumption that literature can mirror reality, and second the assumption that reality is, in fact, an absolute not subject to interpretation. Ezrahi also insists that each piece on the Holocaust be read in comparison to other such works, rather than as an individual statement. In this she fails to recognize the differences that separate more imaginative writing from documentary records—the differences in type and purpose between memoirs and autobiographical accounts on the one hand, and fiction and poetry on the other.

Ezrahi (1980, 213) rejects the work of certain playwrights for the same reason that led Rosenfeld to condemn *Sophie's Choice.* Many writers, she would argue, have merely borrowed the loaded symbols and scenarios of the Holocaust in order either to achieve a kind of instantaneous emotional pitch or to demonstrate the misery of the general human condition by reference to the most abject of its victims. Arthur Miller, who graduated from *Focus* (1945) to more explicit uses of the concentration camp experience, sets out a narrow personal drama in *After the Fall* (1964) amid the ruins of a death camp.

As Alvarez has observed, "Miller thumbed an emotional lift from Dachau" (1964, 67), invoking the horror of violent and anonymous death as a kind of setting for the death of Marilyn Monroe. Miller's *Incident at Vichy* (1965) is related more specifically to the Holocaust, but even here, what transpires among the Jews and one German nobleman gathered in the interrogation room at Vichy is a play of abstract moral forces reduced to stereotypes, "Jew," says the psychiatrist Leduc, "is only the name we give to that stranger, that agony we cannot feel, that death we look at like a cold abstraction. Each man has his Jew—it is the other. And the Jews have their Jews" (84). Miller's play *Broken Glass* (1994) likewise connects two quite remote entities: the shards of the Jewish souls victimized in the Nazi killing fields and an American Jewish wife and husband, struggling with their shattered marriage against the "night of broken glass" occurring overseas. As Miller said of it (Elkin 1996), "This play should make Jewish and non-Jewish audiences ask what is in the soul that allows such things as the Holocaust to happen. What energizes such a thing?"

Unlike most critics of Holocaust literature, Susan Sontag (1961), in her brief comments on the subject, insists that Holocaust literature must meet aesthetic standards. Though admitting that Rolf Hochhuth's drama *The Deputy* shows "fidelity to the truth" and deserves attention because of its "relevance," she argues that "not all works of art which successfully perform a moral function greatly satisfy as art." Setting aside Rosenfeld and Ezrahi's demands for accuracy, she faults the play for its lack of stylistic strength—for Hochhuth's using free verse in a modern play and for incorporating "thick chunks of documentation" into the play. Sontag concludes that if the play is "tremendously moving it is because of the weight of its subject, not because of its style or dramaturgy "(127, 128, 129). Sontag stands almost alone in privileging aesthetic elements that can evoke strong aesthetic responses in works on the Holocaust.

Most critics of Holocaust literature focus chiefly on the contributions of European Jews and devote little attention to American novelists. But since the 1960s dozens of memoirs and novels by survivors have been published in the United States. The rise of Holocaust consciousness and the engagement of American writers with the subject deserves special review.

Further, historians agree that it was the 1961 Eichmann trial in particular that made many Americans aware of the Holocaust. Ezrahi sees the trial as "a watershed in the American perception of the Holocaust, as it provided near-personal contact with survivors and an unprecedented immersion into the facts for those who followed it through the public media" (1980, 180). Ezrahi offers two reasons for this delay in exploring the theme for twenty-five years after Nazism's fall: first, many Jewish American writers were assimilated or acculturated and did not feel direct ties to European Jewry, and second, the enormity of the events had an immobilizing and paralyzing effect.

Interestingly enough, early in the millennium, *The Specialist,* a new film drawn from comprehensive but little known visual records of this trial has been released in New York, and will surely find its way across the country. The story of the "man in the glass both" and his crimes against humanity simply will not fade into oblivion. Thus this theme is ever current in human consciousness.

Information on the Nazi's anti-Jewish program appeared in newspapers late in 1942, but not until the 1960s did American writers confront the Nazi atrocities. And since then a complete reversal has occurred. As Edward Alexander observes, "A number of American Jewish writers, including some of the most gifted, have sought to rediscover for us in the Holocaust our own buried life" (1979, 127). Among these are Philip Roth, Saul Bellow, Isaac Bashevis Singer, Cynthia Ozick, and Bernard Malamud. Even Roth, a merciless satirist of American Jewish culture in *The Ghost Writer* (1979), presents a young writer who discovers his muse and alter ego in a woman he is convinced is Anne Frank, the famous young diarist victim of the Nazis. Roth's subject however is not the Holocaust, but a writer's remarkably imaginative recognition of his relationship to it as an artist. His novel implies that Anne Frank is a kind of ghost of which American Jewish readers are very fond. Roth incorporated his image of Anne Frank into his work at great risk, for the use of any Holocaust figure to enlist automatic sympathy and to charge what appear to be unrelated topics with emotion can easily become vulgar. But he managed to evade this problem in *The Ghost Writer* by analyzing the very circumstances of such fantasies and their ethical implications. Roth raises the very complex issue of using the Holocaust, a symbol of collective trauma, either as a social tool, to bludgeon the Jewish artist into restraining his imagination for the sake of the "common good," or as an artistic tool to evoke sympathy from a critical audience by offering up one of its most sacred subjects. In so doing, he has given us a Jewish version of one of the major strains of modernism—the centrality of art.

Moving beyond Roth's well-known preoccupation with erotica, Kepish, the protagonist in *The Professor of Desire*, while at the grave of Franz Kafka, is struck by the fate of Eastern European Jewry, by the incalculable losses of the Holocaust. Kafka has brought him to this realization. At the novel's end, Roth introduces a new character, and with him a new dimension to the book: Mr. Barbatnik, a Holocaust survivor. His desire to live despite his searing losses is the penultimate scene of the work. He is an inspiration to all those around him, as he 'and Kafka serve as reminders of awesome and unthinkable oppression, internal and external. Roth's turning to the Holocaust survivor and to the diaspora writer whose paranoia was vindicated by the nightmare of history is in keeping with the American Jewish community's tendency to derive its collective identity from the Holocaust (Wirth-Nesher 1983, 266).

Saul Bellow's *Mr. Sammler's Planet* (1970), for Ezrahi (1980, 94), demonstrates the irrecoverability of cataclysmic history. Sammler is a Lazarene figure who literally crawled out of a mass grave alive and then hid in a mausoleum until the war's end. Deprived of all material comforts he has learned to attend to only his barest needs. Sammler adjusts in varying degrees, some bizarre. Langer tells us that history, in the form of a Holocaust encounter with the mass grave, has estranged Sammler from his earlier enthusiasm for the utopian vision of H. G. Wells (1995, 84, 85); it has also alienated him from the student generation of the 1960s, which hoots him off the platform at Columbia, unaware of the genesis of his present condition and, hence, totally unsympathetic to his position. Sammler brings his Holocaust experience into the foreground of his own consciousness throughout the novel, but he can bring it into no one else's, and so must live with his memories and their consequences alone. But he allows himself two luxuries: speculative thought and feeling. His is the simple acceptance of a man's duty to his fellows, for example, in the private eulogy over the body of his nephew Elia Grunter with which the novel ends. Ezrahi suggests that once physical survival has been secured, some other force is needed to keep a man going. She further intimates that the "victim who had a more defined sense of identity as a Jew and located his death or his survival in the spectrum of a community and a history of fellow-sufferers may have been sustained by the sense that his struggle was part of a process larger than himself" (95).

Sammler might have been tempted to believe that he had survived the great cataclysm that should have led either to final dissolution or to final salvation. However, when challenged by the option of a new, space-age alternative to religious apocalypse—Dr. Govinda Lai's proposal for abandoning the teeming, strife-torn earth and colonizing the moon—Sammler replies in the weary yet engaged manner conditioned by the tradition of the Hebrew prophets:

> When you know what pain is, you agree not to have been born is better. But being born one respects the powers of creation, one obeys the will of God—with whatever inner reservations truth imposes. No, I stand by what I first said. There is also an instinct against leaping into Kingdom Come. (220)

Bellow questions "what the reduction of millions of human beings into heaps of bones . . . or clouds of smoke betokened" (1969, 220). This could well allude also to the atomic blasts and not to just the Nazi Holocaust. Hiroshima weighs as heavily on the American conscience of this American Jewish writer as Auschwitz preys on his Jewish sensibilities. Bellow deplores the threat to the self, the loss of identity, represented by both the Nazi and the nuclear forms of mass extermination. For him, this may outweigh even the threat to the entire corpus of Judaism signified by the destruction of European Jewry.

For more than two decades Isaac Bashevis Singer, who had emigrated from Poland to the United States in 1935, seemed to be deliberately avoiding the Holocaust in writing about the *shtetl* as if it still existed. He admitted in an interview with Irving Howe in 1966 that "at the heart of his attitude there is an illusion which is consciously sustained" (60). With the novels *Enemies, A Love Story* (1972) and *Shosha* (1978), however, Singer arrived at a turning point toward a more direct confrontation of the Holocaust and an attempt to incorporate the challenges of mass destruction into his own mythology and cosmology. Edward Alexander (1991, 10) sees Singer as the poet laureate of a Jewish sense of the past that is archetypal and circular rather than historical and linear. His narratives touching on the Holocaust view the Nazis as merely the latest in the long succession of murderous outsiders who have obtruded themselves upon Jewish history. "Yes," sighs the narrator of *The Family Moskat* (1950), "every generation had its Pharaohs and Hamans and Chmielnickis. Now it was Hitler." The stunning paradox of Singer's work is that, by treating all these destroyers as indistinct repetitions of one another, he suggests that a nation that has been dying for thousands of years is a living nation.

Janet Hadda, as quoted by Joseph Sherman, cogently argues that Singer, like his narrators, feels guilty about having survived the Holocaust, "about having avoided the catastrophe. These unhappy responses are without question severely exacerbated by the fact that Singer's own ascent as a popular writer cannot be separated from the very fact of his having lived to describe the perished heritage of Jewish Eastern Europe" (1994, 106). Following this line, Sherman is convinced that *Enemies* and *Shosha* must be read as acts of confessional atonement whose subtext is guilt (1994, 107). He is merciless in attacking what he sees as "a ruthless self-regard," that informs in equal degree Singer's presentation of Herman Broder in *Enemies* and his presentation of Aaron Greidinger in *Shosha*. The problem as Sherman sees it is the moral ambiguity of an author who strives to create responsible fiction out of the guilt of living an irresponsible life. Singer never permits history to detain the progress of his story for long, according to this critic, and that is lamentable.

In the 1980s a number of studies set out to chart the differences that separated Cynthia Ozick from the reigning quartet of Bellow, Malamud, Roth, and Singer. Most concluded that in her insistence on the inextricable relationship of history and memory, law and restraint, what Jewishly lasts and what is Jewishly "important," she represented a mode of thinking and writing that would radically change the way American Jewish writing is defined, and perhaps more crucial, the way American Jewish writing defines itself (Pinsker 1994, 94). In *The Cannibal Galaxy* (1983), *The Shawl* (1989), and even *The Messiah of Stockholm* (1987), Ozick reveals her strong feelings for Orthodox Jewish traditions and beliefs. These she incorporates into fiction involving the struggle of the transplanted Jew in America, the survivor in exile in Scandinavia, the preservation of Jewish culture and identity, the plight of the Jewish people during the Holocaust, the challenge of meeting mass murder unflinchingly, and the problem of facing the destructive as well as creative aftermath.

The Shawl and its sequel *Rosa* (1989) reverse the situation Ozick develops in *The Cannibal Galaxy;* for in *The Shawl* she follows the life of a woman victimized by the Holocaust. Unlike Joseph Brill (*The Cannibal Galaxy*), Rosa Lublin was imprisoned in a concentration camp and forced to witness the murder of her infant. In *Rosa,* set thirty years later in Florida, we find a Rosa Lublin who is still alive, but at a terrible cost. Thus, whereas *The Shawl* ultimately celebrates the human will to survive, Rosa portrays the abiding anguish of the survivor. Both tales mirror themes that obsess *The Cannibal Galaxy* to which the stories are wed. The idea of hell as well as the psychological consequences unleashed by intense rage haunt all three works. Hidden in the cellar of a convent, Joseph Brill escaped the butchery of the death camps, but never makes his peace with American culture; incarcerated in a camp, Rosa Lublin experienced the horrors of a demonic world of unparalleled proportions (Kauver 1993, 179). The former envisions the middle ground as a particular kind of hell. The latter ponders the coldness of hell in the death camp, and in *Rosa,* under the blazing Miami sun, she "felt she was in hell" (14). In late middle age, the schoolmaster and his secretary-bride are melancholiacs, counters of losses, worshipers at altars of death. *The Shawl* is enormously important for Holocaust literature: the events in the German abattoir become searingly

real as their effects merge in Rosa Lublin's thoughts, record-
ing her torment. Ozick not only incorporates into her tales
facts gleaned from history and memoirs, but the storyteller
also lays bare the intricacies of the human mind, at the same
time affirming the courage displayed and unyielding faith of
the sufferers in their efforts to vanquish the powers of darkness. Ozick poses and answers ultimate questions in *The
Shawl*—how far will a person go in order to survive? to prolong
another's life? to insure and to protect the existence of one's
people?

In *The Messiah of Stockholm*, not a Holocaust tale per se,
there is an ever-present smell of something roasting. Puzzling
at first to Lars Andemening, the protagonist, the odor finally
becomes inescapable—it is the smoke from the chimneys of
the death camps. He identifies the stench with the man whom
Adela, presumed daughter and heir of Bruno Schulz, claimed
rescued the infamous lost Schulz manuscript but who, before
he could reclaim it, perished like "All the Jews, all the Hassidim in their long black coats" in Drohobycz (74). And it is
that man, "hurrying and hurrying toward the chimneys," for
whom Lars grieves at the end of the novel. That man replaces
Bruno Schulz in Lars's mind as a metaphor for the Six
Million—tragically all that remains of Lars's chosen history as
he can neither discover his origins nor escape and ascend into
the nimbus of *The Cannibal Galaxy*. His is an orphanhood of
the future as well as of the past. The Holocaust theme as a
threshold and not as a terminus is ever-present in Ozick—a
morally serious writer with a strong sense of historical
consciousness.

The Holocaust and World War II had a deep impact on Bernard Malamud, motivating and intensifying his personal notion that he had something to say as a writer and as a Jew.
"The suffering of the Jews is a distinct thing for me," he once
explained. "I for one believe that not enough has been made of
the tragedy of the destruction of six million Jews. Somebody
has to cry even if it's a writer twenty years later" (quoted in
Langer 1995, 145).

The Fixer is important to this discussion because of its implied evocation of the Holocaust and because a similarly indirect treatment of this theme is skillfully utilized in the poems

of Gerald Stern. Malamud has said that the historical account of Mendel Beiliss was paradigmatic for him in writing his novel. "Somewhere along the line what had happened in Nazi Germany began to be important to me in terms of the book, and that too is part of Yacov's story" (146). To incorporate the Jewish catastrophe, Malamud confronts it obliquely, in microcosm, in the past. The Blood Libel (the notion prevalent from the Middle Ages up to modern times that Jews murdered Christian children and utilized their blood to ritualistically prepare the unleavened bread for the Passover) gave him, as Robert Alter (1966) suggests, "a way of approaching the European Holocaust on a scale that is imaginable, susceptible of fictional representation. For the Beiliss trial transparently holds within it the core of the cultural sickness around which the Nazi madness grew" (74). But Langer (1995, 147) objects: "By reducing the scale of that event from the extermination of a people to the persecution of a person, Malamud does more than make that momentous atrocity manageable: he transforms it into a story of the affirmation of private dignity that elevates the ordeal to tragic dimensions." He continues doggedly, "Alter's very language echoes a vision and a tradition that fall comfortably into a familiar literary stance, but settle uneasily on the circumstantial dilemmas confronting the Holocaust victim" (147). The jailed Yakov Bok, Alter says, forced "to summon up all his inner resources of survival in order to stay sane and alive in solitary confinement, recapitulates the darkest, most heroic aspects of Jewish existence in the diaspora" (74). But how can we use such language to describe that final expression of diaspora in Europe called deportation to the death camps? Malamud's indirect, tentative, circumscribed inroads on Holocaust reality leave untouched vast areas of harsh and unbearable experience requiring fresh explorations of the bond linking the world and the spirit. Malamud's dream-made-real characters, not unlike Kafka's, resemble Langer's European survivors (1975). In *The Fixer,* where the dream is a nightmare, indeed, Malamud's world contains the horrors that Langer includes in the aesthetics of atrocity.

Thus many American authors are committed to confronting the Holocaust in the novel, drama, or poetry. Susan Fromberg

Shaeffer's *Anya* (1974), the story of a survivor's death camp experience and later life in America, was so well researched and consequently so convincing that she had to insist the book was strictly fiction. Ezrahi explains that "the realistic fiction written by American Jewish writers especially in the sixties and seventies tries to make up for the lack of empirical resources by a thoroughly researched representation of events which were still unknown and by literary models which had not yet been established in the 1940s" (180). Perhaps what is also operating is a subconscious feeling of guilt that the author was spared the Holocaust and did not endure this heinous "rite of passage." Such guilt and possibly perverse feelings of envy are likely to lead to an effort to compensate by doing full justice to the subject through exhaustive research into the author's own work.

The novels and plays just cited are indicative of how Auschwitz has become part of the American literary climate. Likewise this timeless horror has become a major theme in American poetry. Furthermore, it is in part through poets' struggles with this theme that certain poetic conventions have lost their former status.

In the remainder of this chapter I will offer an account of the recent fate of some traditional poetic modes and devices by inquiring into the various treatments of atrocity in poetry, and by examining some of the most striking examples of the American poetic response to the Holocaust.

In fact, responses to the Holocaust in poetry have been more varied than those in fiction, perhaps because of flexibility of the length of a poem, which affords the poet tremendous freedom in theme and in structure. Many poets' obsession with the Holocaust—unlike the novelists'—parallels their breaking away from romantic conventions and metamorphosing what was perceived to be the traditional role of the poet as balladeer, lyricist, eroticist, and historical chronicler into something quite stark.

These departures are not peculiar to Holocaust poetry. Poems protesting the war in Vietnam and the oppression of blacks and other cultures in America represent even greater disruptions in poetic conventions. The poet's growing consciousness of the post-Hitler world—a world born and nurtured in Germany where the height of European culture had fallen into evil hands—and his daily exposure to the news and the media about the Vietnam War, as well as the Black and Hispanic struggle in America for equality and humane treatment, brought about innovation and redefinition in poetry.

Years after the Vietnam War, the breadth of poetry protesting that war remains limited, whereas the poetry on the Holocaust suggests that images of Prussian forests littered with graves and a sky clouded daily by the ashes of ten thousand human beings have imposed themselves on the poetic imagination. Nature in this poetry is no longer pristine and sacramental; it is beleaguered by the devouring force of human carnivores and their followers. European and religious identification appears to grip the poetic imagination.

Florence Howe (1993) poses the question: "Why these [Holocaust] poems now? I ask myself as I read enough of them to fill a book by themselves" (11). A long poem of twenty-three parts, "Sources" by Adrienne Rich (1986), suggestive of renaming, rediscovery, and recognition, suggests one possible answer—"the immense silence of the Holocaust" itself. Among the big questions running through "Sources" is how we ground ourselves in this historical moment when the memory of the Holocaust recedes from us in "immense silence," while torture is still a daily threat in prisons and interrogation cells. She probes further: how do we teach ancestral roots that have scarred us painfully in our own families? In exploring her own persona, Rich struggles to lay claim to a Jewish identity that her parents' social world despised. How, she asks, do we find the historical perspective that allows us the compassion to understand, if not simply to forgive, the awfulness of being lied to as children and as adults? Thus Rich moves her personal search for identity back to her own family and also to wider American roots, embracing all outsiders and seeking to reconcile her roots with the present. The poet ponders her own rootlessness, acknowledging multiple biographical threads—that part of her related to the southern Jews of Vicksburg and Birmingham, and that part of her attached to the *Ashkenazim* (German Jews), the *Halutzim* (pioneer land reclaimers in Israel), and the pogroms of World War II that wiped out the Six Million. Rich forces her readers to question whether any poet can exist untouched by all she cannot help but know?

Mary Oliver's poem "1945–1985: Poem for the Anniversary" frames brief glimpses of "films of Dachau and Auschwitz and Bergen-Belsen" (line 28) and "the face of Mengele" (line 58) within the embrace of an idyllic "good leafy place" (line 40) in which the poet observes a lost fawn. Oliver is haunted by the Holocaust, her personal inheritance as a descendant of survivors, and the history of Germany's "iron claw" (line 33). Her poem, wonderfully shaped and painted, draws the strong connection between the aesthetic attentiveness that produces an elegant still life, anchored in nature, and a keen awareness of the history of lives that are both human and nonhuman. At poem's end, the doe finds her fawn and smells the previous danger. Oliver juxtaposes the silence of the planet to the silence of the Holocaust world, and maternal concern for a doe/child to the children who were lost forever

"There Will Be Animals," a recent poem by the young African American Thylias Moss, offers a view of a world after destruction, in which animals "teach us / what we can't teach ourselves." Surreal images—comic, morbid, and shocking—inform the poem, with two allusions to the Holocaust:

> The coast horned lizard still won't be found
> without a bag of tricks, it will inflate and the first
> of six million Jewfish will emerge from its mouth.
> We will all be richer.
>
> . . . .
> . . . Then once and for all we will know it is no illusion.
> The lion lying with the lamb, the grandmother and
>   Little Red Riding Hood
> walking out of a wolf named Dachau.
>
> (23–26, 30–33)

These poems by Rich, Oliver, and Moss are not only about saving the planet and ourselves. In them the Holocaust as historical event becomes a trope, a touchstone signaling danger to all humanity, insisting on the power of memory and feeling to wage war on violence and injustice.

The internalization of a real event by people who did not directly experience it is something relatively new. The First World War, by contrast, produced poetry written in the main by the trench poets, British and American, who tried to make sense of the war they had personally lived through. They quite obviously were not confronted by the existential absurdity of the A-bomb and the death camps. Yes trench warfare raised the horrors of war, but it did not raise questions of man's fundamental nature. As James Mersman argues, "Whether or not the war was presented as heroic or terrible, the poetry of World War I commonly accepted war as unavoidable, or readily pointed the blame to specific persons or classes of persons" (1974, 12).

The poetry of World War I also did not depart radically from traditional verse. Mersman writes that poetry was either "naively heroic-romantic, starkly realistic, or radically socialistic" and that all but the latter "for the most part adhered to rhymes and traditional meters" (12). Paul Fussell is more pointed about the relationship between form and underlying theme, observing that "high" diction dominated the poetry at the beginning of the First World War, revealing "an attempt to make sense of the war as it related to inherited tradition" (1975, 57).

The poets of the 1930s generally shifted from the nineteenth-century romantic conception of poetry. They also rejected the notion of art for art's sake. Additionally, they broke away from the nineteenth- and early-twentieth-century view of the role of the poet and the function of structure. At the same time they held to a persistent belief that love and its artistic expression could save the world. Fascist victories consequently brought disillusionment, although each poet reacted in a different way.

The poets who came into their own after the Second World War had no faith in any particular philosophy or in the power of art. They faced a world in ruins that rendered humanism obsolete and meaningless. This defined their challenge and set them apart from earlier poetry. As the critic Daniel Hoffman observes, although modern and postmodern poetry are part of the "great groundswell of the Romantic movement, the chief difference between the contemporary and the Romantic and modernist generation is, we recognize the past is lost"

(1975, 104). As a result of the Second World War and the destruction of European cities, part of the past was lost in a very real physical sense. But an idea of civilization was lost as well in the aftermath of Nazi brutality and genocide—an innocent belief in man's goodness or the power of reason. Violence had infected the heart of civilization. The security of the individual, too, was also undermined, as he was abandoned to the mercy of a government that exacted mindless obedience and engaged in mass destruction. Evidence of the individual was obliterated.

Such conditions necessarily challenge all humanistic concepts of order. Karl Malkoff contends that because our sense of order had been lost in World War I, "the need to discover [an] order that might not be apparent, but that existed nevertheless, became the dominant literary concern of American poets following the war. But after World War II, by contrast, "the quest for order was no longer dominant. Perhaps it is a matter of exhaustion" (1973, 12).

I would argue, however, that the end of the Second World War was not marked by the emergence of more chaotic poetry. The type of abandonment of order that Malkoff describes is more obvious in poems written during the 1960s, after the Eichmann trial had revealed the full horror of Auschwitz. But unlike Malkoff's view, Holocaust poetry of the immediate postwar period brought its own wholly different call for order. Whereas World War I had threatened the *social* order, the Holocaust challenged something far deeper in us and in our civilization. After the Holocaust, then, order was pursued far more desperately than before.

Some poets rethought their concept of history, the story of the rise and fall of civilizations. T. S. Eliot, already well established before the Second World War, looked to history as a model for contemporary values in art, and to poetic traditions of the past for present practice in poetry. Anthony Hecht (1967), clearly under Eliot's influence in "Rites and Ceremonies," focuses on the Holocaust. He recites there a litany of past atrocities (38–47). Whereas Eliot in *The Waste Land* (1930) delineates the spiritual sterility of modern man in contrast to his status in previous ages, Hecht extends iniquitous man's alienation from God from the Crusades through to the Holocaust.

The works of other poets imply that their perspective on history and civilization, diametrically opposed to Eliot's, contributed to their embracing an innovative poetic style. So-called "confessional" poetry is the uninhibited voice that not only names but also simply admits; it describes not order in the world but rather some disorder in the persona of the poet and in the world. Still, most confessional poetry is not totally autobiographical, since it includes images and allusions from the world outside of the poet's psyche. This kind of poetry exemplifies a radical departure from Eliot's reliance on history and tradition.

One of the first confessional poets, Karl Shapiro, had earlier been influenced by Eliot, but with the appearance of his confessional poems in the late 1950s, he also attacked Eliot's anti-Semitism and his premise that modern poetry should be evaluated in terms of tradition in British poetry. At this time, Shapiro identified himself as a poet conscious of his Judaism; beyond that, he associated Judaism with the Holocaust. The Jew, wrote Shapiro (1958), "is man essentially himself, beyond nationality, defenseless against the crushing impersonality of history." This image, he continues, was revived by the "hideous blood purge of the Jews by Germany in the twentieth century" (x). His rejection of Eliot, he suggests, is connected to his acceptance of a new poetry and the Holocaust.

Holocaust images emerge, too, in the confessional poetry of Sylvia Plath and William Heyen. These poets do not try to seek reason in the world but instead focus on the disorder in their own consciousnesses. Thus Plath vividly defines her relationship to her dominating father in terms of the Nazi brutality that literally consumed the Jews. Heyen calls into question his German heritage. A distinction may be made between poems that make direct statements on the Holocaust and center on Auschwitz and poems in which Auschwitz is a mere metaphor for something else. Yet many of Heyen's poems utilize similar imagery to Plath's such as metaphors of castration and engulfment signaling the grave ending. This implies a single response to the Holocaust in the imagination. The poets' inclusion of similar images for the Holocaust suggests first, that the Nazi reign of destruction has been one of the reasons for a new view of the world, of personality, and of poetry, and second, that the poets who perceive or simply feel some relationship between their awareness of being a poet and the Nazi terror can call themselves Holocaust poets.

Malkoff asserts in his study of confessional poetry that after the Second World War the poet replaced the search for external order with an exploration of the interior world. "Contemporary American poetry," he argues, "can be understood as a series of attempts to reintegrate the relation of man's inner world to the perceptual universe" (1977, 40). Implied in this reorientation is a dismissal of Eliot's insistence that poetry be impersonal and intellectual. Relying on his emotions and interior world, the confessional poet surrenders the organizing principle, the ego, the powerful "poetic voice," and speaks with a personal voice of an outside world that has no more order than the quirks of individual consciousness.

Malkoff believes that a "disintegration of the self is crucial to the Confessional vision of reality" and that the poet's function thus becomes "almost sacrificial." Furthermore, he declares that it is a "descent into the underworld that seems almost a defining characteristic of modern Confessional poetry" (1977, 95). The confessional poet is not a spokesman for man but a survivor of an internal personal holocaust. He suffers from within and not from without and is filled with self-contempt.

The common subject of confessional poetry, as Malkoff sees it, is "the myth of the self, which reaches inward to the archetypal patterns of the unconscious and outward to the shared experiences of the poet's society, rather than the objective actions of the arbitrary isolated individual" (1977, 126). The regularity with which the Holocaust appears in contemporary poetry implies a common consciousness of it. The cataclysmic Nazi devastation of the Jews has assumed a mythic significance that parallels other poetic archetypes.

There are analogies not only between the role of the survivor and the psychological underpinnings of the poet's relationship to his poems but also between the survivor and the poet's persona, the particular voice through which he speaks. Indeed the image of the survivor has become an increasingly important symbol of the twentieth-century hero, or actually antihero, who endures a rite of passage involving the loss of home and family, only to be left mutilated, in existential crisis. This image has recently been appropriated to characterize the AIDS epidemic in our society, as well as the condition of struggling minority groups. This situation is beginning to find expression in drama, and also in poetry. A figure drawn from history is portrayed as the antihero and, in some works, comes to symbolize the human situation.

Death and violence, too, figure as the subjects of many contemporary poems. Lawrence R. Ries studies the poetry of Sylvia Plath, John Wain, Ted Hughes, and Thomas Gunn. He notes two types of violence: that of the forces of nature and that inflicted by men upon one another. Almost all of the poetry after the Second World War that deals with violence, he asserts, takes its "impetus from the perception of human violence, those immediate historical conditions that weighed so heavily upon the artist's sensitivity" (1977, 7). Violence, Ries suggests, is such an all-encompassing feature of the collective consciousness that even when a reader does not completely understand a poem, he accepts it because he senses its source. One is driven to conclude, however reluctantly, that it is the spirit of the age.

The Second World War and the Holocaust have brought yet another change as subjects and images that had never before appeared in poetry crop up. All semblance of decorum has been swept away, it would seem. Some critics consider pornographic and violent elements in poetry as signs of a failed imagination or even of neurosis. But Ries argues against this notion: such language and imagery does not indicate a deficiency on the part of the poet but rather represents an appropriate response to what man has done to his world. He argues further that after the Second World War, man was "left with a feeling of impotency and anonymity with which he was unable to cope. To compensate for this feeling of loss, he must assert himself in whatever way possible, the more violent and extreme the better" (12).

This is what one finds in poems written in the sixties. For the poets of that era, poetry that directly expresses a hatred of violence is outdated and futile. This approach, Ries asserts, has "worn thin after the poetry of World War I, the Spanish Civil War, and World War II" (1977, 13).

Plath, says Ries, "may rightly be called the most natural child of the postwar temperament, and he vehemently disagrees with those who fault her for trivializing the Holocaust. Rather, Ries argues, she accepts a "guilt by association . . . because of her participation in this imperfect humanity," and this is "central to her consciousness" (1977, 13, 14). While she appropriates this guilt, she is also a victim of sorts: "Perhaps no modern poet has been more aware of the forces of power and violence in the contemporary world," he contends, "and their disintegrating effect on human identity" (1977, 34).

Ries, like Malkoff, perceives in contemporary poetry a stripping away of the authority of the self. But whereas Malkoff views it almost as a voluntary act aimed at exposing the interior ordering of reality, Ries sees it more as the rough, intense outer world chipping at the identity and authority of the individual.

Once again the concentration camp inmate is the poet. In a discussion of Plath's "Daddy," Ries, following Alvarez, argues that as a result of her awful relationship with her father, she directs her violence inward, upon herself, like some of the camp inmates who achieved a sense of identity by self-inflicted pain or by planning suicide. Plath, after all, did both.

M. L. Rosenthal, discussing postmodern poetry, also praises Plath and contends that *Ariel*, which includes most of her poems with Holocaust imagery, is her best. Rosenthal, too, identifies a change in poetry since the Second World War. In its most striking form, he suggests it "has taken on a new coloration, in effect a new sense of unease and disorder" (1967, 5). Our blighted culture, he contends, finds many vital poets assuming "an almost helpless identification and sympathy with the victimized psyche of the present cultural moment" as they "seek the way to transcendent meaning" (1967, 322). Although Rosenthal does not see in postmodern poetry as radical a break with tradition as do Ries and Malkoff, clearly he perceives that many poets are grappling with a world fundamentally changed by the Holocaust.

In the following chapters I will discuss the Holocaust poetry of Sylvia Plath, William Heyen, Gerald Stern, and Jerome Rothenberg. Of these poets, only Plath has entered the canon of Holocaust poetry. I will compare her work with that of William Heyen, first as different modes of confessional poetry, and second as poetically sensitive treatments of this tragic era by non-Jews. But in my view, Heyen, Stern, and Rothenberg evince a compelling compassion most certainly deserving of inclusion in this specialized body of literature. In their poetry, the individual perception of events, individual personalities, and individual confessions are as varied as the writers themselves. It seems reasonable to assert that Rothenberg would concur with Heyen and Stern's view of the purpose of poetry, and specifically Holocaust poetry: "to help us live our lives" (Heyen) and "to teach us how to live, how to survive" (Stern).

Overarching this inquiry is the issue of identity and the concomitant tensions as expressed in the different manifestations of the poetic form. What is unique in artists' approaches to Holocaust material? What is the nature of their poetic responses to tragedy? Who are the mourners? How does evil resonate in this poetry? How do these poets address the question of the accountability of Western culture and humanism? Is the tear in our trust in the last two hundred years of civilized behavior and religious sanctions reparable? How is the particularity of victimized Jewish suffering juxtaposed with the universality of humankind's pain? What is the nature of martyrdom and does it in any way convey the sense of ethical rightness, of dying for a just cause? Does this poetry affirm the outstanding British writer of the Renaissance Sir Philip Sidney's notion that the validity and effectiveness of history may be recounted in the poetic genre? "Is their poetry characterized explicitly by a different attitude toward history that rejects any violation or mitigation of reality by the mediation of the creative imagination, but that often contains implicit premises about the transcendent significance to be extracted from historical processes?" (Ezrahi 1980, 23).

The searing questions raised by critics about the aesthetics of Holocaust poetry will be applied to the works of these four poets. The evidence of the Holocaust's moral enormity will be examined to see how it affects the act of poetic representation. What constraints, whether in the use of fact or in the reach of the imagination, does this subject impose on authors and readers? How does the Holocaust shape the perspectives from which it is viewed? Is it possible for a poet to achieve aesthetic distance on this subject? In "Unwilled 'Chaos': In Poem We Trust" (Lang 1988, 9), Heyen points to a formal division in his own poetry—between those of his Holocaust poems that are willed and "controlled" and others that "rave or hallucinate or speak in tongues." The latter, Heyen claims, come closer to reflecting the "opacity" of the Holocaust itself. And so a strange reverberation is set up for the poet: he must resist the impulse to try to understand fully the working of his own poem insofar as its subject from the start first references that limitation. If he achieves this goal, it is through a certain power of perception and understanding—a power that he has developed in response to certain previously accomplished critical work. For it is the critics who by their own intellectual and imaginative struggles with the Holocaust have somehow rendered its dreadful enormity morally and intellectually accessible to those among whom and to whom that enormity occurred.

Holocaust poetry is a body of poetry like no other, centered on a historical event like no other. Part of its reason for being lies in the hope that there will be no other. Knowing and remembering the evil in history, and in each of us, might not prevent a recurrence of genocide. But ignorance of history or suppression of memory removes the surest defense we have, however inadequate, against such mammoth cruelty and indifference. While engaging in this scholarly examination of Holocaust poetry, I must confront the gnawing question of whether there is any ethical system or intellectual tool strong enough to assure us that future barbaric destruction will be impossible. The modern reader, exhorted by the power of the poetry of Sylvia Plath, William Heyen, Gerald Stern, and Jerome Rothenberg, responds to the Holocaust with renewed respect and understanding for humankind, an accounting of those years, and a sense that like the prophets and psalmists of old we must not give in to despair.

2

The Confessional Poetry of Sylvia Plath and William Heyen: Searching for Expiation, Identification, and Communion with the Victims

In the 1960s images of Auschwitz began to appear in the work of many American poets. The images either evoke the Holocaust explicitly, or are used as metaphors for other horrors—abuse, AIDS, abortion, victimization, and so on. Confessional poets such as Sylvia Plath and Anne Sexton first employed images of the world of the death camps extensively. Other poets with a strong political or social orientation such as Denise Levertov and Adrienne Rich express atrocity in terms of the Holocaust. Additionally the Holocaust is a major theme in the poetry of Van Brock, William Heyen, W. D. Snodgrass, and Charles Reznikoff.

Confessional poetry became a main current in American poetry in the late 1950s and has continued into the present century. The critic M. L. Rosenthal takes at least partial credit for naming "The Confessional Poets" in a 1959 review of Robert Lowell's *Life Studies* (Phillips 1973, 1). He used the term to distinguish Lowell's later poems from earlier ones that reflected the poetics of the New Critics and T. S. Eliot. Rosenthal elaborated on the theme in *The New Poets* (1967) in discussing the works of Robert Lowell, Allen Ginsberg, Theodore Roethke, Sylvia Plath, Anne Sexton, and John Berryman.

The year 1959 is most often associated with the birth of confessional poetry because that was when *Life Studies* and W. D. Snodgrass's *Heart's Needle* appeared. But Ginsberg was already writing what was later to be designated as confes-

sional poetry earlier in the decade. Younger poets were profoundly affected by this type of poetry. Anne Sexton, who had
been one of Lowell's students at Boston University, claimed
that Snodgrass's painful exploration of his separation from
his daughter because of his divorce, a central theme in *Heart's
Needle,* opened up new possibilities in poetry. Plath, who
sometimes sat in on Lowell's classes, was inspired by his four-
part *Life Studies,* which merges private and public experience
in its treatment of war, the return home after the war, art, and
the poet's subsequent madness.

In addition to its attention to private experience, confessional poetry departs from the New Critical approach in other
ways: structure is more relaxed, the individual poem is often
meant to be read as part of a series, not in isolation, and, last,
the poet's ordered voice gives way to outburst. This deviation
is interesting because it was not the result of one poet's domi-
nance but, as Malkoff (1977, 89) observes, "a series of nearly
contemporary discoveries."

The evolution of this way of writing poetry predates American awareness of the Holocaust. Nevertheless, except for
Lowell, the earlier major poets in this group—Sexton, Plath,
and Snodgrass—and many later poets have drawn heavily
upon the horrifying film images that documented the Final
Solution and upon the reportage from the Nuremberg and
Eichmann trials. A convention of Holocaust poetry had been
established in short order. Brian Murdoch points out that
many of these poets utilize similar imagery (1974, 124). This
overlap of the confessional poets and poets making use of
Holocaust imagery is not accidental but rather stems from a
potent need to write about the dark side of the unconscious,
about man's inherent evil. Indeed, both confessional poetry
and Holocaust poetry demand like images.

How to define confessional poetry is a difficult question.
Phillips sets out to list characteristics of the postmodern confessional poetry currently written in America:

It is highly subjective.
It is an expression of personality, not an escape from it.
It is therapeutic and/or purgative.
Its emotional content is personal rather than impersonal.

It is most often narrative.
It portrays unbalanced, afflicted, or alienated protagonists.
It employs irony and understatement for detachment.
It uses the self as a poetic symbol around which is woven a personal anthology.
There are no barriers of subject matter.
There are no barriers between the reader and the poet.
The poetry is written in the open language of ordinary speech.
It is written in open forms.
It displays moral courage.
It is antiestablishment in content, with alienation a common theme.
Personal failure is also a favorite theme, as is mental illness.
The poet strives for personalization, rather than universalization.
(If totally successful, the personal is expressed so intimately, we can all identify and empathize.)

(1973, 16, 17)

All of this undercuts Eliot's early position vis-à-vis impersonal poetry and his acrimonious attack against poetry such as Whitman's, which he considered to be mere personal utterance. Some even consider the nineteenth-century Whitman to be a confessional poet. He may be in some respects, but there is an important difference between his poetry and that of mid-twentieth-century American poets: the Whitman "I" is not so much the expression of the feelings peculiar to the poet as it is the expression of what the poet deems to be true of "us." Although this is a result of his individual view, the emphasis is on "us."

One might even be tempted, as Malkoff suggests, to name the Roman poet of love, Catullus, and the seventeenth-century English poet John Donne as confessional poets. However, here, too, there are critical distinctions. The Roman lyric poets, and to an even greater extent the seventeenth-century lyric poets, assumed personae, more often than not as characters in easily recognizable and typical situations, such as the young man who attempts to seduce a modest woman, young or old, married or not. The puns, elaborate metaphors, and verbal dexterity—the wit of Herrick, Donne, and Marvell—are as compelling as their subject matter. Mid-century confessional American poetry, by contrast, is not structurally complex, and its emphasis is typically on the poet's distinctive life and vision. Thus a confessional poet writing about seduction would focus not on the ingenuity of the argument presented by a man in this situation but on the "I's" private yearnings and anxieties.

Some critics argue that confessional poetry is severely constrained by the poet's obsession with self. In this view, even when the poem alludes to something outside the poet, such as a historical event, it is revealing something about the "I" and has no other significance. Other critics who are more sympathetic to this type of poetry contend that historical allusions disclose not only something relative to the persona but also the poet's idea and point of view concerning these events. Thus these two factions divide on Plath: when she calls herself a Jew and her father a Nazi in "Daddy," is she offering merely a self-indulgent presentation of herself, or is this how she sees the Nazi-Jew relationship? James Young suggests that Plath incorporates allegory and personal pain very deeply and fits them together, simultaneously representing them and using them to represent herself (1987, 134).

Malkoff compromises: the relationship between the speaker and the images in poems by Plath and others, he argues, is open to interpretation. Confessional poets differ from other poets who write on personal subjects in that the confessional poet's identity is lost in the web of images. Ironically, perhaps, though the poems are written in the first person, they chart the poet's loss and the disintegration of self. The legitimacy of confessional poetry for Malkoff is that "the boundaries between the self and the outer reality have themselves been brought into question" (1973, 89). Such poetry is egocentric but not egoistic: self is central, and the manifestation of its disintegration results from the poet's candor. Rosenthal says that the best confessional poetry rises above its subject matter to achieve some sort of victory over pain and defeat, as glosses on the triumph of life. To which Phillips adds, "The best confessional poems are more than conceptions. They are revelations" (1973, 17).

It is possible that so many poets writing in this mode draw on the Holocaust because they intuit that the Nazi threat to humanity and humanism is the most powerful recent historical analogue to the outer world's incursion on the self. History has penetrated consciousness. Even if one has difficulty with Malkoff's view of the underlying psychology of the poet's honesty and abandonment of the irrational, the choice to include images of the Holocaust in so many poems is indicative of their immediate impact. There seems to be a correlation between the personal subjective voice and the consideration of this violent epoch in contemporary history. Sylvia Plath (1932–63) and William Heyen (1940–) are exemplars of the confessional school of poetry. Plath and Heyen, from the same generation, emerge as significant poets from the geographic safety of America. Both poets' lives were emotionally and psychologically scarred by the Holocaust, though neither was in any way implicated in the actual event. And though neither is Jewish, their Holocaust poems culminate in identification, and total communion with the tortured and annihilated. These are dark poems of intensity, candor, and dramatic authority.

While most critics claim that the self in Plath, so very personal, swallows up the reality of the Holocaust, A. L. Alvarez (1964, 1969, 1972), literary critic and a close friend of Plath, offers a different reading, as one of the first critics to argue that the poetry of the confessional poets is not simply an art of self-indulgence. Basically, he argues that Plath adopted and internalized the Holocaust in response to a hostile external world; she becomes a "Jew," persecuted and ultimately condemned by an unappeasable, malignant external force. The artist, that is, sacrifices herself for her poetry and offers a personalized vision of history for the world.

In broader terms, Alvarez holds that there is an analogous relationship between the artist and the surrounding society—the artist's suicidal impulses parallel a societal death wish. Like Freud, Alvarez considers man and his civilization torn between the desire for life and the desire for death. The concentration camp Jew epitomizes this dilemma—yearning for life but trapped in a manmade web of death. Plath, who becomes a Jew in "Lady Lazarus" (*The Collected Poems*, 244–47), achieves a kind of psychological verisimilitude with the perils of modern existence. For Alvarez, then, her death wish is indicative not of a disturbed eccentric but of a poet who is peculiarly sensitive to contemporary life.

But many others would disagree, despite the wealth of laudatory reviews. Major controversy has existed since the mid-1960s as to whether Plath's greatness is compromised by a disturbed personality obsessed with self. Beyond the evidence contained in her poems and their interpretation, additional evidence suggests that Plath was not purely egocentric. She said, for example, in a tape that was made to be broadcast (but apparently never was),

> I think my poems immediately came out of sensuous and emotional experiences, ... I think that personal experience is very important, but certainly it shouldn't be . . . a narcissistic experience. I believe it should be relevant, and relevant to the larger things such as Hiroshima and Dachau and so on. (*The Poet Speaks*, 1967, 179–80)

Her husband, Ted Hughes, claimed that "the chemical poisoning of nature, the pile-up of atomic waste, were horrors that pursued her like an illness" (Mazzaro 1979, 228).

Those critics who censure Plath for excessive self-indulgence arrive at their judgments for very different reasons. Thus Alvin Rosenfeld objects to her work on moral grounds, finding in her poems the "imaginative misappropriation of atrocity": bad art. "Daddy," he asserts, is "her boldest effort to manipulate the language of the Holocaust for private ends and, for that reason, her most problematic and distorted poem" (1980, 181, 179). Edward Butscher in his own way echoes Rosenfeld's sentiments: "There is no way that the poetry of an American girl writing from the remote perspective of the 1950s could ever capture the actual brutal reality of the Holocaust" (1976, 327). But then, this would also be true of any young American poet, male or female, Jewish or non-Jewish, writing safely in the 1970s, including Heyen and Snodgrass, who have responded to the Holocaust eloquently and viscerally. Unlike the poets who attempt to capture this history of the Holocaust, Plath has not tried to reimagine or to represent these events in any way. The Holocaust exists for her, not as an experience to be retold or described, but as an event or image available to her (as it was to all who followed) to express another brutal reality, her own internal pain. And

Gloria Young still faults Plath for this use of personal metaphor and finds her poetry most inappropriate (1990, 61).

Defending Plath, Jon Rosenblatt takes issue with the claim that art and life are inseparable in Plath's case and that confession was the ultimate goal of her poetic career. Rosenblatt writes that her poems exist by themselves and can be read and understood in most cases without biographical information. Whereas the term "confessional poetry" suggests that the poet has revealed his actual experience directly to his audience. Plath, according to Rosenblatt, uses elements from her life only as the starting point for imagistic and thematic elaboration (1979, 14, 15). To read Plath in confessional terms is to confuse the point of departure in the poems with their transformed and completed state. Plath thus reorders personal experience into patterns that attain an objective character through repetition, allusion, and symbolic enactment. But Rosenblatt undermines his own line of reasoning with the statement that "the personal elements in her work—the characters who are based upon her friends and relatives; the obsessive personal images of fear, love and death; the autobiographical incidents—serve the same function that the 'impersonal' elements of history, politics and myth do in other poetry." In fact, this only strengthens the case for the "confessional" label.

As noted, Phillips contends that the purpose of confessional poetry is "self-therapy and a certain purgation." Critics have called Plath's work a poetry of annihilation, poetry in which her own suicidal impulses are set against the larger framework of a world that deliberately destroys—the genocide of the Jews, the Kamikazes, Hiroshima. Plath was psychologically disturbed, he contends, and drew "no distinction between her tragedy and those of Auschwitz and Nagasaki" (1973, 8, 128). As for James Young he writes, "She is not a Holocaust poet, simply because she does not write about the Holocaust. She writes about herself figured as a Holocaust Jew, among other contemporary images of suffering" (1987, 117). Plath cannot separate her nature from her poetry.

During the months preceding Plath's suicide, the images of the Holocaust took hold of her imaginative world, and taking root there, evoked in her images of mass suffering in the face of every domestic scene, every daily trauma. It was also in this period that the events of the Holocaust broke into the public domain. Plath was pregnant and moved to Devon from London with her husband between April and December 1961, as the Eichmann trial in Jerusalem riveted public and media attention on the heretofore neglected details of the Holocaust. At the time of Eichmann's conviction in December 1961 and his subsequent execution in April 1962, Plath lived and wrote in their new country home, which she left in September after discovering Hughes's infidelity. At the peak of her unhappiness, in the mid-1960s, Plath wrote her Holocaust poems, "Mary's Song," "Lady Lazarus," and "Daddy." Historical events serve as the objective correlatives for her consciousness as the psychology of the poems parallels the ambiguities in the fascist-victim relationship.

Plath's poems should not be dismissed because she may have suffered from mental illness, however; so did many of her contemporaries, such as Sexton and Lowell. The obsession with the death images of the Holocaust transcends the warped consciousness of one poet. Plath does not confine the subject of the Holocaust to poems written from a particular point of view or on a particular theme, but rather uses it as image and metaphor for the mortal battle between the self and the deadly enemy. Certain image clusters do emerge, however. Most frequently, the annihilation of the Jews is associated with eating. But death is also often associated with the image of the black telephone, "The black telephone's off at the root" ("Daddy," *Ariel*, 69); blackness, "I see your voice / Black and leafy as childhood" ("Little Fugue," *The Collected Poems*, 188, 23–24); . . . black phones on hooks / glittering and digesting / Voicelessness" ("The Munich Mannequins," 263, 24–27); and the Phoenix myth of resurrection, "Out of the ash / I rise with my red hair" ("Lady Lazarus," 247, 82–84). Plath ties the themes of perfection, purity, and Christian salvation to the Holocaust.

In the early poems, the speaker describes something outside herself. In later poems, the speaker considers herself part of the irreducible signs of the liquidation of millions. One of the first poems on this subject, "The Thin People," in *Colossus* (1962), is a meditation on the Holocaust survivors. A father's renunciation of his daughter is equated with the Nazi destruction of Jewry. "The Thin People" are at once the Jews and the ghosts of the past that haunt her. The human landscape imitates Eliot's "The Hollow Men." Here it is not that "We are the stuffed men / We are the hollow men" who are spiritually sterile but that "they [the survivors] are always with us, the thin people / Meager of dimension as the grey people" (1–2). These scapegoats in human history are Christlike, since they are ". . . forever / Drinking vinegar from tin cups: [and] they wore / the insufferable nimbus of the lot-drawn / Scapegoat" (19–22). The Jews, historically persecuted by Christians and blamed for the death of Christ, are compared to Christ, himself a Jew, in his suffering. Another one of the poem's arguments is highly ironic—that of the survivors inexorably intruding into reality and consciousness: "So weedy a race could not remain in dreams, could not remain outlandish victims" (23–24).

"In the contracted country of the head" (25) is compared to an "old woman in her / mud hut / . . . cutting fat meat" (26–27). "Out of the side of the generous moon space when it / Set foot nightly in her yard / Until her knife had pared / The moon to a rind of little light" (29–31). Ironically, starved, ghost-like people are associated with a woman's fatty dinner. Plath continues: they linger "in the sunlit room" (36) and even ". . . the trees flatten / And lose their golden browns / If the thin people simply stand in the forest" (43–45). The poem is ambiguous: it presents the brutality the survivors have suffered, but it also reveals the speaker's resentment at her inability to escape personal awareness of their suffering. Their presence overwhelms her. In later poems the intrusion is no longer simply external, but the victims' experience is transferred to the speaker so that she herself is haunted by guilt and the craving for vengeance. This theme first appears in "The Thin People." The survivors are likened to Christ: they make ". . . the world go thin as a wasp's nest" (46). But unlike Christ, these sufferers find no salvation. And all are guilty; the survival of the remnant is a constant reminder to a complacent world.

In the early poems, Plath is ambivalent not only about the survivors, but also about Christ and the notion of salvation. In "Brasilia," which appeared in *Winter Trees* (published posthumously in 1972), after describing the destruction of masses of people as their bones are "nosing for distances," she invokes a powerful force: "O You who eat / People like light rays," "[leave my son safe,] unredeemed by the dove's annihilation, / The glory / The power, the glory" (17–23). To be unredeemed, ironically, is to be saved. That God is evil, another reading, is also ironic: the bondage of human beings and all organic life to death signals, inevitably, a perpetual war against the nonliving universe. For Plath, God is man's greatest enemy, because he either controls or is the exterior inanimate blackness. The speaker assumes the fearful universal role of the mother begging for her child's life as she addresses God—a collective role rather than an individual one.

"Mary's Song" from *Ariel* (1966), Plath's best known book, also presents an equivocal speaker. Perhaps the title suggests the poem expresses the thoughts of the Virgin Mary recounting the destruction of the Jews in images suggestive of both medieval scourges and the Holocaust. The poem employs fire as its central image. It begins, "The Sunday lamb crackles in its fat" (1), and moves to "The same fire / Melting the tallow heretics, / Ousting the Jews. / Their thick palls float / Over the cicatrix of Poland" (6–10). The speaker continues, "Mouth-ash, ash of eye. They settle. On the high / Precipice / That emptied one man into space. / The ovens glowed like heavens incandescent" (14–18). The speaker has no actual role in the slaughter in Poland, but symbolically she resides at its center: "It is a heart, this holocaust I walk in, / O golden child the world will kill and eat" (19–21). As in "Brasilia," the Christian imagery is ambiguous. It may be argued that Plath is suggesting that the Jews, like Christ, were sacrificed, for the Holocaust is compared to a heart, an emblem for Christ's sacrifice. But there are no images of salvation; the image of fire (often used to represent the Paraclete) here symbolizes the Holocaust and man's killing Christ rather than Christ's saving man. In this way the Christian concept of sacrifice is rendered ironic. Or, as James Young suggests, it is not the personal pain of the victims that Plath draws upon, or the mass murder, or the history of Jewish persecution, but rather an idea of victimhood and sacrifice of innocents that constitutes the core of her figure (1987, 133). She did not suffer "as a Jew" so much as she represented her suffering through her own grasp of how (even why) Jews suffered.

Sacrifice, devouring, persecution, the randomness and violence of contemporary life—these are major themes in "Mary's Song." Christ is alluded to in "The Sunday Lamb [that] crackles in its fat" (1), and in the ending, "O golden child, the world will kill and eat" (21). The way to salvation is the total annihilation and consumption of Christ. Plath also associates the destruction of the Jews with images of devouring. Therefore she associates the sacrifice of Christ with the death of the Jews not only through the juxtaposition of heart and Holocaust, but also in their sharing this consumption imagery. There is also the possibility that in treating Christ as a Jew, rather than as a Christian savior, the Christian myth becomes an early example of the horror of the commodification of humanity. In other poems the speaker is sacrificed, though what is accomplished by these acts of oblation is not clear.

Jerome Mazzaro contends that Plath's concept of history, like Yeats's, is characterized by stages and that purgation is necessary for the movement from one to the other. The Jews in "Mary's Song," according to Mazzaro,

> are presented in language that deliberately recalls the "sages standing in God's holy fire" of Yeats's "Sailing to Byzantium" (1927). They burn until their being made translucent comes to be equated to Christ, and the speaker, like the Communion Host, is killed and eaten. The "meal is possible" Plath maintains, because the world has not had its heart consumed away. The residual heart is the oven and holocaust through which the Jews and the poem's speaker must both proceed. (1979, 230)

Mazzaro's explanation of the meal is not grounded in the poem however. It is sufficient to say that these sacrifices do represent a kind of Yeatsian purgation; but without salvation or an affirmation, purgation is meaningless.

Another critic, Caroline Barnard, does not stretch the poem as far as Mazzaro, nor does she see the influence of Yeats. She agrees, however, that Plath is prophetic, and in "Mary's Song" the devouring of Christ "suggests the sacrament of communion" (1978, 83). In addition, she argues, many of the later poems, often masochistic in tone, intimate that through the speaker's sacrifice will come purgation and then improvement. This view, though defensible, has its pitfalls. For example, the imagery and diction in "Mary's Song" suggest an ironic reading, so that instead of an image of communion and grace, the reader is left figuratively holding a Host that will be fried in its own grease and devoured. But Butscher persists in saying that this vision is necessarily Christian: like the victims of Hiroshima, Plath suffers innocently for the crimes of others (Young 1988, 322, quoting Butscher). That is, she suffers, martyrlike, Christlike, and in her mind, Jewlike, for others' sins. Through this figure, Plath's Holocaust seems to imply a kind of Calvary. But by making herself the sacrifice in "this holocaust I walk in," she also betrays her own understanding of the figure of Jewish suffering itself. Again, it is a particularly Christian remembrance of events automatically figured by her idea of a holocaust as a sacrifice, however innocent. So even as she uses a knowledge of the Holocaust to figure her pain, her own victimhood, this knowledge itself is necessarily configured in an essentially Christian frame. This is the mournful message of the poem: the meaning of the Holocaust lies in the contrast between its horror and its lack of consequence.

A number of poems in *Ariel* present a speaker, tormented and suffering, who is sacrificed and thereby purified. In "Getting There" the speaker describes her journey to a concentration camp. The wheels of the train appall her, and she asks: "What do wheels eat?" (13). Then, "How far is it?" (34) and "Will there be fire, will there be bread?" (20). These images—fire and bread—play off against each other. Fire symbolizes devouring, but it is also the catalyst for the burning of incense, and bread is consumed in communion with Christ. Both are inextricably tied to purification and are complementary elements in the sacrificial act. Plath also treats two other ideas as complementary—birth and death. Stretchers for the dead "are cradles." The speaker, apparently on the verge of death, concludes, "And I stepping from this skin / Of old bandages, boredoms, old faces / Step to you from the black car of Lethe / Pure as baby" (65–68). Just as these complements are well balanced, so too are image and theme. The poem supports two interpretations: its subject is the persona's self-concept, but is also death at the camps.

Perfection and purity are associated with Nazism in "The Munich Mannequins," also in *Ariel*. The poem begins, "Perfection is terrible, it cannot have children. / Cold as snow breath, it tamps the womb" (1–2). Perfection is associated with menses—the continuity of human life as well as its antithesis—when the moons are unloosed ". . . month after month, to no purpose" (5). The women in the camps who serviced the pleasure of the commandant and others were medicated so that they did not menstruate during the entire time of their incarceration. The "tamping" negates the potential for creativity and fecundity, rendering the woman as fruitful as a barren mannequin or corpse. The poem concludes with the image of ". . . black phones on hooks / Glittering / Glittering and digesting / Voicelessness" suggestive of death and infertility. As the Nazis sterilized their victims, the fascist birthplace, Munich, also became deadly and lifeless.

The image of the telephone also appears in "Daddy," Plath's most widely discussed and controversial poem. "Daddy" and "Little Fugue" deal with Plath's relationship to her father, and images of the Holocaust dominate both poems. "Daddy" in particular reveals a love-hate relationship and seems to be based on the poet's autobiography. Plath's father, who died when she was a child, was a German American, and her mother very possibly part Jewish. The love-hate relationship between daughter and father defines the role of each and is analogous to the relationship between the Nazi and Jew, where the oppressor's role is defined by his victim and vice versa. The dynamics of this relationship also parallel that between vampire and prey, the image that concludes the poem. The relationship between the speaker and her father, resembling a deadly marriage, is horrible yet almost mystical. Addressing her father, the speaker says:

> I made a model of you,
> A man in black with a Meinkampf look
>
> And a love of the rack and screw.
> And I said I do, I do.

> So daddy, I'm finally through.
> The black telephone's off at the root,
>
> . . . .
>
> If I've killed one man, I've killed two—
> The vampire who said he was you
>
> . . . .
>
> There's a stake in your fat black heart.
>
> . . . .
>
> Daddy, daddy, you bastard, I'm through.
>   (64–69, 71–72, 75, 80)

Some critics have argued that the speaker changes places with her father as she becomes a Nazi and he a Jew. This interpretation seems to be undercut by the ambiguity of the last word of the poem: "through." She is through with the poem, yet more importantly she is through living because the vampire has been destroyed; their relationship was symbiotic in a sick way. He tortured her, and she adored it. The madness of their relationship, the subject of the piece, parodies the Nazi-Jewish one. The insanity is accentuated both through Plath's choice of images and in the driving overuse of end-line rhymes that are inconsistent from stanza to stanza. The "oo" sound dominates the poem. The lines of the first stanza end in "do," "shoe," "foot," "white," and "Achoo." "Jew" ends three out of six lines in a middle stanza, and in practically every stanza "you" is an end word at least twice. This repetition affects the poem's tone so that the speaker, aside from the relationship she describes, sounds demented. Plath thereby suggests that this particular daughter-father relationship and the Nazi-Jew relationship are alike in their sickness. The poetic dissection of her personal pain illustrates the confessional aspect critics have found objectionable.

In "Daddy" Plath treats some of the perverted qualities of the Nazi mind, such as the meticulous care taken in the destruction and elimination of human bodies and the use of human bodies as resources. Extracting the gold fillings from the dead, making soap from human fat, and finally the bizarre storage of the shoes and hair of the dead are overt physical signs of the Nazi madness. "Daddy" opens with the image of a black shoe that apparently stands for the speaker's father. Addressing it, she begins, "You do not do, you do not do / Any more black shoe" (1–2). The shoe is also a symbol of the speaker's confinement: at the end of the poem she will surrender that shoe which she has "lived in like a foot" when she is "through." Here lies one of the main ironies of the poem: being free of restriction and of the shoe implies death. The speaker, like the Jew in the camp, is trapped, release is found only in suicide.

For Sophie B. Blaydes (1977, 497) the rhythm suggests a nursery rhyme—we are in the world of the old lady who lived in a shoe, a world where one's father is "Daddy." But "black shoe" quickly becomes part of the sinister Nazi motif that builds throughout the poem. The black shoe—black is Plath's emblem for death or evil—is the fascist boot, the Nazi shoes, the black goose-steppers, the black shirts. The Fuehrer is that father who, even dead, has controlled her for thirty years. Seen this way the black shoe becomes a metaphor for her past, her suffocated spirit, or for the Prussian / German parent she cannot escape. The black shoe, also a metaphor for fascism, focuses the argument of the poem. Plath selects words with Germanic sounds. Even though she begins with a kind of nursery innocence with "Achoo," a word that carries a double suggestion. It is the child's word for sneeze, but it also hints at the heavier, more sinister sounds used in the poem: "Ach, du," "Ich, ich, ich," "luftwaffe," "Panzerman," "Mein-kampf," "Achtung."

Abandoning her childlike tone, the poet becomes a Jew, and the basic metaphor becomes threatening, more violent. The figurative language includes "Polack," "barb wire snare," "Dachau, Auschwitz, Belsen," "gypsy," and "Jew," "Jew," "Jew." As we move with her through the poem and observe her as she assumes these identities, Plath becomes a victim, without will, without identity. She was abandoned by her father; the Jews were abandoned by the Fuehrer. As they were destroyed by him, their father, so she continues the parallel; she too is carried off by a wave of murder and destruction. Plath herself emphasized the confessional nature of "Daddy": "The poem is spoken by a girl with an Electra complex. Her father died while she thought he was God. Her case is complicated by the fact that her father was also a Nazi and her mother very possibly part Jewish. In the daughter, or in her imagination, the two strains marry and paralyze each other—she has to act

out the awful little allegory once over before she is free of it"
(introduction to *The Collected Poems,* 65).

By the end of the poem she becomes violent as she rejects
and kills, but her actions are part of a mass response in which
she loses her individuality. The violence is propelled by the
incantatory tone and form of the poem—she is part of a self-
less motion that builds hypnotically with frenzy, until she is
driven to an act of passion. At the poem's end she joins a
village in a primitive ritual. This last stanza is repeated in full:

> There's a stake in your fat black heart
> And the villagers never liked you,
> They are dancing and stomping on you.
> They always knew it was you,
> Daddy, daddy, you bastard, I'm through.
>   (76–80)

Thus the poem concludes without hope—unless death is
hope. The counterpoint of the child's cry with its bitter accusation is hideous, startling, compelling. The conclusion not only
misappropriates the historical event but also mitigates Plath's
authenticity. She has assumed the role of a concentration
camp victim with all of the attendant racial and psychological
credentials—but she has not earned them.

In "Little Fugue," addressed to her father, the speaker refers
to him as "A yew hedge of orders" (25) and describes herself
and him as a series of unconnected parts. She says of herself,
"These are my fingers" (51), and of him, "You had one leg, and
a Prussian mind" (44). Plath's father, Otto Plath, of Prussian
descent, was born in 1885. He came to America when he was
fifteen. He died when his daughter was nine. Had he remained
in Germany, he could have become a Nazi. By implication her
father is a Nazi in this poem. Otto Plath's left leg (to which the
poet refers) was amputated before he died, and when "death
opened, like a black tree, blackly" (48), it leaves only a black
frightening silence, similar to the absence of a limb.

The poem contains no direct references to the camps; they
are suggested instead by the standard death images that control the poem: cold, dark clouds, the black yew tree. Both are
often associated with her father. The father is black, authori-
tarian, Germanic. The daughter, faced with a negative image,

declares: "I am guilty of nothing" (28). She then presents her father as a black yew tree:

> I see your voice
> Black and leafy, as in my childhood,
> A yew hedge of orders,
> Gothic and barbarous, pure German.
> Dead men cry from it.
>
> (23–27)

The poem opens, "The Yew's black fingers wag; / Cold clouds go over" (1–2), and the father's blindness is then compared to the "featurelessness of that cloud" (6). Music is also associated with her father and the image of the tree and the cloud. "He could hear Beethoven; / Black yew, white cloud" (13–14) begins one of the early stanzas, proposing that her father, like some of the Nazi leaders, valued the perfection and drama of music. The conclusion of the poem focuses on the speaker:

> She survived the while,
> Arranging my morning.
> These are my fingers, this my baby.
> The clouds are a marriage dress, of that pallor.
>
> (49–52)

The speaker's emotional obsession with her father is no less evident here than in "Daddy," because its images, dark, Germanic and harsh, are also associated with her father and death.

These images, central to "Little Fugue," had similar associations in "Todesfuge" [Fugue of Death] by Paul Celan, a camp survivor who also committed suicide. He describes sunrise in the camps as the "Black milk of day break" (1). The focus then shifts to the Nazi commander, who "whistles his Jews forth" (8) out of the barracks to perform in the camp orchestra (Hamburger and Middleton 1962, 318–21). The commander shouts to the musicians: "Stroke darker the strings and as smoke you shall climb to the sky / Then you'll have a grave in the clouds." As in Plath's poem, blackness, clouds, and music evoke the Nazi death force.

The similarity between a poem written by an American living in London in the mid-1960s and one by a camp survivor

causes one to think. The images created by the American
poet's imagination and by the memory of a camp victim overlap strikingly. It is entirely possible that Plath had read
Celan's poem because it was published in 1962. But even if
she had read "Todesfuge," it is not likely that she consciously
tried to imitate it; more likely these images and associations in
Celan's poem struck in her a broad, empathic note. Assuredly,
the Holocaust weighed heavily on the consciousness of the
young American writer.

"Lady Lazarus," another of Plath's poems in this vein, is
about suicide and is like "Daddy" in its excessive and inconsistent end-rhyming. The middle two stanzas end in "hell," "real,"
"call," "cell," "put," and "theatrical" (*The Collected Poems,* 244,
45–50). One of the main subjects is the speaker's view of her
body as an object she describes part by part. "I am," she says,
"A sort of walking miracle, my skin / Bright as Nazi lampshade, / My right foot / A paperweight, / My face featureless,
fine / Jew linen" (4–9). Toward the end of the poem, the
speaker describes herself in similar terms while addressing a
sinister force:

> Herr Doktor.
> So, Herr Enemy.
> I am your opus,
> I am your valuable,
> The pure golden baby
> Ash, ash—
>
> . . . .
> . . . There is nothing there—
> A cake of soap,
> A wedding ring,
> A gold filling.
> (23–28, 30–33)

Thus the speaker defines herself not only in the frightening
images of what the Nazis appropriated from the dead, but also
in terms of the ultimate result of their handiwork—burning
linen to ash. Twentieth-century historical atrocities become
emblems of death. The speaker's bizarre confrontation with
death is conveyed through the juxtaposition of her reduction
into a series of objects with the incomprehensibly huge num-

ber of people murdered and turned into commodities. "Lady Lazarus," like "Daddy," is addressed to an evil force, although here it is not clear that it is the speaker's father. As in "Daddy," there is a shift in the speaker's attitude toward this figure; first he is God, then he is the Devil: "Herr God, Herr Lucifer / . . . Beware / . . . / I rise with my red hair / And I eat men like air" (34–38). The obtrusive rhyme calls attention to the lines and emphasizes the speaker's madness. The surprise ending is consonant with the contradictions in the poem: while living, the speaker is dying; she is pure baby turned to death object; God and Lucifer are one. The poem embodies a series of opposites, and the reader has no time to pause or draw a single conclusion. Both reader and poet are driven—without rest, impelled by contradiction, tormented like the souls in Dante's *Purgatorio.* Four basic sequences of images define the lady's identity: she begins as cloth or material (lampshade, linen, napkin); in the middle she is only body (knees, skin and bone, hair); toward the end, she becomes a physical object (gold, ash, a cake of soap); and finally, she is resurrected as a red-haired demon.

Each of these states is dramatically connected to an observer or observers through direct address: first to her unnamed "enemy"; then, to the "gentlemen and ladies"; next to the Herr Dokter; and, finally, to Herr God and Herr Lucifer cited above. In addressing these "audiences," Plath is able to characterize Lady Lazarus's fragmented identities with great precision. A passage near the end of the poem incorporates the transition from a sequence of body images (scars-heart-hair) to a series of physical images (opus-valuable-gold baby) as it shifts its address from the voyeuristic crowd to the Nazi Doktor:

> And there is a charge, a very large charge,
> For a word or a touch
> Or a bit of blood
>
> Or a piece of my hair or my clothes.
> So, so, Herr Doktor.
> So, Herr Enemy.

I am your opus,
I am your valuable,
The pure gold baby

That melts to shriek.

                              (61–70)

With this inventive language Plath creates an oral medium
appropriate to the distorted mental states of the speaker. The
sexual pun on "charge" (discharge, ejaculate) in the first line;
the bastardization of German ("Herr Enemy"); the combination of Latinate diction ("opus") and colloquial phrasing
("charge," "So, so")—these linguistic elements reveal a character grotesquely split into multiple warring selves. Lady
Lazarus is a different person for each of her audiences, and yet
none of her identities is bearable for her. For the Nazi Doktor,
she is a Jew, whose body must be burned; for the "peanut-
crunching crowd," she is a stripteaser; for the medical audience she is a wonder, whose scars and heartbeat are astonishing; for the religious audience, she is a miraculous figure,
whose hair and clothes are as valuable as saints' relics. And
when she turns to her audience in the middle of the poem to
describe her career in suicide, she becomes a self-conscious
performer. Each of her deaths, she says, is done "excep-
tionally well. / I do it so it feels like hell" (44–55). When the
lady undergoes total immolation of self and body, she emerges
in a demonic form. The "Doktor" burns her down to ash, and
she is reborn. She is the phoenix, a pure spirit rising against
the imprisoning others around her: gods, doctors, men, and
Nazis. After an ordeal of mutilation, torture, and immolation,
this translation of the self into spirit is a kind of triumph.

While the poet couches the speaker's predicament in terms
of the images of the Holocaust, the quest for a reasonable
explanation for the Nazi-Jew relationship leads into a similar
tailspin. Although the poem is ostensibly about the speaker's
suicidal tendencies, it focuses on her being driven by a mad
force, like the one behind the Nazi machine and its victims.
Finally, "Lady Lazarus," like "Daddy," incorporates historical
material into incantatory, metaphoric, and imagistic patterns. These elements of Plath's method have generated much
discussion, including the charge leveled by Irving Howe and

others that her references to Nazism and to Jewishness are not authentic (1974, 92). Yet it is possible to view these allusions to historical events as part of the speaker's fragmented identity, allowing Plath to portray a kind of eternal victim. The title of the poem lays the groundwork for a semicomic historical and cultural allusiveness. The lady is a legendary figure, a sufferer, who has endured it all. Thus can Plath include among Lady Lazarus's experiences the greatest contemporary examples of brutality and persecution—the sadistic medical experiments on Jews by Nazi doctors and the Nazis' use of their victims' bodies in the production of lampshades and other objects. But these allusions are not meant to establish a realistic historic norm in the poem any more than the allusions to the striptease are intended to establish a realistic social context. Rather the references in the poem—biblical, historical, political, personal—draw the reader into the center of a personality and its defining mental processes. And the reality of the poem lies in the convulsions of the narrating consciousness as the drama of external persecution, self-destructiveness, and renewal, with its horror and its grotesque comedy, which is played out through social and historical contexts that symbolize the inner struggle of Lady Lazarus.

The claim that Plath misuses particular historical experiences is therefore open to challenge. Hers is a contemporary consciousness obsessed with historical and personal demons. The demonic character of the Nazi Doktor and of the risen Lady Lazarus is more central to the poem's tone and intent than is the historicity of these figures. Thus setting this demonization against the backdrop of Nazism, Plath universalizes a personal conflict. The fact that Plath herself was not Jewish has no bearing on the legitimacy of her use of a Jewish persona—the Holocaust serves her metaphorically on many levels. "Lady Lazarus" is one of the most powerful and successful of the poems in which life's enemy appears as the sadistic force of Nazism.

It is well to consider, as Alvarez reminds us, that the "Holocaust Jew" was not Plath's only figure for victimhood (1969, 17). Mixing her figures in an early version of "Lady Lazarus," Plath also drew upon the Japanese victims of the atomic bomb. It was not for any actual correspondence or even any implied parallel between these kinds of suffering, but as Alvarez suggests in the case of the Japanese, it may have been for the rhyme; the figure of victimized Japanese was presumed already to be part of an available figural lexicon, which she now chose for the right sound:

> Gentleman, ladies
> These are my hands,
> My knees
> I may be skin and bone,
> I may be Japanese.
> (quoted by Alvarez, 17)

"Why Japanese?" Alvarez prodded her. "Do you just need the rhyme? Or are you trying to hitch an easy lift by dragging in the atomic victims? If you're going to use this kind of violent material, you've got to play it cool." "She argued back sharply, but later, when the poem was finally published after her death the line had gone" (1969, 17). As Alvarez acknowledges in retrospect, despite the fact that this line seems to diminish the poem, she did need the rhyme, even if her allusion to the Japanese was not quite relevant. Form and sound may have influenced her choice of words at this point, as well as the meaning created in such allusions.

Both the Japanese and Jewish references recall massive, anonymous suffering from the war period, an era contemporary with her own life. Her historical memory consisted of both history books and classical poetry, as well as images from the mass media, newsreels, newspapers, and radio, which invent public figures and icons by saturating the imagination with them. It may have been important for Plath to draw on events from her own era, if not from the experience of her own life. In this way, she shared the age of victimhood, victimized by modern life at large, as the Jews and Japanese had been victimized by specific events.

Throughout her poetry, her focus on the Holocaust is expressed in the signs of death, the human remains, the crematory smoke, and the infernal trains, the mechanical object in the procedure that brought inmates' destruction. Plath's poems employing this imagery change over the course of her work. The images become increasingly internalized so that they are eventually integrated into the persona's consciousness. In early poems such as "The Thin People," Plath's main subject is the survivors and a conscious response to them. In *Ariel*, which includes poems written in a desperate rush late at night a few months before she died, the poet creates a persona and dramatizes the relationship between herself and her father, her relationship to death, and finally her relationship to madness in the Nazi-Jew nexus.

Via the emotional load of Holocaust symbols in her poetry, Sylvia Plath came to regard herself as "an imaginary Jew from the concentration camps of the Mind" (Alvarez, 1969, 19). Howe is harsh in his moral and literary judgment about Plath's use of these images:

> That dreadful events in the individual's psyche may approximate the sufferings of a people is indeed possible, but again it might be good to remember that Jews in the camps didn't merely "suffer": They were gassed and burned. Anyone—poet, novelist, commentator—who uses images of the camps in order to evoke personal traumas ought to have a very precise sense of the enormity of what he or she is suggesting. He or she ought to have enough moral awareness and literary control to ask whether the object and the image have any congruence.
>
> Is it possible that the condition of the Jews in the camps can be duplicated? Yes. . . . But it is decidedly unlikely that it was duplicated in a middle-class family living in Wellesley, Massachusetts, even if it had a very bad daddy indeed.
>
> To condone such a confusion is to delude ourselves as to the nature of our personal miseries and their relationship to—or relative magnitude when placed against—the most dreadful event in the history of mankind. (1979, 12)

What then are the rightful and credible claims that can be made upon the memory and the images of the Holocaust? On the one hand, Plath's use of those symbols is testimony to the widespread diffusion of the Holocaust images, their common currency in Western culture. On the other hand, as Ezrahi (1980, 214) so poignantly reminds us, her appropriation of them to express personal suffering represents a kind of devaluation of both the particularity and the enormity of the historical experience. However, it is well to consider that those

self-appointed guardians of the culture and destiny of a mar-
tyred people—who insist on considering the Holocaust as a
unique horror, totally unrelated to any other acts of organized
brutality or to any form of personal suffering—are in fact
denying the legitimacy of the very process by which events of
the past become the shared heritage of humanity.

Yet when the vocabulary of the history of 1933–45 is applied
to any situation of intense emotional or social privation, the
enormity and the moral inadmissibility of the concentration
camp experience are diluted, even as widespread symbolic
assimilation of the experience is achieved. As a poet whose
world is expressed in terms of a God-Lucifer creator, of a love-
hate relationship with her father, and of the conflicting desires
to live and to die, Plath is obviously tormented by extremes of
oppressive dilemmas, unable to make peace with herself,
caught between passivity and aggression. She seems to have
intuited parallels between the madness in her consciousness
and that of the death factories where humankind was busy
killing and being killed. Their lives were ironically affirmed by
the machine of death. Similarly, Sylvia Plath busied herself
considering death and was ultimately successful in finding it.
Hypothesizing, she was her own Nazi executioner, gassing
herself in her own gas chamber on 16 February 1963 in her
London flat.

Writing of the horrific images of Sylvia Plath's poetic "over-
draft," George Steiner asks:

> Does any writer other than an actual survivor have the right to put
> on this death rig? Auschwitz and Belsen lodge at the center of our
> current lives and sensibilities like the energized, malignant void of
> a Gnostic vision of damnation. The imagination touches on them
> at its peril. . . . What extraterritorial right had Sylvia Plath to draw
> on the reserves of animate horror in the ash and the children's
> shoes? Do any of us have license to locate our personal disasters,
> raw as these may be, in Auschwitz? (305)

This is really not the problem for viewing Plath's Holocaust
poetry as specious. It is the conversion of personal pain to
larger crimes against humanity that disturbs us. Plath thus
evokes, at least to me, an ambivalent reaction—dismay that
she compares her paternal impasse with the Holocaust, an

event so much larger than herself, but acceptance that her poems are better than no word at all.

Despite Steiner's contention that the notion of Holocaust poetry is an oxymoron, William Heyen, though not a survivor, has a compelling right, a qualified affirmation to his specialized poetry. He, like Plath, is a confessional poet and a non-Jew, but he comes to write Holocaust poetry with a different agenda. Born in Brooklyn in 1940 to German parents, he has researched documentary evidence and fused it with autobiography and family history. He had two German uncles who died in battle for Hitler and a Nazi father-in-law who had worked for Goebbels in the Propaganda Ministry in Berlin. Thus his biographical link to the Holocaust, unlike Plath's, is authentic—which should merit Steiner's approval.

In *Depth of Field* (1970), a brilliant first volume with a broad, coherent, and deeply moving design, Heyen begins in a confessional vein, confronting in separate poems the images of two uncles, one a German infantry man, the other the pilot of a Stuka, killed in the Second World War. The poet is driven to wrathful confrontation with his personal heritage, but is mollified when he finds that there is a common heritage. Thus the uncles, Wilhelm and Hermann, foreshadow the poet's more complete exploration of his German ties in his later poems. Heyen addresses his uncles directly. As images of Wilhelm's life and sudden death are cinematically spun on the screen of the page, Heyen writes in *Erika* (1984), "Wilhelm, your face is a shadow / under your helmet" (pt. 4, l. 1). To Hermann, he says, "My Nazi uncle, you received the letters / My father still talks and wonders about—/ the ones in which he told you to bail out / over England and plead insanity" (8–11). Heyen probes the characteristic confessional theme of man's animality and its consequences:

> Because the cause is never just,
> Rest, my twenty-year-old uncle, rest.
> All the oppressors are oppressed
> The dog's heart is his only beast.
> . . . These are all your wars. . . .
> Asia trembles. You are never dead.
> (pt. 3, ll. 1–2, 7–8; pt. 4, ll. 9–10,
> "For Wilhelm Heyen")

In these moving pieces, Heyen calls upon memory to help him explore his relationship to his family. Even in their differences he claims identity, finding his place among other Heyens. But even as Robert von Hallberg concedes (1980, 121) Heyen's personal stake in his subject, he nonetheless still finds Heyen guilty of posturing, his lineage notwithstanding. In *Erika* ("Letter to Hansjörg Greiner"), the poet writes to his dead father-in-law:

> Has no one written you? Then I. You're
> Another one. I don't know how
> to talk to, but have to.
> (pt. 2, ll. 1–3)

Personal destiny, in Heyen's sense, resides in the ordinary, in the same way that Eichmann was perceived to be an ordinary murderer (1980, 121). Whether or not he agrees intellectually with Hannah Arendt's controversial thesis on the banality of evil (1963) is not relevant. In it Arendt claimed that European Jewish leadership had failed, that the victims were partly responsible for their own slaughter by their failure to resist against the Nazis, and that Eichmann represents the "banality of evil." Emotionally certainly, Heyen does not seem to accept this proposition. Perhaps this accounts for the energy behind his Holocaust poems and his relentless drive to portray who the victims really were outside of his German uncles. There are times when the poet's presence in his poems is felt as an intrusion, before we are fully aware of why he is doing all this. This is apparent in this capsule apologia, also from "Letter to Hansjörg Greiner" in *Erika:*

> Born in America of German immigrants
> a mother who dismisses guilt,
> a father whose two brothers
> died on your side,
> whose graves he has never seen,
> all these years to hover speechless
> over the bed of his four sons to try
> to make them over to Wilhelm and Hermann
> in the gracious dark—.
> I have a stake in this.
> (1–10)

Michael McFee reacts: "No one would deny Heyen his 'stake,' his involuntary involvement in the War, but the specter of his father hovering 'in the gracious dark,' trying to reconcile a quartet of sons to his Nazi brothers is pathetic. It may be accurate as fact, but as poetry it overcompensates for the guilt Heyen feels" (1982, 161). However, the reason for this sort of thing is important. For at its source Heyen's motive in writing Holocaust poetry is to expiate his own sense of personal guilt over the atrocities.

As a child during the war Heyen found swastikas painted on his family's home on Long Island. "I remember the persecution we suffered because we were Germans, the swastikas my father scraped from our windows or painted over when they appeared suddenly in the mornings on our steps or doors" (*The Georgia Review*, 206). Then as a young man he became obsessed with the Nazi extermination of the Jews and the realization "that people of my own blood flushed the ashes of millions of people into the pond at Auschwitz" (1995, 123). William Meredith is especially perceptive about *The Swastika Poems:*

> A number of poets in the middle generation poets between 30 and 40—seem to face a special predicament: They are not at home in recent history. It is not their nightmare (as it is the familiar nightmare of those of us who lived as adults through World War II), it is their parents' nightmare. To come of age as poets, they need to imagine their parents' history and to establish a continuity with an older violence . . . they need to come to grips with their heritage of violence, now that they are mature. Further acts of praise and insight, further poems, depend on this. (1977, 26)

Impelled by his German background, Heyen confronts in *The Swastika Poems* (1977) and in much of his other poetry the hell created by his father's generation and takes himself and his readers through a rite of passage—facing the nightmare of the Holocaust. The issue of Gentile-Jewish relations and Heyen's exploration of its meaning for Gentiles in a post-Auschwitz world looms large in his consciousness and informs his writing. Memory, too, propels his poetry. His verse techniques mimic riddles, biblical poetic incantations, and utterly bewildered and bewildering discourse. One of his sc lected epigraphs is a passage from Susan Sontag's preface to *The Swastika Poems*. She says of the atrocities: "Ultimately, the only response is to continue to hold the event in the mind, to remember it." The other quotation from Heinrich Heine calls forth the dream of "a lovely fatherland" and "a German kiss" on his brow. But he awoke and the dream was over for the poet as well as for the rest of humankind. But memory is not the only response; for Heyen there is this poetry, a magnificent vessel for holding memory. With his multiplicity of perspectives Heyen orchestrates an anthem that gives voice to victim and perpetrator alike—to all voices. And it is the responsibility of the reader to listen to them. Heyen's hope is that through the ritual singing of his verse, he can somehow save himself and us from the heavy moral strain of our collective past: "Reader," he says in "A Visit to Belzec," "all words are a dream. / You have wandered into mine." He dreams of peace, innocence, and salvation:

> This happened only once, but happened:
> One Belzec morning, a boy in deathline
> composed a poem and spoke it.
> The words seemed true, and saved him.
> The guard's mouth fell open to wonder.
>   (Section 5, ll. 5–9)

The specter of Walt Whitman emerges in both Heyen's poetry and random writings. "Although the sources and strategies of poetry must necessarily be oblique, on a slant, somewhat mysterious, indirect, I have always believed, simply, what Walt Whitman said—that 'literature is a means of morally influencing the world'" (1976, 103). Whitman's ghost is not manifested in parallel imagery and meter in Heyen's poetry, but rather is felt in the poet's exploration of nature and man, in his view of the relationship between language and reality, and finally in the heightened sense of his role as a poet. The Whitman legacy is palpable.

But Heyen is painfully cognizant of the enormous historical atrocity that comes between Whitman and himself. In the essay "What Do the Trees Say" (1976), he speaks of one of the death camps: "We would never be the same. It might be that today, with our knowledge, none of us can enter totally or even partly for very long the transcendentalist faith in the beneficence of man, God, the world that Whitman felt" (102). Heyen, admittedly, in an interview with Stanley Rubin, said that the Holocaust is "at the center of everything" he knows and feels "about this century" and "about himself" (Heyen and Rubin 1978, 41). Within a period of a few years, Heyen published *The Swastika Poems* (1977) and two short chap books, *My Holocaust Songs* (1980) and *The Trains* (1981). This productivity has continued with the publication of *The City Parables* (1980), *Lord Dragonfly: Five Sequences* (1981), *Erika: Poems of the Holocaust* (1984), (1991), and *Falling from Heaven: Holocaust Poems of a Jew and a Gentile* with Louis Daniel Brodsky (1991) . Many of the earlier poems reappear in the later volumes. To Heyen, the Holocaust is not a metaphor for something else; it is an entity unto itself, a mystery, an obsession. All of the volumes plot the imaginative course of one man's emotional descent into the Nazi hell.

Heyen is consumed by his subject, by the morality of writing on the subject: "To write a bad poem about the Holocaust" "seemed/seems to me somehow worse than writing a bad poem about something else," he says to Rubin (39). As an artist writing on the suffering of others, he feels that he "was making morally important choices each time in regard to what poem followed what poem" in the book (43).

In this key interview with Rubin, Heyen's remarks show that he is capable of relieving the heavy burden of moral responsibility by manipulating the subject of his poems, the Holocaust, one speaker's reaction to it, and the reader's potential reaction to these poems. In discussing the speaker in his poems as though he were another person, Heyen discourages the reader from taking the poems to represent the poet's conclusions on the Holocaust. His purpose, unlike Pound's or Eliot's, is not to present his personal criticism of Western culture through his poetry. Instead, he treats the poems as though someone else had written them and makes the same kind of observations readers might make about the speaker and his subject. He says, "As I see the poems now . . . they are primarily about the speaker. My interest is in him . . . during the course of the book he strains to find out who he is" (37).

The poems thus attempt to explore, almost equally, the meaning of the Holocaust and the speaker's reaction to it; they seem to have a preconscious source. Heyen notes: "Holocaust poems come to me, and I write them, and they exhaust me. I think, for a time, I'm free of all that forever. And then, maybe even when I'm in the middle of other work, that rhythm begins again" (37).

Heyen is plagued by the possibility that the narrator can go either way—wearing jack boots or wearing the striped rags of the death camps. His own potential for evil obsesses him, and he fears becoming lax in his personal assessment of the situation. "I am tall, I was a blonde youth, an athlete—if I had been born in Germany in 1920 instead of Brooklyn in 1940, might I not have aspired to membership in the SS?" (1982, 128). He can never know with certainty what he might have done had he been there in 1934 or 1943. George Clare's *Last Waltz in Vienna* (1982) tells the story of the rise and fall of the Clare family from 1842 to 1942, of the seductiveness of the scene upon his young sensibilities. "The men themselves were tall, smart and polished . . . the young and handsome soldiers of the Wehrmacht. If I had not been born a Jew, could I not have been a Nazi at seventeen? Could I have been one of them, attracted by the power and glory of Hitler's Reich? I was racially immune to Nazism, but to this day my judgment about those youths who succumbed to Hitler is beclouded by the memory of my own sensations on that day" (90). Heyen has said ("What Do the Trees Say?"), echoing his lectures, that *Erika*, which includes *The Swastika Poems*, came to him in dreams, and the fragmented, vivid, unwilled flash of these voices and scenes confirms that origin. His dream simply will not go away.

The first speaker in "Three Relations" is a German who is aware of the evil of Nazism and fearful of the fuehrer. The time is 1935, and our speaker sees Hitler even then as the "incarnation of death"; those who worshiped him "cried for Death." But during the rally our citizen feels, in his dread and fear, helpless:

> His look froze my heart,
> and I raised my arm,

> and I cried Heil.
> (Section 1, ll. 22–24)

This is the testimony of the skeptic in the revival meeting, making eye contact with the charismatic leader, finding that he has spoken in tongues. So, too, the German discovers himself succumbing to forces he hardly understands. That is both the monstrousness and the thrill of such primitive, passionate behavior: it is not conscious but rather seems to well up from blood and memory of the ancient love of authority and feeling of tribal unity. Suddenly one belongs. In a broken world the participant feels a rush of kinship, the triumph over an uncertain, humiliating reality.

"Darkness" explores the love of a fuehrer figure, of a death lust. The reader in some sense feels a twinge of identification: we, too, are in some way responsible. Heyen stretches the notion of being his brother's keeper to include the enemy. "Lord help me to rid myself of the desire to kill other people, for my spirit wants to declare that spirit alien," he writes in his notes, insisting that "they are all with us now: all of those impulses, this sensibility, moral and murderous and sexual at the same time." (112, 113).

In trying to make poetry out of atrocities, Heyen takes a tremendous artistic and emotional risk. On the whole, he pulls it off, a testament to his large talent. Though he does not always avoid the pitfalls inherent in the attempt, he does in the main avoid them. One danger is overwriting, apparent in "Darkness," where an emotionally charged dream monologue reinforces its imagery through the reiteration of the word "darker": ". . . darker / Doctor, help me kill / the Goebbels children. Darker" (45–47). The sensitivity of this subject demands instead unusual restraint; in this instance, the author has overfueled his fire.

The Swastika Poems has its learned dimension—Heyen has read widely in the primary and secondary sources and has traveled to the particular sites of atrocity. At times, he uses quotations in his poems, which gives rise to another artistic danger: some of the material is so powerful that the words of the poet pale beside it. Can Heyen compete with a passage such as this: "The bodies were tossed out, blue, wet with sweat and urine, the legs soiled with feces and menstrual blood. A couple of dozen workers checked the mouths of the dead, which they tore open with iron hooks?" (McPherson, 31). The reader may be sickened or be left numb; whichever, though, the lines that follow can hardly be expected to register as the prose overwhelms the poetic.

In evaluating some of Heyen's poetic skills one finds unity in his poetry. Not only are the poems on the Holocaust unified, but even his poems on other subjects often employ similar images that relate them thematically to the poems on the Holocaust. In a series of poems, *The Chestnut Rain: A Poem in Progress* (1979–81), the central image of the tree symbolizing life and its destruction was prefigured by "The Tree" in *The Swastika Poems* (1977), a prose poem about a Czechoslovakian village that the Germans completely destroyed (47). Similarly, "Pigeons" in *Long Island Night: Poems and a Memoir,* (1979), deals with the slaughter of an overpopulation of pigeons in Kentucky. While implicitly alluding to the Jews, the speaker says that the dead birds seemed "to return the pulse of your thumb"—suggestive of genocidal guilt (35, 1. 24). That which is gone—the extinguished life—somehow returns to haunt the murderer. This theme is echoed in "Numinous," which is restrained, documentary, anguished.

This poem from *Erika* contains an epigraph from Rudolph Otto: "Our language has no truth that can isolate distinctly and gather into one word the total numinous impression a thing may make on the mind." The poem traces the poet's walk in the streets of a German city, "watching gray smoke / gutter along the roofs / just as it must have / from other terrible chimneys" (3–6). The poet seems to be walking "almost into a dream / only those with blue numbers along their wrists / can truly imagine" (10–13). Then something "bursts into the air," frightening the poet. But it is only pigeons, ". . . an explosion / of beautiful blue-gray pigeons" (19–20). The pigeons circling over the buildings metamorphose into "a hundred hearts / beating in the air. / Beautiful blue-gray pigeons. / we will always remember" (32–35). The suddenness of the flight of hundreds of pigeons in a present-day German city suggests both the souls of the Jewish dead and the speaker's awareness of the life and death of those Jews. The juxtaposition

of the pigeons with the smoke of the chimneys is subtle—
the images of the pigeons in both poems have a haunting
similarity.

"Pigeons" poured from the wellspring of a personal experience. As Heyen wrote in his 1976 essay:

> One day a couple of years ago my wife and I drove to Bergen-
> Belsen, in northern Germany. Walking that camp was a frighten-
> ing experience. We would never be the same. The idea of the total
> numinous impression of a thing reaches toward the idea of the
> glory of God within all objects, bottomless, endless, mysterious.
> But . . . my wife and I walked the sidewalks of a German city,
> Hanover, one day . . . after our experience and the camp, and
> those beautiful pigeons burst in the air in front of us, we stopped
> in our tracks, shocked and afraid. My own emotion was complex,
> had been building up. . . . [I]t was fear. Belsen entered the
> pigeons' wingbeats . . . Belsen is pure atrocity and nightmare . . .
> the whole world is still there in Whitman's blade of grass, William
> Blake's worm and grain of sand. The total numinous impression
> of those beautiful pigeons . . . sight, emotion, speech, silence.
> (104)

In relating his poem to personal experience, Heyen enhances
our understanding. Nevertheless, the poem can stand on its
own merit even without this narrative.

In another poem, "Simple Truths" in *The Swastika Poems*,
the poet cites atrocities, stanza by stanza, concluding each
stanza with an ironic, stark, understated "simple truth." Each
stanza describes an aspect of a man's life. The poem begins
naively:

> When a man has grown a body,
> a body to carry with him
> through nature for as long as he can.
> (1–3)

But men do not grow bodies in the same manner that farmers
grow and tend their plants. The second stanza continues:

> and when a man has a wife,
> a wife to love for as long as he lives,
> when this wife is marked with a yellow star

and driven into a chamber she will never leave alive
then this is murder
so much is clear.

(9–14)

Love is forever, but not under the conditions of the Third
Reich, where the yellow badge is the ticket to oblivion.
    The fourth stanza states:

it is clear that where we are
is Europe, in our century, during the years
from nineteen-hundred and thirty-five
to nineteen-hundred and forty-five
after the death of Jesus, who spoke of a different order,
but whose father,who is our father,
if he is our father,
if we must speak of him as father,
watched, and witnessed, and knew.

(25–33)

Not an enumeration of the atrocities of the Holocaust, this is a
biblical incantation ending in anger as the poet rails against
God.
    The concluding stanza is followed with the "simple truth"
that "it is clear that this is the German Reich, / during approximately ten years of our lord's time." And the perpetrators are
also victims:

When we read these things or see them,
then it is clear to us that this
happened, and within the lord's allowance, this
work of his minions, his poor
vicious dumb German victims twisted
into the swastika shapes of trees struck by lightning,
. . . .
this unfathomable oceanic ignorance of ourselves,
this automatic Aryan swerve this

fortune that you and I were not the victims, this
luck that you and I were not the murderers, this
sense that you and I are clean and understand
. . . as we kill them all.

(65–70, 76–81)

There are no simple truths. There is no paternalistic God; God does not perform according to Heyen's expectations. Heyen accepts his German past and proclaims both global and individual responsibility.

Heyen's other poetry connects thematically with his poems on the Holocaust in their exploration of death. Thus he considers the loss of a farmer's land that is sold and paved over, or the necessity behind a farmer's killing a ewe or the impulse of a boy hunter to shoot a cat. His childhood associations and the adult fear of nuclear holocaust are thematically linked to the mystery of the death camps. This is a post-Holocaust man who resists the temptation to be sentimental or judgmental.

Heyen may not have unlocked the mystery of unwarranted death in *The Swastika Poems* (1977) or *The Trains* (1981) or *My Holocaust Songs* (1980) or *Erika* (1984), but his poems force him and his reader to remember. In the interview with Rubin (Heyen and Rubin 1984), the poet points out that the last word in *The Swastika Poems* is "remember," and he adds:

> I know that the theme of remembrance comes up often—I wasn't conscious of how much it was coming up as the poems were being written, but it comes up again and again. It seems important to me that as human beings bear this experience with us in some sort of way that we can handle it without going crazy. . . . The Holocaust is a part of the twentieth-century consciousness, and has to be. (49)

The Swastika Poems is divided into three parts: in the first, the speaker meditates on his German heritage, especially his relatives' roles in the Second World War, and his American neighbors' hostility toward his family during the war because of his family's German roots; in the second he meditates, in a combination of poetry and quotations from trial documents, on the gas chambers in Bergen-Belsen; finally, in the third part he recapitulates the first two parts with the experienced speaker pressing to assimilate the facts of Auschwitz. *My Holocaust Songs* is more optimistic; it is the affirmative voice of someone who has endured the trial represented in the first book. *The Trains* is bleak, mainly meditations on Nazi barbarism. In addition, it explores the relationship between reality and language. A meditation on Treblinka states, "the camp's three syllables still sound like freight cars / straining around a curve Treblinka" (21). Heyen also includes a piece from his journal that considers the effect of language on understanding and reiterates his belief that "moral works of art can actually help to build a consensus for moral action" (19).

In another passage from the journal, Heyen reveals his ambivalence about God. Just as the camps baffle, so God's role is equally confusing. It is difficult to believe, he writes, that man is not "an ongoing experiment in whom God is uninterested," but he also calls on God's goodness when he asks God to help him rid himself "of the desire to kill other people." Unlike Plath, Heyen does not offer a Christological approach to the Holocaust. In his essay "Of Providence" (1976), Heyen writes, "I've tried to imagine what it would be like to hold a different kind of knowledge, an almost cellular Truth about the world" (99). And "Nature itself is the Zen master who sends us back day after day for as long as we live to study perhaps one inexhaustible leaf or sound or angle of sunlight. And Nature sends us back, in our time, not only to God, but to ourselves" (102). As Sandra McPherson notes, Heyen employs several literary techniques for handling the Holocaust, including consistency of tone and enumeration of the Nazi crimes. Words and phrases are often repeated, but the most important unifying factor is his original imagery (1977, 31).

Color imagery infused with multiple meanings permeates the poems. Blue symbolizes not only Jewish suffering but also the Nordic myth and the mystery behind the Holocaust. Blue is introduced in "Darkness." The themes of the Holocaust's receding in the collective memory and the increasing likelihood that Hitler is still alive or that similar evil still exists are at the heart of this poem. It considers atrocity and time:

> Thirty, fifty, eighty years later
> it's getting darker.
> The books read, the testimonies all taken,
> the films seen through the eye's black lens,
> darker. The words
> remember: Treblinka green,
> Nordhausen red,
> Auschwitz blue, Mauthausen
> orange, Belsen white—

colors considered
before those places named themselves.
(1–11)

Blue reemerges several pages later and is the core of a poem of that title, based on an account by Elie Wiesel of a truckload of burning babies. Heyen, the poem proclaims, considers God and the Holocaust equally impenetrable. He considers them in the same context:

"Blue"

Thcy were burning something. A lorry drew up at the pit and delivered its load—little children. Babies! Ycs, I saw it –saw it with my own eyes . . . those children in the flames. . . . I pinched my face. Was I still alive? Was I awake? I could not believe it. . . . Never shall I forget the little faces of the children, whose bodies I saw turned into wreaths of smoke beneath a silent blue sky.
—Elie Wiesel

To witness, to
enter this
essence, this
silence, this
blue, color
of sky, wreaths
of smoke, bodies
of children blue
in their nets
of veins: a lorry
draws up at the pit
under the blue sky where
wreaths rise. These
are the children's bodies, this
our earth. Blue. A lorry
draws up at the pit
where children smolder. The sky
deepens into blue, its
meditation, a blue
flame, the children
smolder. Lord of blue,
blue chest and blue brain.
a lorry of murdered children

          draws up at the pit. This
             happened, this
          happens, Your
       sign, children
       flaming in their rags, children
          of bone- smolder, scroll
             of wreaths on Your blue
                bottomless sky, children
                rising wreathed
                   to Your blue lips.
                                    (1–33)

Blue is the end of life for the children. God, the creator of the
blue sky, receives the children to His blue lips, a symbol of cold
death. Perhaps God is dead as well. Blue—the intangible quality of smoke, the mystery of the Holocaust. God's presence is
difficult to locate in *The Swastika Poems* because Heyen drops
the capital "y" of Your (referring to God) after the first use, but
returns to the capitalization in *Erika* published later. Also, this
is the only poem in which the left margin forms a wavering
line: the poem is smoke. Smoke—as difficult to define as is the
reason for the Holocaust, which literally entailed smoke and
fire. One recalls Nelly Sachs's chimneys (1967), which dominate not only her poetry but also her plays. They are the last
stage of the "Final Solution."

    Heyen's poetry is paralleled by that of another contempo-
rary American poet who is also a non-Jew, W. D. Snodgrass.
But Snodgrass does not turn to the iconography of smoke,
suffering children, distraught families, and victims. Instead
he explores the families surrounding the fuehrer himself, revealing the history, motives, and the texture of lives in this
most dreadful epoch. *The Fuehrer Bunker Poems* (1995) deals
with events centered on Hitler's last headquarters. It employs
a collage format. Heinrich Himmler speaks in a memo-
telegram printed on graph paper. There are snippets of
folksongs—notably "Tea for Two," spoken by Eva Braun, but
the effect is one of cuteness rather than irony. Albert Speer in
one of his monologues offers some ostensibly digressive comments about chimneys, indicating that Speer knows more
than he admits to himself. There is too much reliance on
kitsch to really move the reader. Stephen Yenser sees Snod-

grass as "confessional" in two senses, though different from Heyen. First, as Snodgrass notes in his afterward, his characters "are much more open and direct about their destructive feelings and intentions than their historical counterparts ever were . . . the Nazis—like some others one may have encountered—often did or said things to disguise from the world, sometimes from themselves, their real actions and intentions. . . . my poems, then, must include voices they would hide from others, even from themselves" (89). This comment also gives us a glimpse of the second sense in which these poems are confessional. As Richard Wilbur (Wilbur, Snodgrass, and Mathew 1986) remarked, "I don't know of anything which is absolutely not myself, including Adolph Hitler," or, as Snodgrass said it in "A Visitation," the poem about Adolph Eichmann in *After Experience,* "There's something beats the same in opposed hearts." Not to understand that, not to acknowledge our human kinship with the likes of the Nazis, is to incubate in us the potential for evil. That is the conviction behind the book, as it was behind "A Visitation," in which Snodgrass remarked, "How subtle all that chokes us with disgust / Moves in implacably to rule us unaware" (Yenser 1978, 87). How very like Heyen this sounds. Indeed, *The Fuehrer Bunker Poems* was published the same year as *The Swastika Poems.*

Snodgrass, finally, does not move us as Heyen does, because the latter concentrates on facts rather than on the emotions evoked by such immediate sensations as color. Multiple meanings of blue are also to be found in "This Night," a poem published several years later in *My Holocaust Songs:* it appears in *The Swastika Poems* as well and is cited from that work. It opens "Which is our star this night?" and closes, "Which was our star this night?" Between the first and last lines is a meditation on blue and Belsen:

> Belsen is bathed in blue,
> every foot worn lane, every
> strand of wire, pale blue.
> The guards' bodies,
> the prisoners' bodies—
>
> . . . .
> Which eyes are yours,

> which are mine? Even
> blue-eyed crows
> drift overhead.
> Even blue-eyed words
> sip dew from the weeping leaves.
>   (2–6, 14–19)

Blue signifies the victims, the guards, the crows, worms—man and nature. The speaker quests for a reason for the existence of places such as Belsen. We are, it is emphasized, simultaneously victims and guards, a theme prefigured in an earlier poem, "Two Walks" in *The Swastika Poems*. The first part opens:

> *One of them is yours*, my father said
>
> . . . .
>
> *It's exactly overhead,*
>
> *and always will be . . .*
> . . . . I saw it burning near
> (planet born when I was born), and blue.
>   (1, 4–7)

Part 2 suddenly makes the startling leap to a description of Bergen-Belsen. Within the context of later poems, however, it represents a logical shift. The combination of the star and color imagery here suggests that the speaker's destiny is to consider the Holocaust, and this is borne out by the fact that so many of his later poems are on this subject. Moreover, there is a unifying continuity to Heyen's imagery.

In addition to imagery, Heyen uses mockery to great effect. *The Swastika Poems* opens with a poem about his father, "A Snapshot of My Father, 1928." It begins:

> His hick tie
> flares out into the granular wind
> his thick kraut hair sprouts from under a cap you
> wouldn't be caught dead in.
>
> But he's smiling.
>   (1–5)

Other poems convey serious themes through a light ironic tone. "Riddle" in the same volume combines three and four strong stresses per line and the four-line ballad stanza, a b c b repetition. It reads like a nursery rhyme and indeed is based on "Who Killed Cock Robin?" This same technique we have observed in Plath's "Daddy." Heyen modulates his form carefully. The first stanza sets the pattern and begins the questioning in this well-structured poem:

> From Belsen a crate of gold teeth,
> from Dachau a mountain of shoes,
> from Auschwitz a lampshade.
> Who killed the Jews?
>
> (1–4)

Consonant with folk songs, "The Riddle" summons the stars, the sun, and the moon to remember the dead Jews and the way that they died. But human memory flawed as it is, cannot totally accomplish this mandate to remember or to answer the final question.

The second stanza consists of four negative answers, all having the same form: "not I," cries the typist, then the engineer, then Adolph Eichmann, then Albert Speer. So far it is familiar. But in the third and fourth stanzas, Heyen turns to examples of people who were actually killed. A new rhetorical pattern emerges at the end of the fourth stanza ("Some men signed their papers, / And some stood guard" [15–16]) and continues forward for eight more lines. In his catalog, Heyen moves from those most directly responsible, workers in the death camps themselves, to peripheral characters—farmers, steelworkers. The concluding two stanzas move further outward, enlarging on Heyen's original question:

> Some smelled the smoke,
> some just heard the news.
> Were they Germans? Were they Nazis?
> Were they human? Who killed the Jews?
>
> The stars will remember the gold,
> the sun will remember the shoes,
> the moon will remember the skin.
> But who killed the Jews?
>
> (25–32)

Whatever reservations we may have had about this nursery rhyme at the outset, it has by poem's end become a tremendously powerful question, full of moral reverberations.

In "The Legacy" (*Erika*), Heyen juxtaposes himself, writing in the first person to the victims. He begins simply enough until he announces the death of one nameless Jewish couple. Life is pitted against its antithesis—death. Verbs are repeated again and again, invoking the senses of hearing and of listening, as well as of thought. "R" sounds prevail in the almost dead and in the act of the dying couple. They also sing (a Heyen technique), and after the speaker smells of almond, the Jews smell of almond. And then the roles are reversed: "I die with them. They live with me." And Heyen responds to memory:

> I am dying. They are living.
> I am dying. They are singing.
> I am dead. They are living.
> . . . .
> I am dead. They are dead.
> I am dead. They are dead.
> I am dead. They are dead.
> I am dead. They are dead.
> (28–30, 33–36)

Repetition imitates the process of grief in this chant of and for the dead. There is the wish to die, the feeling of having died, and the desire to negotiate one's own life to save the dying or to return them to life.

Elsewhere, Heyen's style is less rhetorically charged; quieter passages more clearly reveal his lyrical talent as in this segment from "Three Fragments from Dreams" in *Erika:*

> Again I walked that Freiburg corner
> under the frieze
> where a unicorn has stabbed the air
> since Luther. The years
> have worn its stone horn
> down, down.
> Imagine the rains.
> Imagine the wars.
> How many women?
> It is almost impossible to remember

> Imagine the flowers in their hair.
> (9–19)

Before the line "down, down" the words are strikingly flat, but from there the poem flows with lovely imaginative images.

As in poems by Plath, the signs of death take on almost mythological significance, and childlike statements convey terrible facts that defy sophisticated sociological or psychological analysis. "Dark in the Reich of the Blonde," in *My Holocaust Songs*, also is riddlelike with its rhyme and frequent end-rhyme repetition. Spoken from the point of view of a German, it, like "Riddle," is a series of enumerations.

Many of Heyen's poems list Nazi war crimes. In "I Dream of Justice" (*Erika*), in end-stopped parallel lines the speaker says, "You who are poor, take back your coins. / You who are Jews, take back your teeth. / You who are shorn, take back your hair" (1–3). Similarly, in parallel and mainly end-stopped lines, "Simple Truths," previously discussed, recites a litany of infamous barbarities.

Heyen returns to the Holocaust repeatedly. Perhaps, in writing of such painful material, he is purging himself. Unlike Snodgrass, who holds to dramatic conventions and thereby manages to veil his own presence, Heyen prefers to address his reader directly and not in the foul, bizarre monologues of *The Fuehrer Bunker Poems*. His repetition of German war crimes in poem after poem remains almost compulsive, phobic. "Poem Touching the Gestapo" in *The Trains*, his longest poem on this subject, "tries to say everything at once, strains for relief from incidents that still burden the speaker after years of dwelling on them" (10). In an article entitled "Unwilled Chaos: In Poem We Trust," Heyen writes, "I will trust a poem to be what I need it to be now, a vessel to hold within its form, at least for a little while, my whirling thoughts and feelings about writing about the Holocaust." This is the didactic and dispassionate Heyen who recounts history and names not only the players but also their roles. As if all of this were too much, he continues, "Even the poem's method calls an end, for now (or so it appears to me), to these poems" (10).

After having written so copiously, Heyen is left in greater doubt than ever about the Holocaust. *The Trains* is simpler

and shorter than the previous volumes, concluding with a riddlelike poem, "The Trains," which imitates the actual rhythm
of the sound of the boxcars and the psychic rhythm of the
facts. Obtusely and insensitively the poem begins:

> Signed by Franz Paul Stangl, Commandant,
> there is in Berlin a document,
> an order of transmittal from Treblinka:
>
> (1–3)

Two middle stanzas itemize the trains' contents and the uses
made thereof:

> 248 freight cars of clothing,
> 400,000 gold watches
> 25 freight cars of women's hair
>
> Some clothing was kept, some pulped for paper.
> Most of the finest watches were never melted down.
> All the women's hair was used for mattresses, or dolls.
>
> (4–9)

The reader enters the poem with the poet's interrogation in the
fourth stanza:

> Would these words like to use some of that same paper?
> One of those watches may pulse in your own wrist.
> Does someone you know collect dolls, or sleep on human hair?
>
> (10–12)

The poem suggests that much is tied to that train, to its things
and its terrors. Not so benignly does Heyen point the accusing
finger at the readers' culpability for the stolen watches. Even
collecting dolls is no longer innocent. And who among us may
be sleeping on a bed of evil? Trains have been a dominant
image in Holocaust poetry almost from its inception, and both
historical and poetical reasons account for the emergence of
this motif as central. It is both a contextual symbol and a
rhythmic one, with its eternal running of the wheels. The repetition might also signal a general inevitability, an eternal return of suffering, particularly in a Jewish context.

Erika is a book of eulogies, many of which have been re-
printed, for uncles and a father-in-law, for a grandfather, for

the six million Jews and the thousands of gypsies, and for the German people. Once again, Heyen invokes a return to origins. Lines from the title poem of *Erika* echo the refrain from the opening of "little Gidding," T. S. Eliot's poem of return to family sources:

If you come this way, taking the route you would be likely to take from the place you would be likely to come from, If you came this way in may [sic] time, you would find white hedges again in May, with voluptuary sweetness.

(21–25)

Erika reads as follows:

You are not likely to visit that place, but if you do, and if you are there in December, as I was, you will walk into a single big room.

(paragraph 7, ll. 1–3)

This return, however, does not bring the pilgrim to the reassurance of spiritual roots but rather brings him to the terrors of the Third Reich and yet again to the recognition of one's potential for evil. It would be hyperbole to write that the *Erika* poems are an indictment of romantic culture, but the suspicion is planted and reinforced in poem after poem that the grandiose and passionate may be just the flip side of brutality and bestiality.

The poems in *Erika*, similar to *The Swastika Poems*, are divisible into those presenting historical events and those placing the poet among such events. "The Uncertainty Principle" is a poem that relates history by referencing an event presented through other media. In this, Heyen attempts to recreate and comment upon Jacob Bronowski's "whole hour of film," a television presentation where Bronowski walks into the pond at Auschwitz, the mud of the dead. Heyen invokes the Divine at the beginning of the poem in italicized text:

Lord, must this end in prayer or
does the Lord enter secular words?
What is in the wind? Does the wind's
red trail ever end? What is certain?
By the time Jacob Bronowski walked

into the pond—is it Your pond?
is it our pond?—what had he learned?
                                    (1–7)

Bronowski, the scientist, cups water in his right hand and
commingles it with the residue of human ashes. He bows at
the pond respectfully and submissively. The Lord of this pond
at Auschwitz is a God of silence. The infamy of the place has
also clogged up nature. Bronowski and his camera help the
reader touch the watery remnants of the dead with his tears.
"Stories," also in this volume, recounts the futile search for a
place of peace and belonging: stories abound, of ancestors and
of the war, but they "solve nothing," he writes, "lead nowhere"
(18). Still there is a Wordsworthian recompense: "But the
spruce / appears again, / . . . its own true story, yours, /
mine, ours to tell" (pt. 3, ll. 8–12).

One singular feature of *Erika* is that it offers neither help nor
hope from science. Much American poetry is fascinated, however indirectly, by science and its applications. From Emerson
through Gary Snyder, a cult of scientific accuracy, terminol-
ogy, metaphor, higher truth evolved. Whether in physics or
botany, anthropology or psychoanalysis, science has supplied
much of the metaphoric lore worked by our poets. But from
the perspective of the Holocaust, science is no antidote for
history. In this case, after all, men of science perverted science. Although Heyen does not mention it explicitly, the backdrop for these testimonials and meditations is inevitably the
present nuclear age.

"The Spire," a prose poem, probably one of the finest pieces
in the collection, is here quoted in its entirety:

The Spire
    Wherever I am, I am not supposed to be here. I am above the
street, above cobblestones shining the black shine of night and
rain. It is cold, but in this dream I cannot feel the cold, and wherever I am, I know, I have been here a long time. Great dark shapes
hang in the air behind me. Bells. A spire, a fretwork of porous red
stone rises above me. Bodiless, I am in the belltower of the cathedral above the square at Freiburg. I have been here for centuries. I am breathing the air that flows around the still clappers of
the great bells. The square below is empty. I have lived in this air, I
know, since before the spire.

Something is about to happen. A straining of ropes, chains. The bells' clappers begin to slam against cold iron. Pigeons lift their black bodies into the air. It is as though the bells are inside me, as though they are echoing deeply and mournfully the sounds for dead, dead.

It is winter here, a drizzle of sleet sifting through the dark red fretwork of the spire, through the sound of the bells. In the east, toward the forest, the horizon whitens with dawn. Lord, help me, I cry, and awaken. (69)

"I have been here for centuries" reverberates in the silence, as the bells will do a few lines later. The power and the helpless terror of this dream move one more than the explicit recitation of atrocities in some of the other poems. Its power is in indirection, in ambiguity. And thus it is a poem of terror more than of horror. The subject is bodiless, unseen. The bells are about to sound, mourning the dead of Europe and the death of a once-great nation. But in this dream the clappers "slam against cold iron." No tolling is adequate. In the bell tower above the square at Freiburg this bodiless consciousness and conscience is terrified of itself and its metallic music. This poem is almost medieval, a dream vision smack in the center of the volume toward which the other poems before and after point. Its forceful thrust is in its extreme economy combined with symbolic suggestion. It is a poem of dread, distrust of self, genes, and species. At its end it is a prayer for help and awakening.

In this bleak and searching book all of Heyen's preoccupations are transfigured in a radically different perspective. "To the Onlookers"—a work after Nelly Sachs, German escapee, poet of the Holocaust and Nobel laureate, whose influence permeates much Holocaust poetry—addresses the Germans as ". . . you / who could have been changed / into light" (20–22), and suggests both the deep mystical heritage of the people and the likelihood that dissenters would have been burnt in the ovens also. In "The Trench" (74), the enemy soldier to be killed is ". . . the first black shape / to fill the trench light" (20–21). The Nazi consciousness is imagination turned inside out, exploited into evil. Heyen's translation of Celan's "Death Fugue" is wonderfully crafted, partly because he has found American equivalents for the very rich German and biblical textures of the original. His notes tell us: "I'm familiar with translations of Celan's poem by Michael Hamburger, Christopher Middleton, and Joachim Neugroschel. While many of my words must of necessity be theirs, I've brought into my translation emphases and rhythms different from theirs that I feel in the original German" (113).

Additional examples of the poet's imagination at work include "Nocturne: The Reichfuehrer at Stutthof" (34), "The Car" (35), and "Kotov" (39). In the first, Himmler is heard meditating at night on his success: "you are so happy / your heart wants to burst" (15–16). The second tells, as if it were a joke, the story of how doomed people will grasp at the most unlikely straws:

> He said he'd save
> just enough Jews
> to fill one car.
>
> He said he'd drive
> that car himself
> through the cities.
>
> Last stop: Berlin.
> Citizens throng
> to see the Jews
>
> his mercy spared
> Berliners count:
> one, two . . . three, four.
>
> Each Jew thinks he
> or she will be
> among the four.
>   (1–15)

"Kotov" relates the story of a man who saved himself from the gas by soaking his sleeve in his own urine and covering his nose and mouth.

One of the most gripping verse poems is "The Children" with its refrain: "I don't think we can save them" (106–7). Heyen, the father of two children, has said, "For a while I thought I was done with the subject, i.e., the Holocaust, completely, that I'd written all I knew and felt. Then I had a dream, and wrote a poem, 'The Children' about that." Here history is comprehensible to anyone who has ever held a child. Later, something brutal happened, of course,

> but as to this life I had to, I woke,
> and cannot, or will not, remember.
> But the children, of course, were murdered,
> their graves lost, their names lost,
>
> even those two faces lost to me. Still,
> this morning, inside the engine of my body,
> for once, as I wept and breathed deep,
> relief, waves of relief, as though the dreamed
>
> rose would spill its petals forever.
> I prayed thanks. For one night, at least,
> I tried to save the children,
> to keep them safe in my own body,
> and knew I would again. Amen.
>   (quoted in Heyen and Rubin, 51, ll. 50–62)

Is this poem overly sentimental? Is it not too easy a response to a very complex dream? Are the prayers at the end meant to stroke the poet's ego? Does the act of dreaming offer protection? One can certainly empathize with the vulnerability and helplessness of children for all that their use as a subject might be clichéd.

Heyen tells us that the poems "write themselves" through him or are the record of a mind in the "act of discovering what it knows." And although the book is a record of the strengths and ambitions of such a method, it also becomes, according to Jorie Graham (1985), the most evident source of failure.

> The poems come to feel out of control, the imagery weak, vague or banal just when we most need to be made to see. Especially at those junctures where it is the natural world against which man's horrifying acts are measured or made to resonate, we need more than the endless mists, ironic blue skies filled with crematorium smoke, ash-beds over which new flowers grow. We need more than the easy, received ironies of "skin lampshades darkening under varnish" which along with numbered wrists are the key imagery. (30)

Graham continues:

> Where 40,00 huddle in a freezing field, dying of exposure, the poet
> tells us he wants "to be led there, where they were." But the imag-
> inative tools he employs to reach them—"in their threadbare
> coats, or coatless / some shoeless," planes droning overhead, the
> light "milky"—can't take him "there." If the world of things is
> vague, or stock, the emotion tends to grow generalized until we are
> left with a dangerous passivity which is not spiritual openness but
> formlessness, not a redemptive recognition of complicity as much
> as a dilution of all acts to the same status. . . . In the strongest
> poems, one feels what one needs to feel: the battle between the
> desire to transform and the resistance of the facts; the frailty and
> perhaps even the immorality of those horrifying facts becoming a
> story. (30)

But, in fact, Heyen's imagery has much greater range and
effect than Graham credits it with. A close reading of the *Erica*
poems shows the subtlety and delicacy of his approach. Moreover, the imagery is convincing, strong, and compelling. The
reader is reminded of the horse in Picasso's *Guernica*—dying,
stifling a scream. While Heyen cannot cleanse us of the blood
of the crimes depicted, he brings us face to face with the
eternal agonizing question: what is man? And his poetry born
of courage—but written with discipline, honesty, and restraint—helps.

Hayden Carruth reminds us: "History is the problem always. It attaches itself to us, sucks our lives, yet it continually
fades; we despise it, fear it, yet cannot do without it; and we
continually worry about it, like dogs with a dead rat. At least
part of the artist's job, is to keep history alive and some way
make it serve us." Carruth credits Heyen for knowing what
history can do, even at its worst, especially if cast in aesthetic
form. "His poems are fine ones, clear, modest, yet powerful in
their very unpretentiousness and at the same time poetically
acute, their tones, textures and rhythms all working sub-
liminally, below the surface of shock to reinforce our sympathetic perceptions. In the end Heyen says, the death camps
can keep us human. And his poems prove it" (1978, 97, 98).

We cannot help but respond to the haunting beauty of the
long prose poem "Erika," which recounts the history of

Bergen-Belsen, a name that "whines like a missile or jet engine" (paragraph 1). The poem counterpoints the unnatural deeds at Bergen-Belsen and the natural beauty of the mounds of graves covered with Erika. "Erika, bell-heather, *heide*, a heath plant, wild and strong. Wild and strong, and beautiful. . . . Erika over the graves, the *heide*'s billions of flowerlets veiling the open spaces in shifting mauves and orchids and blue-purple shadows. It must be very beautiful and very terrible at Belsen when each fall the Erika blossoms" (paragraph 10). On the white marble shaft memorializing the thirty thousand Jews who were exterminated at Bergen-Belsen are the words, "Earth Conceal Not the Blood Shed on Thee!" (paragraph 11). For Heyen, Erika becomes "the blossom of memory" (paragraph 11), itself a memorial. Beneath it can still be found twisted eyeglass frames or the casing of a bullet or a wedding ring. "Bergen-Belsen is a simple place but more eloquent than the cathedral at Koln" (paragraph 11).

In "The Baron's Tour" a high born German ponders the ancient tide of blood engulfing his family's castle. The antecedents are unavoidable: "We have always lived in this castle" (4). German destiny and racial memory are part of the narrator's history. There is an unsettling insanity about this poem. The reader is enjoined to

> Come, see where kings entered
> the grained wood of the oak bed
> where you will sleep tonight.
> One said he'd dreamed
>
> of his whole courtyard filled with heads
> whose eyes mirrored
> fields inside of fields inside
> of fields forever.
> We have always
> lived in this castle.
>
> (25–34)

No matter the ruler, all of history's genocides were contained in the eyes of the corpses. This castle was one with the German evil mentality. Heyen's repetitive "castle" and "we" is his way of defining the obscenity of the German culture. Hence both the castle and the tour are defining metaphors for German history and culture.

Falling from Heaven: The Holocaust Poems of a Gentile and a Jew (1991) is a collaborative effort, composed of poems by Louis Daniel Brodsky and William Heyen presented in alternation. The poems, selected and revised from previously published works, are an invaluable collection of evocative thoughts from two poetic sensibilities who share, as nonsurvivor American poets, the "sharpness of distance" from the horrible events about which they write. Heyen and Brodsky dedicate their collection to Elie Wiesel and Harry James Cargas, another Jewish-Gentile team of authors who have cooperated on essays and Holocaust projects for many years. The Heyen-Brodsky collaboration, too, is impressive (Cohn 1991, 12a).

Of the two writers, Heyen emerges as the more consistently elegant and formal; his writing, even in its simplicity, has more range. Brodsky aims more often than not at outspoken grandeur. However, the two are not collaborating to be compared one with the other, and they work well in counterpoint. Moreover, it is apparent that they share a religious dimension, a sense that whatever can be said is simultaneously too much and not enough, and we are left ultimately with the wish that hope is not finally less illusive than understanding. Strains of Zionism are present; a continual theme is the historical and political transformation of the swastika into the star of David, the ever-threatened flag of the state of Israel. Nonetheless, politics is only secondary. Heyen and Brodsky emphasize the irreducible fact of suffering, the complications of history, and the psychic complexities—even chaos—that lie beyond theatrical facades of brutality, militarism, and the presumption that knowledge is secure.

Divided into five sections of ten poems each, the book switches between Brodsky's and Heyen's visions, probing personal memory, history, human frailty and endurance, introspection, and the poets' power to record, atone, and provide sanctuary for the victims about whom they write. Neither bitter nor resigned, these poems are determined to reckon with one's heritage and place in this world. At first the poet, then the reader, becomes observer, survivor, curator of historical events. An unexpected grace is also present, as in *The Swastika Poems*, where Heyen's father's house is attacked by vandals. Heyen's prose statement of this happening, already discussed, is included in the collaborative volume.

> They appeared, overnight,
> on our steps, like frost stars
> on our windows, their strict
> crooked arms pointing
>
> this way and that . . .
> my father cursed in his other tongue
> and scraped them off.
>
> (1–4, 7–9)

Brodsky, across the page in "For the Time Being," sets a serene scene of father and daughter reading side by side on a porch ("She, *The Diary of Anne Frank*, / I, *Death of a Salesman*" [5–6]). Never taking the present for granted, he muses:

> The two of us, Jewish waifs,
> Cocooned in affluence
>
> .   .   .   .
> Quietly reading,
> Safe from the past and the future—
> For the time being.
>
> (24–25, 28–30)

Many poems place the reader in situations of astonishing immediacy, with detail and insights. In Heyen's "Men in History," we move from the fuehrer's crumbling bunker to the ". . . Chancellery's upper rooms, / where walls peeled, drapes were down, / and paintings he'd insisted on / were long since packed away" (pt. 2, ll. 8–12). Brodsky gives us a sensual and tragic scenario in "Lovers' Last Evening in the Warsaw Ghetto," where two faceless lovers celebrate each other before the anticipated annihilation:

> Tonight, partaking of pleasure's cadences,
> We devote our anonymous lives
> To these few, fleet moments possessing us,
>
> .   .   .   .

For these few precious hours left us,

. . . .

. . . Your palpating breasts pressed to my chest,
My penis, itself a blessed Torah,
Nestled in your dark Ark, eternally sealed.

(22–24, 36, 40–42)

Horror is evident in the simple listing of events and facts and in questions, Heyen says, must be asked in "Coin":

What was a Jewish child worth, summer, 1944
when the Nazis halved the dosage of *Zyklon B*
from 12 boxes to six boxes for each gassing?

(1–3)

The poet calculates the meager savings that multiplies the victims' agony, and answers himself: "A Jewish child / was not worth a ½ cent to the Reich" (17–18).

Other poems recount the emotional scars of survivors in deft character studies of victims (including "Windchill Factors," "Friday Night Out," and "Bert Jacobs Furrier," by Brodsky) and of villains ("The Baron's Tour" and "Poem Touching the Gestapo," by Heyen). Among these are poems that try to defy cruelty and to correct history. In one instance, in "The Power," Heyen signs a book for a survivor whose mother was designated for death by Mengele, and he urges both son and mother in short, breathless lines "to keep walking" as he imagines himself in the role of an SS officer distracting Mengele and letting them escape.

Some poems focus on more abstractly resonant images: trains, the names of Eastern European *shtetls*, the finely wrought dreams of survivors. Heyen's remarkable prose poem "Canada" catalogs the articles stolen from murdered Jews and kept in warehouses, the "wealth" of the Third Reich. Primo Levi has said in the epigraph preceding the poem that these stories "are simple and incomprehensible, like stories in the Bible" (in epigraph to "A New Bible"). Incomprehensible, yet necessary; one of the strengths of this volume is that it never attributes anything so simple as a meaning to these deaths. So Heyen writes, "We turn the page. It is three o'clock. So many trains converge on the station, so many stories" (20–21).

Sylvia Plath and William Heyen show several similarities in their treatment of this most dreadful event in the history of humankind. Timeless concerns for both of them are illusion and disillusion, victims and victimizers, eater and eaten, powerless capitulation and rebellion of both the intellect and the soul against monolithic authority and the hopelessness of situations from which there is no escape. Their poetry transcends time and place—it is not geographically limited to the death camps of Germany and Eastern Europe—since the Holocaust is a subject for all time to come. Both poets remind us that the evil that was the Third Reich is in all men and is the shared heritage of all humanity. Their poetry, confessional by design, probes the darker realms of the unconscious. Confessional poetry must emphasize its personal authenticity and link to its subject over all else. As testimony to the poet's private pain, confessional poetry depends for its potency on personal accountability.

Both poets rely on like imagery to tell their story: trains, wheels, chimneys, children, parents, wedding rings, gold fillings, soap, ash, fire and smoke, concentration and death camps. There is also stylistic kinship, in that both resort to the nursery rhyme to bring this unfathomable story to its most understandable level. While Plath does not attempt to recapture history, Heyen is driven to remember and to teach the supreme madness of the twentieth century. To keep this memory alive is at the center of his life. Thus in his poetry as he codifies, contextualizes, and clarifies his own understanding of memory, he simultaneously creates memory for his reader. Expiation of guilt in Heyen's personal history is his route to confronting the particular and universal tragedy of the Holocaust. This he does as an American of German descent who lost family members in World War II and as one who is tortured by familial involvement. Plath attempts to work her way out of her private turmoil through the utilization of the Holocaust as metaphor. It is precisely these figurative claims that may forever be read as patent and somewhat illegitimate hyperbole and therefore lacking in authority. It is not a matter of Plath's having been Jewish or not, for as a Jewish writer she would not have used her figures as she did—for purely personal suffering (Young 1987, 132). For both poets God and the Holocaust are equally impenetrable and unfathomable, even though Plath often has recourse to Christian symbolism. For Plath, God is dark and evil. Heyen suggests that God was dead, especially when it came to the children, or if not dead, ominously silent.

The poets individually respond to the seminal poetry of the Holocaust matriarch Nelly Sachs and patriarch Paul Celan, Plath through unconscious imitative poetry and Heyen via a superb translation of "Todesfuge." Though Celan bared his pain at the height of his poetic powers, it did not spare him from despair (as Camus suggested) but may have only deepened it. The generation of non-Jewish poets who identified in their work with Holocaust Jews—John Berryman, Randall Jarrell, Anne Sexton, and Sylvia Plath—all killed themselves after using the Holocaust as image in their poetry. It is difficult to speculate how Plath would have utilized Holocaust poetry had she lived to continue writing. For Heyen, there is no surcease in this domain of writing. For him, throughout his work on the Holocaust, empathy and poetic identification are total.

The differences that emerge in the Holocaust poetry of Plath and Heyen are enormous but subtle. Plath's emotional yet indirect experience contrasts with Heyen's palpable, close, familially bonded connection. As we have observed, the critics are divided in their assessment of the honesty of Plath's Holocaust poetry, with Alvarez standing in opposition to Rosenfeld, Steiner, and Howe. The middle ground advocated by Young seems to be the best path to take:

> Rather than attempting to constrain the Holocaust's impact on our understanding and current representations of the world, the critic's task is to examine how the Holocaust has mattered. For by allowing these images to figure current experiences, writers and critics sustain events in consciousness and measure their impact at the same time. To remove the Holocaust from the realm of the imagination, however, to sanctify it and place it off limits is to risk excluding it from public consciousness. (146)

And this seems to be "too high a price to pay for saving it from those who would abuse its memory in inequitable metaphor" (146). Better abused memory, even if critically qualified, than no memory at all. Sylvia Plath and William Heyen force us to come to grips with the unthinkable. At the same time we are admonished that all cruelties, even the most bizarre and incredible, are within the realm of possibility.

3

Gerald Stern Weeps and Mourns and Eulogizes: Holocaust Poetry as Catharsis for Guilt

IN GERALD STERN'S HOLOCAUST POETRY, THE ENCOUNTERS between the imagination and traumatic history move from a reverence for facts to the creation of a mythical literature. His Holocaust poetry emerges from his lifelong affair with Judaism and the emotional weight this carries. Stern's Holocaust poetry requires a comprehension of and an appreciation of the interwoven strands of Judaism.

The Judaic concepts of confession and remembrance link Stern's Holocaust poems to some extent with the school of confessional poetry. But given the extensive Jewish background on which he draws and his general restlessness with the confessional mode, Stern's poetry on the Holocaust breaks free of the confessional tradition of Plath, Heyen or Lowell. Rigorously trained as a child in the Hebrew *Siddur* (prayer book) and the liturgy of the High Holy Days, Stern absorbed their litany of confessions and eventually brought that sensibility to his poetry.

Equally important for Stern is the Jewish legacy of remembrance. Already in the Bible Jews (Israelites) are enjoined to "remember" what Israel's ancient enemy, the Amalekites, perpetrated against the children of Israel (Deut. 25: 17–19). In Jewish history, Amalek often serves as a metaphor, a shorthand, for all suffering endured by the Jewish people throughout the ages. Stern uses nostalgia to evoke and perpetuate memory. But paradoxically opposing these notions of confession and remembrance is Stern's preoccupation with a third Jewish strand: kabbalistic secrecy—that which is not revealed. To these threads of the Jewish past Stern adds in his poems historic facts about the Holocaust. His more figurative references to the Holocaust reflect his concept of poetry as a means of preserving the life of the body and the life of the spirit. Thus, a multifaceted Judaism stands at the core of Stern's sense of poetry, as well as of his meditative essays, and his interviews.

Quite aside from Stern's incomplete fidelity to the confessional mode, Judaic or secular, confessional poetry itself is not easily reconciled with contemporary poetic theory, even though the two developed simultaneously. It was an inevitable conflict, given that modernist poetic theory rejected inward-facing romanticism, forswore the exploration of the poet's personal psychology, and sought to present the self's objective response to an autonomous exterior world. In the confessional poem, of course, self-expression becomes self-exposure, the self as subject. Stern himself is ambivalent about confessional poetry, and looks to a time when "perhaps the pain in the life of the poet will stop being the main subject" (Somerville, quoting Gerald Stern 1988, 15). Yet he also claims that preoccupation with the self is inevitable, for "we don't have a common history in this country, a common culture, we're all separate from each other" (Glaser 1982, 27).

Stern's poetry, unlike that of many confessional poets, is marked by the absence of the rage and negativity or the desperate embrace of suffering of say a Plath or a Heyen. If Plath consorts with Lucifer, Stern more likely looks forward to Paradise. Though pain and suffering cannot be overlooked in his poetry, it is more likely to be the transformative suffering of the hero or a suffering tempered by comedy. Moreover, Stern's speaker is not engaged in humble self-searching or self-accusation. Rather, his speaker presents himself flagrantly, shamelessly, without humility or contrition, without the psychological stress of the typical confessional speaker. We feel we know not only his personality, but his character as well. Yet we see Stern only peripherally, from the outside in—not from the inside out—again the antithesis of what we get in the confessional mode. His half-mocking "confessions" are playful, either a joke on confessional poets or on himself as in "My First Kinglet":

I ate my sandwich
and waited for a signal, then I began
my own confession; I walked on the stones, I sighed
under a hemlock, I whistled under a pine,
and reached my own house almost out of breath
from walking too fast—from talking too loud—
from waving my arms and beating my palms; I was,
for five or ten minutes, one of the madmen you see
forcing their way down Broadway reasoning with themselves
the way a squirrel does.

                                        (1990, 34–43)

"Confession" moreover implies an admission of guilt and an acknowledged need for forgiveness. The confessional poem is strongly rooted in Freudian theory: "Pay attention to what they've done [the other in society] to me" (Thompson 1994, 30). On the contrary, Stern in his confessional poems, while pleading for forgiveness, does so comically: "Please forgive me, my old friends" (1984, 40); "Forgive me ten times, but this is what I did" (1979, 87); "dreaming of my weaknesses / and praying to the ducks for forgiveness" (1981, 64); "forgive me / for turning into a tree, forgive me, you lovers / of life for leaving you suddenly" (1984a, 61); "I sit in the sun forgiving myself" (1987, 74). These entreaties sound like lighthearted, tongue-in-cheek formalities. Stern has perfected his own confessional performance to placate his audience.

Stern does acknowledge a kind of self-pity that finds echoes in all confessional poetry. But there is a tonal difference: confessional poets may sometimes seem consumed by self-pity, but do not state it overtly, whereas Stern openly jests about it, thereby acknowledging his own weakness. At one point the speaker in *Paradise Poems* (1984), is looking for his kidney along the road:

I want to see it
weeping with pure self pity, wringing its hands
the way a kidney wrings its hands, much better
than the liver, much better than the heart.
                ("One Bird to Love Forever," 77–80)

In the largest sense, his self-pity is part of the encompassing pity at the heart of his work.

He shares the emotion of the confessional poems of Plath and Heyen but not their frank disclosure. In Stern, effusive feeling is often eclipsed; critical personal information, including early failure as a writer, is only marginally visible. Thus the poem is never imprisoned by fact. Stern, that is, does not write poems "about" these subjects but instead bathes references to them in historic, mythic, or fantastic encounters. Sometimes only a nugget of the actual situation that motivated the poem remains, as if he were recalling a passionate sexual engagement or a scene of anguish by describing only skeletal details. In another instance in *Lovesick* (1987), Stern denies such concealed meaning:

> here is my yellow tablet, there are no
> magic thumb prints, nothing that is not there,
> only the hum, and I have buried that
> on this piece of paper.
> ("It Was in Houston," 24–27)

A few lines following, he retracts this denial, writing that his words are created to be hidden away in a hip pocket or wallet, "and there are broken words, / or torn, hanging onto threads, the deep ones / underneath the flap, the dark ones forever creased" (41). These "dark ones" may be remnants of private material, or they may signal Stern's preoccupation with mystical Judaism, with what he terms "the secret text" in "What Is This Poet?" (153).

Kabbalah is the most common term for the esoteric teachings of Judaism and for Jewish mysticism. It seeks an apprehension of God and creation whose intrinsic elements are beyond intellectual grasp. In essence, the *Kabbalah* is far removed from a rational approach to religion; by its very nature mystical knowledge cannot be communicated directly but may be expressed only through symbol and metaphor. In theory esoteric knowledge can be transmitted, but those who possess it are either forbidden to pass it on or do not wish to do so. The Kabbalists emphasized this occult aspect by circumscribing the promulgation of their teachings. They set a minimum age for initiates, demanded ethical qualities, and limited the number of students to whom these teachings could be expounded. Hence the secrecy and the silence (Scholem 1977, 489, 490). These elements of *Kabbalah* fascinate Stern, who creates his own ecstatic *Kabbalah,* as seen in "Burst of Wind between Broadway and the River," in *Rejoicings* (1984):

> There at the little chairs and the round tables
> the rebbes read and eat.
> I walk between them like a learned soul,
> nodding my head and smiling,
> doing the secret steps and making the signs,
> following the path of authority and silence,
> I and the dust, in the black soup and the herring.
>
> (8–14)

Secrets abound in Stern, as do paradoxes. Stealthiness trumps confessional outbursts in his work and tension prevails between concealment and disclosure, internal and external, subconscious and conscious. Secrecy wages war against the religious-Freudian workings of confession—the revelation of that which is most intimate. But such quotidian problems may seem trivial in the shadow of the killing grounds of the concentration camps. Stern's secretiveness is also at odds with that stratum of postmodernism that prefers openness. A secretive poem is inaccessible. Concealed meaning is not without value, though. It creates a substratum to put pressure on the poem's compressed surface, and intensify it beyond its apparent meaning, even as ordinary events are intensified by hidden meanings in dreams.

Stern's private material causes us to look constantly at the speaker as he struts on the stage of the poem. We are compelled to listen to his distinctive descriptions of his own actions. The speaker often proclaims "I am here" or "here I am," again, insisting that we acknowledge his physicality. This pronouncement is similar to the biblical *hineni:* here am I. His continual self-description creates the effect of dramatic presence. It establishes that kind of sympathy or identification that we give to a fictional character, quite different from the type that a confessional poem demands. Yet Stern's need for recognition does survive under this exterior. He wants to be visible:

In my left hand is a bottle of Tango,
In my right hand are the old weeds and power lines
                    ("On the Far Edge of Kilmer," 10–11)

I bend my face and cock my head. My eyes
Are open wide listening to the sound.
My hand goes up and down like a hummingbird.
                    ("Weeping and Wailing," 6–8)

His dramatic posturing on the stage notwithstanding, Stern
talks about his secrecy to Sanford Pinsker (1990):

I do think that in my recent poems the speech may get
plainer, but the experience gets more 'secret' or complicated.
I suppose the plainness of speech is simply a result of my
giving more public readings in the last couple years. I don't
really know what accounts for the 'secret' part, except that
I'm getting older and possibly more secret. (192)

This secrecy encourages a formalist approach to reading, also
termed the "quest" reading: initial impenetrability or confusion, an engagement like wrestling with an angel, and final
illumination. This reading style is controversial, however, because traditionally this mode looked for a single meaning supported by every aspect of the text. Nor does Stern's work respond to a demand for consistency. Paradoxes in the text
must be accepted on their own terms or on faith. However, the
quest reading opens multiple possibilities; in fact, the process
itself, as with any quest, is valuable. Stern's poetry has a
strong tendency to draw the reader away from interpretation,
at the same time keeping him poised on the poem's surface,
which does not seem to militate against the quest reading.

In its self-absorbed focus on one life, the confessional poem
tends to differentiate that life, to set it apart, though it may be
used as an example. But in Stern, the poet's experience is not
the main subject of the work—his self is, despite its oddness, a
representative figure, whether poet or man. With Stern, it is
not, finally, "look how I have suffered," but "look how we suffer." This is consonant with the Judaic practice of confessing
in the plural. Underlying the pluralization is a compulsive

longing to connect like E. M. Forster's characters in *Howard's End*, to make oneself part of the whole. This movement toward union is a traditional function of literature, sometimes missing in contemporary writing centered on the effort to separate, to differentiate rather than unite.

In a 1996 interview with me, Stern refused the label of confessional poet. A personal life for Stern is a resource offering shameless lies as well as imaginative and literal truths. He claims that "one's biography is the occasion for the poem but not the poem itself." He protests: "'my personal poems' are not necessarily confessional." (He does not deny absolutely the possibility of this label.) For Stern, myth is the essence of what he creates from his own life, a raising of the domestic onto another plain. The self-glorification associated with confessional poetry is not for him. Jane Somerville even claims that Stern does not see himself as "accountable," except in very obvious ways, to external influences. "He is less inclined to identify literary antecedents than aspects of his 'personal accidental history' such as Judaism, the Depression, the political Left, the crucial childhood loss of his sister—even being left-handed. Ultimately, he believes his own loss and failure became his subject" (1988, 12). Despite his objections, then, the confessional motif is intrinsic to Stern's poetry.

Far more important to Stern than any labeling of his work is the impact of Judaism upon his life. The repetitive rhythms of prayer, the theory of history, the philosophical way of looking at life (all human existence), the prophetic model—all these provide the basis for his Holocaust poetry. Stern was born in 1925 in Pittsburgh to a second-generation East European working-class family. His maternal grandfather, whose childhood influence on him was very strong, accounted for many of his Jewish attitudes. The grandfather, born in Bialystok, Poland, had been a rabbi and a *shochet*, a kosher, ritual animal slaughterer. He moved to Pittsburgh after immigrating to the United States. Grandfather Barach never found a place for himself within American culture, never mastered English, and stubbornly clung to religious orthodoxy, to superstitions, and to the ways of the ghetto. Stern saw him as a holy man who killed chickens and taught boys (Hillringhouse 1984, 27), the personification of alienation and exile. The religious character of his familial experience defined Stern's Judaic education, and the memory never left him.

The death of his only sibling, Sylvia, at the age of nine from spinal meningitis irrevocably affected Stern, who was eight years old at the time. After a prolonged and excessive period of grieving, his mother still refused to accept her daughter's death and became chronically depressed. Stern became the outlet for Ida Stern's shattered affection and feelings of irreparable loss. The poet tells of his mother taking him to her bed, weeping and crying, "Sylvia, Sylvia, Sylvia." He did not reject this role, but embodied her loss while searching for an outlet for his own grief. To this day, the memory of Sylvia's untimely end will not go away. This episode continues to haunt him and is dominant in his personal poetry. Poetic expression for Sylvia's passing is found in "Joseph's Pockets" in *Leaving Another Kingdom* (1990, 85–87), "Sylvia" in *Bread Without Sugar* (1992, 3), and in "The Expulsion" (*Leaving Another Kingdom*, 180–82). Stern echoes the talmudic dictum, "Whoever saves one life saves the world entire, and conversely he who destroys one life destroys the world entire" (*Sanhedrin, Mishneh* 4:37a, 233). The one loss he forcibly takes beyond familial boundaries in his poetry—to the afflicted family at large—is the annihilation of his brethren, the six million European Jews. "I think I have a bone somewhere in my spine," he confesses, "or a wire somewhere in my system, or a feather, that attracts me endlessly to the ruined and fallen" (Parmet 1996).

Thus continuity, tradition, and loss, in their full, tangibly Judaic interconnectedness, comprise Stern's central themes, which are expressed as death, burial, rebirth, the angel, music, exile, prayer, and the Holocaust. The Jewish sources of his affectionate reverence for heritage, culture, and learning are accented by powerful Hebrew biblical reverberations in the phrasing and structure of his poems. Mystical and spiritual overtones dominate his poetry. In an interview with Pinsker (1984), Stern says that he wants to teach "about how to live, how to survive" (65). His is a subtle social, psychological, and political agenda. Overarching these issues is spiritual survival. For him, however, the past does provide a transcendence beyond the minimalism of surviving through spiritual connection. Stern spoke to me in our interview (Parmet 1996) of the cultural, emotional quality of being a Jew, asserting that the sense of compassion and a quest for justice were among the elements pulling him to writing Holocaust poetry.

Nostalgia, like confession, a vital component of Judaism, surfaces in Stern's Holocaust poetry, providing the keys to unlock a "redemptive past," as Stern defines it in one of his *American Poetry Review* essays. The Judaic mode of nostalgia distinguishes his confessional poems from most modernist confession. This essential nostalgia is "a search for the permanent." It is "a combination of absence and presence, the far and the near, the lost and found. In that charged memory are found the unbearable pain of separation and the sweetness of remembered union" (1984d, "Notes from the River,"17–19). It is "the weeping mouth / that will not let you go, the sweet smell drifting / through the alley" ("Poem of Liberation," 1981, 60). The definitive feature of Stern's voice is the amalgam of joy and sorrow permeating his work (Somerville 1984, 102).

Stern tells Elizabeth Knight in an interview in 1987, "Nostalgia means longing for a home. . . . If you lose the culture you lose everything. With a Jew it's . . . religion and culture" (38). In Stern's "Romania, Romania," in *Leaving Another Kingdom* (1990), written outside the Lower East Side's Romanian synagogue, he imagines himself playing the violin:

> I stand like some country crow across the street
> from the Romanian Synagogue on Rivington Street
> singing songs about Moldavia and Bukovina.
> I am a walking violin, screeching
> at the depths, plucking sadly on my rubber guts.
> It's only music that saves me. Otherwise
> I would be keeping the skulls forever, otherwise
> I would be pulling red feathers from my bloody neck.
> It's only music, otherwise I would be white
> with anger or giving in to hatred
> or turning back to logic and religion—
>
> . . . .
>   Yehudi Menuhin
> wandering through the hemlocks,
> Jascha Heifetz

> bending down over the tables,
> the great Stern himself
> dragging his heart from one ruined soul to another.
>   (1–11, 29–34)

The poem's title recalls a world extinct: Stern's Romania no longer exists—only the music remains. The violin, with its powerful Jewish associations (from Chagall, to the *Klezmorim* [the itinerant musicians of the *shtetl*], to classical artists), makes a subtle reference to the Holocaust. That instrument, which imitates the crying human voice, intensifies the poem's poignancy. It lures Stern back to the European *shtetl*, a fallen world, a lost world, a world of death signified by the skulls. How many Jewish musicians perished in that world? And each ruined soul has known his portion of the hemlock, that classic symbol of finality.

Nostalgia also propels the reader toward a promise of lost perfection, embraced by garden beginnings and messianic finality. Often at the heart of a Stern poem, the garden is emblematic of both the permanent perfection of Eden and its cyclical appearance in death and rebirth. Here the gardener-poet recognizes that he is not primordial Adam but common man: "I walk / like man, like a human being, through the curled flowers, / I almost can't stand the beauty" ("Two Trees," *Paradise Poems,* 1984a, 20–22). Yet Stern does not see himself as a melancholic; he is not always in mourning. He claims not to lament the lost Eden, not to be angry with time, not to be gloomy. However his subject is repeatedly loss, and he is overwhelmed by separation. Stern recognizes that the Edenic idyll in Gen. 2 is immediately followed by the expulsion in Gen. 3.

Nostalgic sadness pervades "Kovalchik's Garden" *in Leaving Another Kingdom,* an abiding sensitivity to mortality and to history. So strongly does the speaker identify with the cardinal and with the dead pear tree that the poem itself slips easily, almost imperceptibly, from naturalistic description to biblical lament:

> It is dusk, the drive-ins are opening, the balloon is coming to rest.
> Out of the east, so fitting, the cardinal moves into the light.
> It is the female, almost too small and shabby for its splendor.
> Her crest opens out—I watch it blaze up.

She is exploring the dead pear tree.
She moves quickly in and out of the dry branches.
Her cry is part wistful, part mordant.
She is getting rid of corpses.

(1–8)

   This reinvention of paradise offers a redemptive transcendental moment of harmony that annuls the distance between subject and object, past and present, the visible and the invisible. It is a doorway in "the long and brutal corridor / down which we sometimes shuffle, and sometimes run." And it is also a lament offering catharsis: "Lament, lament, my father and I are leaving Paradise" ("The Expulsion," *Leaving Another Kingdom*, 41–42). The poet receives the supranatural, records it, and makes it happen. Stern often achieves transcendence through the fusion of the visible world with the art and culture of the past. His poetic double dances to the tune of Magritte, Oscar Schlemmer, and Picasso:

> I dance on the road and on the river and
> in the wet garden, all the time living in Crete
> and pre-war Poland and outer Zimbabwe,
> as through my fingers and my sparkling hair
> the morning passes, first the three loud calls
> of the bluejay, then the white door slamming,
> then the voices rising and falling in sudden harmony.
> ("Magritte Dancing," 31–37)

Poland before (and after) the Nazi *Anschluss* was part of Stern's legitimate inheritance and beckons to him.
   The nostalgic element in Stern's poems evokes an expansiveness of voice and a range of feeling that invite comparison to Walt Whitman. Yet their worlds are also separated by vast differences. Indeed in his interview with Pinsker (1984, 61), Stern distances himself from Whitman:

Pinsker: Granted you're a romantic of a different stripe (Jewish), but I feel the Whitmanian strain nonetheless. The long lines, the parallelisms, the repetition, the cataloging lists—all these seem very much indebted to Whitman.

Stern: Whitman is certainly a factor, but there's a concreteness in my work, a love of the particular, a clinging to the physical . . . But he didn't know about New York cafeterias.

Jonathan Monroe pushes a modified comparison:

> Whitman's is the voice of unlimited possibility, Stern's of the pos-
> sibilities within a more delineated sphere. If Whitman speaks for
> outwardness, the 'manifest destiny' of self and nation, Stern
> speaks for the recovery and sharing of inwardness. If Whitman is
> able to represent the spirit which in his day was building a new
> nation, Stern is compelled to image the ruins resulting from that
> ceaseless construction. As Whitman speaks for the promise of self
> and for a young country, Stern speaks against the betrayal of that
> promise. His poems are attempts to recover from the wreck of
> culture, and the consequent wreck of self, which is a dominant
> part of life in contemporary America. (1979, 41)

And Edward Hirsch calls Stern a late, ironic Jewish disciple of
Whitman (1985, 56).

Clearly Stern belongs to the tradition that harks back
through Whitman and Blake to the ancient Greeks and most
especially to the Psalms and Proverbs of the Hebrew Bible:

for what I thought was a soggy newspaper
turned out to be the first Book of Concealment, written in English.
and what I thought was a grasshopper in the windshield,
turned out to be the Faithful Shepherd chewing blood,
and what I thought was, finally, the real hand of God
turned out to be only a grey wire and a
pair of broken sunglasses
             ("Blue Skies, White Breasts, Green Trees," 14–20)

Stern often finds correspondences between the ways we
treat plant and animal life and the ways we treat each other,
between the "yellow iris" (1) and "a nest inside a ruined building, / a father hugging his child, / a Jew in Vilna." ("Three
Tears," 10–12). Poland and the special character of that place
are never out of Stern's consciousness. He is an archaeologist
sifting through the ruins of both America and Eastern Europe
to salvage from what has been condemned and neglected what
deserves saving. Like Whitman, he accepts the interdependence and interreliance of all things: plants, animals, human
beings and their objects. Perhaps this awareness and recognition of biology and zoology give scope to his writing, inviting a
comparison of the two poets who had such different back-
grounds and visions.

And how does Stern see himself in his immediate world? In this confession we find strong echoes of a strident nostalgia as he expounds on his self perception as an outsider in exile (Moyers 1989, 379):

> I'm in exile from the Christian world insofar as I'm a Jew and I'm in exile from the Jewish world insofar as I've broken away from Judaism. I'm in exile from the bourgeois Jewish world of Pittsburgh that I was expected to flourish in because when I was nineteen or twenty I rented a room and started to read books and became a crazy poet. . . . And I feel I'm in exile from the connection or community that I had with my sister. . . . So often I feel that I'm writing for her and about her, and that my life is a debt that I owe to her. I'm also in exile from the six million Jews who were killed. Now, at my age, I'm studying Yiddish, which is an expression of that exile and an attempt to redeem that exile simultaneously.

Stern's exile from the six million Jews combines both psychological and geographic distance, and much of his Holocaust writing acts as an atonement for that distance. In studying Yiddish, the lingua franca of Eastern European Jewry, he attempts to reify what has perished. Stern confesses the significant losses that have affected his life and he finds release in his poetry. Within this same conversation (Moyers, 383), Stern speaks of his attitude toward poetry and religion:

> my poetry is a kind of religion for me. It's a way of seeking redemption for myself, but just on the page. It is finally a way of understanding things so that they can be reconciled, explained, justified, redeemed. (Moyers 1989, 383)

Elizabeth Knight asks whether Stern views writing poems, like writing prayers, brings Stern to consider prayer as an embodiment of Jewish concerns and motifs:

> It's a good question, but a hard one to answer . . . because I don't know how to pray. But I do know how to write poetry and I often, even consciously think of poetry as a form of prayer. . . . Yes, there are a lot of Jewish connections in the poems. More than that. There's a rhythm and an incantational quality only partly derived from Whitman. I think it derives from my reading the Old Testament. (1987, 33)

Stern's meditative essay, "What Is the Sabbath?" (*American Poetry Review*), brings his Jewish self into focus. He begins: "I think of lying on my back listening to Brahms and looking at the cracks in the ceiling, Or it could be Vivaldi or Schumann. . . . I am a recumbent angel" (17). The Sabbath foreshadows Paradise, in which Stern's shoes are off, he wears the thinnest of T-shirts, and there are bird sounds, thoughts, lines of poems. But this is the Sabbath he came to only in adulthood:

> If you were raised in Western Pennsylvania, as I was, the Sabbath was forbidding, a day of mostly suffering, particularly if you not only had to undergo the public ordeal, the silent streets, the locked-up stores, the closed movies, but the private ordeal as well, the heavy Sunday of guilt and gloom, almost as the two Johns had planned it. . . . My own Sabbath came a day earlier, of course, since I was a Jew, and though I had to bear the sadness a little of their Sunday, I still had the pleasure of my own Friday night and Saturday, with its attention to feasting and celebration. There was an excitement, a headiness to that Sabbath, and though various things were forbidden, or at least frowned on, that wasn't the critical aspect. On the other hand, I wasn't pure anything. I was for a while bastard Orthodox and for a while liberal Conservative before I became nostalgic Agnostic at the age of thirteen and one day. (17)

Stern announces that the Sabbath is a day for man, a "dream . . . a work of art . . . a poem" (19). His yearning for a more attractive world, his infatuation with messianism (17, 18), his desire to share the fate of his fellow Jews, and most of all his concern with remembering place him squarely within the Jewish experience. The particularity of his Jewishness, his Jewish songs, and his Holocaust poetry, we see are strongly wedded to one another. Jews are mandated to remember by the Decalogue, the Hebrew prayer book, the philosophers, and the holy texts. Stern heeds the moral obligation, selecting nostalgia as his poetic muse. He turns to 1 Samuel for the biblical, cultural, and historic juxtapositions in "Weeping and Wailing" in *Paradise Poems* (1984a):

> I like the way my little harp makes trees
> leap, how putting the metal between my teeth

makes half the animals in my back yard quiver,
how plucking the sweet tongue makes the stars
live together in love and ecstasy

I bend my face and cock my head. My eyes
are open wide listening to the sound.
My hand goes up and down like a humming bird.
My mouth is opening and closing, I am singing
in harmony, I am weeping and wailing.

(1–10)

In some literal sense, Stern is playing a Jew's harp—the lyre of David the psalmist played by plucking its flexible metal tongue. As his hand "goes up and down like a humming bird," he is reminded of Orpheus, whose song made the trees dance and tamed the wild animals, and of the psalms that celebrate creation. The resultant poem is harmonious, declaring a oneness with the world. But it is also filled with minor chords, bespeaking a recognition—however unconscious—that "love and ecstasy" are somehow bound to "weeping and wailing," a quintessential Jewish spin on the romantic/orphic ball.

Stern obeys the prophetic call to do justly; a moment in "The Shirt Poem" in *Leaving Another Kingdom* recalls the political meetings of his childhood, the air thick with hope and brotherhood. Granted, such a poem takes the aesthetic risk of sentimentalizing the past. However, this litany can work—if the vision can be made convincing enough, so that we believe that in this rapture Stern seeks an authentic connection with history:

Gone is the sweetness in that closet, gone is the dream
of brotherhood, the affectionate meeting
of thinkers and workers inside a rented hall.
Gone are the folding chairs, gone forever
the sacred locking of elbows under the two flags.

On Sunday night they used to sing for hours
before the speeches. Once the rabbis joined them
and religion and economics were finally combined in exile.
"Death is a defect," they sang, and threw their hats
on the floor. "We will save nature from death,"

they shouted, and ended up dancing on the sound stage,
the dark crows and the speckled doves finally arm in arm.

(7–18)

Like the strange tune that vibrates from his Jew's harp, this,
too, is a song of lament, a blending of "weeping and wailing"
evocative of the Hebrew prophets. These men of memory—
rabbis and Jewish socialists—can never return. This poem
calls forth the politics early associated with the Bund, the
fiercely secular Jewish socialists in Russia who eventually
transformed themselves and their organization to America.
But the poem is also spiritual. Rav Kook, an eminent religious
Zionist, appears among the mourners in the synagogue:

Give this to Rabbi Kook who always arrived
With his clothes on fire and stood between the mourners
Singing songs against death in all three languages
at the crowded wall, in the dark sunlight.

(77–80)

Stern gathers together people of disparate politics and spirituality, uniting socialists and religious Zionists. He collects
them here in response to the injunction "to remember." Added
to this is the sense of mystery—are the "shirts" dead Jews who
perished in the Holocaust? Are they prisoners? Or are they
some hidden energy that comes to life when the closet door is
open, when they desire to be free? At best, all Stern can do
is keep faith with the eternal moral imperative of Jewish
history—to write and to record. As he puts it, thinking of the
empty-sleeved shirts that haunt his closet in the poem:

What is my life if not a substitute for yours,
and my dream a substitute for your dream?
Lord, how it has changed, how we have
made ourselves strange, how embarrassing the words
sound to us, how clumsy and half-hearted we are.
I want to write it down before it's forgotten,
how we lived, what we believed in;
most of all to remember the giants
and how they walked, always with white hair,
always with long white hair hanging down over their collars,

> always with red faces, always bowing and listening,
> their heads floating as they moved through the small crowd.
>
> (41–52)

Stern packs an entire world into this elegy of remembrance, which conjures up everything from socialism with its "giants" in its religious form to the rhapsodic joy of brotherhood in a world totally destroyed and nearly forgotten. Through this poem, this world is saved from oblivion.

For landscape, secrets, Jewish sadness, and a conversational Holocaust memory, we turn to "Four Sad Poems on the Delaware" in *Lucky Life* (1979), in which Stern writes about four plants growing along the towpath behind his home:

> This is a locust tree, dying of love,
> waiting one more time for its flowers to come,
> regretting its life on the stupid river,
> growing more and more Jewish as its limbs weaken.
>
> (4, 1–4)

Becoming an "old Jew" who can trace his troubles back to the destruction of the temples is to live both in the world and within history. Stern remarks to Mark Hillringhouse (1984, 27): "My identity with that tree has something to do with Judaism, and with persecution. The tree is short-lived—forty years maybe—it's asymmetrical, considered ugly, worthless. It is used for fence posts, torn down, replaced by other trees. I love that tree. I identify with it; it's my poverty tree" (27). Moreover, locusts are used for fence posts because they do not rot in the ground. They are also used to mark territory (possibly cultural). To Stern this is the most beautiful of trees—blooming in extraordinary color and possessing an incomparable smell. "I sometimes see the concentration camp number on the forearm, or forelimb. I don't identify a lot with the oak or the smooth maple" (27). Stern metamorphoses the telling event of the twentieth century into a haunting apparition of the victims. He is the locust "growing more and more Jewish as his limbs weaken" (4). Even though the Jews are no longer locusts, he remembers the "locust tree Jew" (25) abandoned, tested.

An elderly Jew ready for death also knows the "secret of life" that Stern alludes to in "Burying an Animal on the Way to New York," also in *Lucky Life:*

Don't flinch when you come across a dead animal lying on the road;
you are being shown the secret of life.
Drive slowly over the brown flesh,
You are helping to bury it.
If you are the last mourner there will be no caress
at all from the crushed limbs
and you will have to slide over the dark spot imagining
the first suffering all by yourself
Shreds of spirit and little ghost fragments will be spread out
for two miles above the white highway.
Slow down with your radio off and your window open
to hear the twittering as you go by.

                                                    (1–12)

Burial may be the last tangible physical act of remembering.
To see death's face plainly and to understand it—as the young
Moses Herzog understood when his mother rubbed her thumb
against her palm to teach the biblical verse about man emerg-
ing from dust and returning to it—is to eschew sentimentality
for deeper wonder. If the ceremonial of burial—that we "drive
slowly" over the bodies of the dead and that we imagine "the
first suffering," that we permit the "twittering" sounds to flow
through our open windows—strikes some readers as ghoul-
ish, then the juxtaposition of candor and compassion is precisely the "flinch" that his poem means to overcome.

If remembering represents the performance of one's Judaic
duty, then spirituality is the highest rung on the ladder of
feeling and observance. Stern's Jewish identity, while not religious, has a deep spiritual cast to it. Wonderment and mysticism are artfully conveyed in "The Blessed" (1984a, 6) and in
his reference to primordial man, Adam Kadmon, in "On the
Far Edge of Kilmer" (11). "Brain of My Heart" (1992) is a scath-
ing reminder of the Twelfth Crusade, a return to Europe where
murders will take five years to repay (14, 15). "In First Day of
Spring" Stern writes of the herding of Jews on Holy Thursday
to listen to a sermon at II Gesu (31); "Only Elegy" concludes
with a list of Jewish people who have had an impact on his life
(1995, 38). And God as the creator of nature is nice in "Nice
Mountain" (19). The kabbalistic "three" is prevalent in "The
Blessed," "Three Skies" and "Three Tears" (1984, 172–74, 37).
Biblical themes emerge repeatedly in "The Sensitive Knife,"

(28) "Strauss Park,"(24–25) "Joseph's Pockets" (85–87) and "Angel Poem" (90–93).

When interviewed by David Hamilton (1988) on the meaning of "The Red Coal," Stern recalled the story in Isaiah of an angel, one of the seraphim, placing a live coal in Isaiah's mouth to purge him of his sin. Stern also relates the Midrash (Midrash Rabbah, Exod. 1:26) of Moses as a baby in the pharaoh's court. The child is given a choice—between the pharaoh's jeweled crown and a hot coal. An angel intervenes and directs him to choose the coal; had he chosen otherwise, it would have been construed that he wanted to seize the pharaoh's crown, as the magician-priests had warned. This story has psychological and anthropological overtones that Freud has touched on. Moses puts his burned hand into his mouth and burns his tongue, thus his tongue-tiedness (1988, 56). When Mark Hillringhouse (1984, 30) comments, "Your poetry sometimes sounds rabbinical," Stern counters, "Why not? I'm a rabbi." His poetry draws on the literal meaning of "rabbi" as teacher and interpreter of the past.

"Sycamore," in *Leaving Another Kingdom* (1990), projects Stern's strong feeling for diasporic exile, with Apollo representing the danger and seductions of a world alien to Daphne. We are Daphne, and Stern is Israel at the Seder table, praising the sycamore tree and ultimately transforming himself into a tree:

> This year when I sit at the table with bitter bread
> in my hands I'll stop for one full minute to give
> some lovely praise for the sycamore; I'll say,
> let's stop a minute and think of the sycamore,
> let's think of the lovely white branches, let's think of the bark,
> let's think of the leaves, the three great maple lobes.
> What does it know of liberation? I'll say.
> What does it know of slavery, bending over
> the streams of America? How does it serve as a text
> for lives that are pinched or terrified? Were the sycamores
> along the banks of the Rhine or Oder? Tell me
> about its bells again, those most of all,
> the hard gray balls that dangle from the stems,
> tell me about the bark, the large thin flakes,

and the colors, dark at the bottom, light at the top.
And I will go on for an hour storming and raving
before I drink my final cup of wine
and shout to the Egyptians—as I do every year—
you are my Apollo, you are my flesh pot, forgive me
for turning into a tree, forgive me, you lovers
of life for leaving you suddenly, how foolish
and cheated you must have felt, how foolish the body
must feel when it's only a carcass, when the breath
has left it forever, as it always does
in search of something painless; and I'll end
by sprinkling the tree and sprinkling the ground around it
and holding my hand up for a second of silence,
since I am the one who runs the service—I am
the only one in this house, I do my reclining
all alone, I howl when I want.

                                                                (69–98)

He suggests the ugliness of the German world tied to the
Holocaust, the pain inflicted upon the victims; he hints at
slavery and ultimate redemption. Can a tree tell the story of
pinched or terrified lives? The bread of affliction is yoked to the
bitterness of modern history. It is also inextricably tied to the
recounting of the story in the Haggadah (the text of the Passover Seder), except there was no redemption for the European
Jew. This, then, is not only the Seder service, but also a memorial service for the suddenly vanished "carcass": Stern sancti-
fies the ground around his trees with water traditionally associated with purification. And instead of chanting, he howls his
despair and rage. Each one, he counsels, must mourn in his
own way. At Passover, a time for recounting, one remembers
all the atrocities directed against the Jewish people. And his
wandering Jew emerges as symbolic consciousness, continually searching for political and religious security and freedom as he flees the flesh pots, an eternal enemy. History and
modernity are blended.

Time and time again Stern heaps together the disparate
pieces of his life trying to compose the definitive autobiography, his protests to the contrary. Thus the confessional as well
as nostalgic motif may be observed in the concluding lines of

"Knowledge Forwards and Backwards" (1990), which begins with the memory of city boys' street games in the 1930s, spying and maiming. Experience is the best teacher and insulator against pain:

> We were not yet assimilated,
> Nothing fit us, our shoes were rotten; it takes
> time to adjust to our lives, ten and twelve years
> was not enough for us to be comfortable—
> after a while we learn how to talk, how to cry,
> what causes pain, what causes terror.
>
> (9–14)

Self-realization and acceptance of his earlier persona are apparent in "The Same Moon above Us." This poem ostensibly is about Ovid after he was exiled by Caesar. Stern thinks of himself as a bum sleeping over a subway grate and also identifies with Ovid, co-opting his situation, himself in exile, as he ends up on Third Avenue "humming in both languages." His language could be English or Yiddish, or, for Ovid, Latin—the speech of one's old country. The "soft pillow" is an exercise in the poet's imagination. Both poets are the "other" in society, especially Stern:

> the white moon above me, the dirt somewhere beneath me,
> the sidewalks crazy again, the lights in Jersey,
> the lights in Manhattan, like the fires in Rome,
> burning again without me, I on the edge
> of Empire walking west in the snow, my neck
> now raw, my feet now raw, my eyes gone blind,
> the last one on the streets, the last poet left
> who lives like this, the last one who does a dance
> because of the dirty ice and the leather boots,
> alone in the middle of nowhere, no one to see
> his gorgeous retrieval, no one to shake the air
> with loud applause and no one to turn and bow to
> in the middle of his exile ten cold minutes
> before he leaves the street for his soft pillow
> and his other exile, far from Rome's domain,
> and far from New York's domain, now silent and peaceful.
>
> (105–20)

Sometimes, as in "Grapefruit" (1984a), his fragments add up to a wild charity and praise—bittersweet, like the grapefruit itself. Tearing at his breakfast over the sink in who-knows-what brutish frustration, he manages to be inspired and renewed by the food he mangles and eats—"how quickly the day goes, / how full it is of sunshine" (226). But the Divine is very close to Stern, and the relationship is playful; in a final burst of absurd, irreverent yet poignant self-irony he echoes and parodies the formulaic introduction to every Hebrew blessing:

> Blessed art thou oh grapefruit King of the universe,
> Blessed art Thou my sink, oh Blessed art Thou
> Thou milkweed Queen of the sky, burster of seeds,
> Who bringeth forth juice from the earth.
>
> (58–61)

The spirituality and the intellectuality that inhabit places are made clear in "Psalms" (1979, 58), where Stern makes the connection between the "bald hills of Tennessee" and the "rabbis of Brooklyn." In each of them and anywhere, everywhere as well, "the gigantic lips / [move] through the five books of ecstasy, grief and anger." The Divine Presence of the Hassidic tradition exists wherever one stands, for even if the locale is strange, the passions are not. He shares those passions he attributes to the books the rabbis have always read (and therefore to the rabbis themselves)—the ecstasy, the grief, and the anger. He is distant from their world, but also he is so intertwined with it. He is with them, in Brooklyn as in Tennessee. The poem, itself a psalm, rejoices at all his worlds, as well as at the range of embrace in his words:

> When I drove through the little bald hills of Tennessee
> I thought of the rabbis of Brooklyn bent over their psalms.
> I thought of the tufts of hair and the bones and ridges
> and the small cows eating peacefully
> out on the open slopes or in the shadows
> while the forehead wrinkled and the gigantic lips moved
> through the five books of ecstasy, grief and anger.
>
> (1–7)

Stern discusses the importance of presence and place in "In the One Thing No One Else Wanted" (1979):

> If I had to explain my art I would talk about it in terms of staking out a place that no one else wanted. . . . On a most literal level, I am talking about weeds, and waste places, and lovely pockets, and in my poems I mean it on a literal level as well as on a psychological and symbolic level. . . . In one sense there is a battle—or at least a dialogue—going on between light and dark, present and past, city and country, civilization and savagery, power and lack of it, and I would seem to favor the latter. But I don't write from a philosophical point of view, and furthermore I am seized by the contradictions, and I have irony, but most of all I have affection for both sides, if I may call them sides, and move toward reconciliation and forgiveness. I am moved a lot by Jewish mysticism and Hassidism and by the historical idea of the Jews as well in blue holes, shirts, ties, stones, corduroys, spikes, grandfathers; and as with Heyen, in a—from a poetic and mythic point of view. A lot of my poems have as a setting nature or the garden. But I am in no sense of the word a nature poet; I am equally at home in the city and the country and go where my spirit takes me, whether it be Upper Broadway or the Delaware River. (31)

Stern correctly observes that he does not write from a philosophical point of view, because even his relative contradictions do not fall into a logical philosophical construct. Rather, he embraces the idea of paradoxes creating a mystical whole. Placing his multiple references to Poland in this context, the weed and wasteland imagery become obvious.

In "Weeping and Wailing: The Jewish Songs of Gerald Stern" (1990), Pinsker concludes with a statement about Stern and the modern Hassidic movement: "In important though not specific ways, Stern can count himself in their number, just as Stern counts himself in the *Minyan* of those performing the ritual of *Tashlikh* [a ceremony in which one's sins, in the form of bread, are cast into a body of running water on the first day of Rosh Hashanah] along the banks of the Delaware":

> Behind me in the locusts
> . . . are ten or twelve others
> in coats and hats, with books in their hands. We sing
> a song for the year and throw our sticks in the water.

We empty our pockets of paper and lint. . . .
I make a kissing sound with my hand—I guess
we all do. This was a painful year, a painful
two years.

("Tashlikh" *Lovesick*, 5–12)

The rabbis would, no doubt, gloss *Tashlikh* in different terms.
No matter; dance and prayer, prayer and dance—it all adds up
to the same thing. In the Mittel-Europe of the nineteenth century, one who performed a *Mitzvah* (commandment) was
called a *Yiddische Mensch* (Jewish human being with the attributes of goodness). And among the best, the most characteristic, the most "Jewish" of Gerald Stern's songs, this poem
in particular is a subtle indicator of the joy derived from the
diligent pursuit of the Law.

Of the Holocaust specifically, Stern said in his oral interview
with me in 1996, "It belongs to me, the particular tragedy of
the Jewish people, an extension of persecution and man's in-
ane stupidity." One finds in his Holocaust poetry a strong
sense of guilt for having lived in the United States in safety and
in peace during that horrendous time. Some critics, Pinsker
among them, consider "Behaving Like a Jew" (1979) a signature piece that characterizes the indifference and suffering of
the twentieth century. In this poem Stern stops his car for a
"dead opossum" on the road and takes a negative position
against a culture in which "the spirit of Lindbergh" is "Over
everything, / that joy in death, that philosophical / understanding of carnage, that concentration on the species" (11–
14). Stern, protesting, announces, "I am going to be unappeased at the opossum's death / I am going to behave like a
Jew / and touch his face, and stare, into his eyes, / and pull
him off the road" (15–16).

Moyers questions the meaning of "Behaving Like a Jew."
Stern replies,

I'm declaring an act of mourning. In staring into that opossum's
eye, I became that opossum and, identifying with him, I became a
Jew. I identified with his whiskers, his round belly, his little
dancing feet. Maybe I'm also claiming something for Jews that
shouldn't be claimed for them, but for all thinking people, all feeling people. Maybe I'm claiming feeling for the Jew even though

there are as many unfeeling Jews as there are unfeeling Gentiles.
I'm sensitive about arrogating feeling to the Jews, but at that point
in that poem, I was claiming tenderness, elegy, love, memory for
that absurd little animal. (386)

Stern sees the Jew as ethnic victim, and for him Charles
Lindbergh represents the political, even fascist right—as an
isolationist who urged the United States to remain neutral
toward the Nazis before World War II. Lindbergh epitomized
a society that valued machines over life. Reeve Lindbergh
(1998), youngest child of the aviator, took a very different position on her father's public persona. In her memoir, *Under
a Wing,* in which she discusses her father's anti-Semitic
speeches of the1930s, she is convinced that was not his intent. At any rate, there are many negative aspects of his life
that will not disappear. And Stern uses the opossum as an
occasion for reflection, for what can only be called "prayer"—
but not for a metaphysical leap. Instead he seeks to re-
establish contact with his "animal sorrow," in grieving for a
specific opossum, one with a hole "in his back / and the wind
blowing through his hair" (1979, 4–5).

Stern balances the central tension between thought and action, between the things that "sicken" him and those that draw
him to the opossum. With considerable delicacy, he does more
than merely shake a fist at roadways, automobiles, and progress in general: he offers a work with deeper homiletic reso-
nances. Stern utilizes lists to imply that death has dominion
both across and above the landscape, but consider the manner in which the repetition of "I am sick" links these stanzas
together:

> I am sick of the country, the bloodstained
> bumpers, the stiff hairs sticking out of the grilles
> the slimy highways, the heavy birds
> refusing to move;
> I am sick of the spirit of Lindbergh over everything. . . .
> (7–11)

Stern's phrases—"the spirit of Lindbergh" and "the heavy
birds" who no longer fly—are rich in associations, but his
Lindbergh is not the hero associated with the *Spirit of St. Louis*

and the solo flight across the Atlantic. No, this is the man who was enthralled by the Sturm und Drang of German romanticism, by philosophers who equated beauty with death, by the cult of Adolph Hitler, the kind of romanticism that led directly to the death camps, where a "concentration of the species" took a hideous and horrific turn. Stern's charged language challenges the reader to see the dark patterns in our history.

As to Stern's assertion that he will be "unappeased" by the opossum's death, he alludes to Jewish ethics, concerned less with what one believes than with what one does. Stern therefore pulls off the road (in a gesture that seemingly contradicts the imperatives of "Burying an Animal on the Way to New York," in *Leaving Another Kingdom*); touches the opossum's face; stares into his dead eyes. The first poem seems to be bizarre, but what he will not do is simply stand in a wet ditch "and praise the beauty and the balance / And lose myself in the immortal lifestream" (1979, 22–23). That conceivably would be to lose oneself in the Lindbergh philosophy but would not be how to "behave like a Jew" who follows the stringent moral demands on behavior prescribed by Judaism.

Stern concludes by bringing his poem full circle. The dead opossum that was initially compared to "an enormous baby" (2) is now visualized as an old world Eastern European Jew: "his round belly and his curved fingers / and his black whiskers and his little dancing feet" (27–28). If Lindbergh embodies a romantic tradition that conflates joy and death, the "black whiskers and . . . little dancing feet" imply a very different romanticism, one that feels the intrinsic holiness in all things and that dances and prays in an effort to release these "holy sparks" from the vessels in which they are imprisoned. Here Stern's attraction to Hassidic thought and spirit asserts itself.

Another way of looking at this poem is through its tonal blueness. In his book *On Being Blue*, William Gass observes:

Among the ancient elements, blue occurs everywhere:
in ice and water, in the flame as purely as in
the flower, overhead and inside caves, covering
fruit and oozing out of clay. Although green enlivens
the earth and mixes in the ocean, and we find it,

copperish, in fire, green air, green skies are rare
Gray and brown are widely distributed,
but there are no joyful swatches of either, or any exuberant black,
    sullen
pink, or acquiescent orange. Blue is therefore most suitable as the
    color
of interior life. Whether sleek light sharp high bright thin quick
    sour
new and cool or low deep sweet thick dark soft slow smooth heavy
    old and warm
blue moves easily among them all. And all profoundly qualify our
    states of feeling.

                                                              (75–76)

A particular "blueness" permeates this poem, even as it does
in many of Stern's other pieces as well—in blue holes, shirts,
ties, stones, corduroys, spikes, grandfathers; and as with
Heyen, in a vastly different context, God comes up blue. Entering the "blue world" for Stern is a willful act—an act of
survival that orders the multitude of details and events that
occur in the external world. His interior life of thought and
reflection is not one of resigned acceptance. When there is
acceptance, it is usually uneasy or tenuous, as in "Behaving
Like a Jew." His ability simultaneously to grasp an external
event and to come to grips with it internally signals that Stern
knows his interior life—how to use the blueness. At no time
does he cut himself off from the external world, where his
persona's hands shake from handling the opossum; for only in
this world is action possible.

    According to Richard Chess (1988), Stern

is the post-Holocaust Jew standing up against the forces of evil
residing not in man's technological inventions but in the very
spirit of man himself. Stern stands determinedly opposed to a
society that chooses to ignore the consequences of its behavior,
that indulges in a "philosophical understanding of carnage." Perhaps by his moral gesture, he is perpetuating the image of the Jew
as the world's moral guardian. Reading this poem against the
backdrop of the Holocaust, we can recognize the poignancy of
Stern's method of behaving like a Jew. (150)

But Stern is not always as successful at rendering a realism from which he is distant. Sidra Dekoven Ezrahi (1980) questions the authenticity of American Jewish poets who write on this most ungraspable subject—distanced as they are from the Holocaust in every sense: physically, emotionally, intellectually, artistically, and spiritually. Can they approach this subject without sounding trivial or sentimental? She identifies three modes in which American writers have engaged Holocaust history vicariously. First, there has been a tendency to "extract a universal message out of the particularist experience and to explore the relevance of such experience for post-Holocaust man." Next, American writers on the Holocaust have sought to "possess the experience itself . . . through a form of witness or historical reconstruction." And finally, they have attempted to render it "through a leap into fantasy charged with historical possibilities" (216). "Behaving Like a Jew" provides us with what Ezrahi would characterize as an attempt to understand the relevance for post-Holocaust man and, to a limited degree, for post-Holocaust Jewish man.

"The War against the Jews" (1981) also fits Ezrahi's categories. This poem describes a wood carving in a Polish town square, of Jews about to be arrested by a German soldier. Stern begs for a reversal of history for the Jews and for the soldier. Desperate and pitiful though it is, this cry cannot save either. "He was carved while he could still remember his mother's garden. / How glad he was to go to Poland. / How young he felt in his first pair of boots" (8–10), are the innocent words of the young soldier. This unassuming poem is striking for its empathy for both Jew and German, exemplifying Judaism's feeling for all of humankind. But this "leap into fantasy" is finally sentimental and exploitative, for it resolves on a note of historical impossibility, a "wooden cry": "Oh wooden figures, go back, go back" (10). Some readers will surely see the poem as improperly representing the subject matter.

"Soap" (1990) represents another leap into the irreversible fantastic and will no doubt offend those who expect a respectful silence. But when it comes to tone, Stern is the most surprising of poets, typically pursuing a metaphor or an idea as far as possible just to see what it will yield, with the result that his comic inflations often turn out to be serious. Whereas

"Soap" begins as an odd, semihumorous piece about finding small bars of soap in human shape ("Here is a green Jew / with thin black lips" [1–2]), it quickly evolves into a study of the poet's imaginary counterpart who perished in the Holocaust. To write of green Jews and blue Jews, some Austrian, some Hungarian—human beings metamorphosed into fancy beautiful soaps—is to pile grotesquerie on top of grotesquerie. "Soap" in this assessment demands a return to Adorno's claim that after Auschwitz, poetry is barbaric. Is there no better choice of words than Stern's? For the poem has images so stark, so shrill, that Richard Chess (1988, 152) brands the entire poem a selfish act of invention, an easy method of purging oneself of guilt. By contrast, the "weeping and wailing," the song of lament (a constant Stern theme), is for those "who remember the eighteenth century." Those European Jews, born in 1865 or 1870, are the "ones who listened / to heavenly voices, they were lied to and cheated" (152). Stern's alter ego in "Soap," born in 1925 in Poland, is his secret sharer and blood brother, deprived of his books, like the victims of the Holocaust, unable to run away to escape their hideous destiny:

> I don't like to see him born
> in a little village fifty miles from Kiev
> and have to fight so wildly just for access
> to books, I don't want to see him struggle
> half his life to see a painting or just to
> sit in one of the plush chairs listening to music.
> He was dragged away in 1940
> and turned to some use in 1941,
> although he may have fought a little, piled
> some bricks up or poured some dirty gasoline
> over a German truck. . . . I love
> the way he smelled the air, I love how he looked,
> how his eyes lighted up, how his cheeks were almost pink
> when he was happy. I love how he dreamed, how he almost
> disappeared when he was in thought. For him
> I write their poem, for my little brother, if I
> should call him that—maybe he is the ghost
> that lives in the place I have forgotten, that dear one
> that died instead of me—oh ghost, forgive me !—
>
> (62–80)

Stern comments to Gary Pacernick (1996) on his associative way of writing:

> I actually remember starting "Soap" in a little store in Iowa City that was selling soap, and horrified by the kind of graceless accumulation of soap for its own sake. I may have been thinking about something or remembering something or had read something or, in my gruesome, ironic way had connected soap with the camps and the poem came into being.
>
> But as the poem came into being, as I got into that animal, that poem, it took over, my memory took over and my horror and my anger and my pity and, most of all, my guilt as an American Jew of a certain age who, if I'd been in Europe, would probably have been dead but was not because I was American. A very common subject for American Jews in my generation. So in the poem itself, I talk about my other, my spirit, who would have been born in Europe—how I would have thrown gasoline bombs at German trucks. (2)

In the same manner that Wiesel argues there cannot be novels about Auschwitz, we can argue that there is no such thing as a "Holocaust poem," even though we know cognitively that there is nothing in the poetic genre per se to disqualify it as a form of expression for any particular subject matter. Many of us are as uncomfortable with the position of silence as Stern is with the string of negatives ("I don't like to see (62) . . . . I don't want to see." (66)) that provide the counterweight, the tension in "Soap." To visualize such an imaginary brother is to become a witness by imagination as Ezrahi (1980) would put it. One could argue that art itself is vicarious, a way of undergoing another person's experience. If the Holocaust tested the limits of intelligence, of the ability to confer pattern and meaning on our century's most shattering event, it is no less a test and a challenge for imaginative writers. Thus, in criticizing the visceral quality of Stern's images, Chess misses the soft and loving note upon which the poem concludes (1988). Whether or not "Soap" suffices for *all* readers, it is nonetheless a daring, innovative, fully engaged poem about the guilt of having survived.

In "Bread Without Sugar" (1992), a poetic melange of many elements, including an elegy to his father, Stern recounts moments from a trip to Poland replete with the pieces of racial memory that a man shores up against his ruin, his ultimate demise, and his future burial site:

> There are two plots . . .
> the third is in Egypt; I go from country
> to country in search of a plot; I see me
> buried in Poland—what a nightmare *that* is!—
> I go to my mother's city
> and on the second day while waiting
> for Gregor Musial, my Polish translator,
> I am hit by a cab; I'll never
> die of a heart attack in Warsaw,
> I'll never catch pneumonia, not there;
> the cab will lose its steering and jump
> the curb; of course I'll be the one sitting
> closest to the street, I'll be reading
> the newspaper with a dictionary,
> I'll be reading the principal poets
> in Polish and English. . . .
> . . . .
> . . . What a
> fate for a Jew from Pittsburgh, guilt
> and sadness driving him for fifty years,
> to join his brothers and sisters that way.
>   (155–70, 173–75)

Stern does not equivocate about indicting his ancestral home and the killing fields of his people. Poland is not a metaphor for death; it is death itself, inflicted from without.

With the same force, Stern mixes culture, religion, and history in "Hot Dog" (1995), a poem more than forty pages long. It is at once vexing, magical, and special, an experience akin to wandering in a wonderful forest, almost lost, and then feeling immense relief at returning home. Fruit, stone, wind, and wheat are symbols of holiness in the Hebrew Bible, and shapes of a ruined land have something to do with the riddle of how the soul is trapped within heavy flesh. This post-Auschwitz Ezekiel craves mercy, illuminating the banal mystery of memory as he explodes the material objects surrounding him. Where one least expects it we have:

Yiddish driven
into a corner onto some seats in back of
a tiny theater on Second Avenue; I climbed
the stage, we should have turned it into the language
of feeling—we already did—we would have added
more complexity and more profundity
and borrowed less from the Russian and the English
and voices moaning in Polish and Ukranian
as one more coffin floated by: Forgive me,
Jew, Jew, forgive me, kike; forgive me,
. . . Ah, where should we put the bell
now that the goat his throat is slit?

(pt. 5, ll. 41–52)

And I
who didn't shower at Auschwitz—you should forgive me
for mentioning it again—I breathed my fire
wherever I went.

(pt. 6, ll. 94–97)

Two death symbols existing in tandem: the ancient scapegoat
and the gas showers of the twentieth century. The derelict son
eats a pear on Yom Kippur afternoon; his stomach burns with
fear of being found out. As he moves on with his life, he confesses that eating the pear helped him immeasurably to meet
life's difficult moments (84). The poet as Jew identifies with
Elijah the prophet who was to herald the coming of the Messiah. "Hot Dog" is the name of a homeless, beautiful street
person whom Stern watches over and who lives in and around
Tompkins Square Park in New York City. The poem's other
characters are St. Augustine, Walt Whitman, the biblical
Noah, a ninety-year-old black preacher from the Midwest, and
Gerald Stern himself. Birds and flowers are recurrent
motifs—symbols of beauty, fragility, and vulnerability. As articulated by Stern, the birds are kindred spirits of Stern's personal pain. In "Hot Dog," as in "Soap," the connection between
symbols for death and destruction, as in "Soap," turns obsessive, visceral, and grotesque:

I remember the smell
of dead birds when I lived in Pittsburgh, there was

a certain rottenness, a sweetness I would know
somehow long in advance the smell was coming,
and I would see it there, the broken wing,
blood on the neck, a beak gone, or a leg gone;
it was for me my loss.

(pt. 4, ll. 16–22)

Here Stern in recalling his own smaller deaths and their smell,
seeks to identify the horror he cannot know first hand.

In "The Rose Warehouse" (1984b), history matters in ways
that strike one as Eastern European,"Jewish," rather than
American, even though the locale is pure Northeastern U.S.A.
Ostensibly the poem is about the end of a love affair and
Stern's sadness at leaving New York and returning home to
Pennsylvania. The warehouse used to be a meat-processing
plant, and there are sheep and cattle—in stone—projecting
from the top floor. The building, a hangout for prostitutes,
stands near one of the entrances to the Lincoln Tunnel. When
Stern writes of loss, it is chillingly immediate, no matter how
far removed from his present. He does not recapture the past
as much as relive it, and his memory is burdensome as well as
comforting. The opening of "The Rose Warehouse" is chatty
and ironic, but its ending is sinister, as he binds the Jewish
customs of mourning to the Holocaust:

Ah tunnel cows
watching over my goings out
and my comings in,
you preside, like me, over your own butchery.

I always look for you
when I go back to Pennsylvania,
driving under the rusty piers
and up Fortieth Street.

All of New York must be laid out for you up there,
the slope on Park Avenue,
the moon on the river,
the roof of the Port Authority.

I feel like putting up my own head,
the head of Gerald Stern,

on the side of the Rose Warehouse, his glasses slipping off,
His tears falling one by one on Eleventh Avenue.

I want to see if he will sing
or if he will stare out at the blue sky forever and forever.
I want to see if he's a god
and feels like murmuring a little in the lost tongue

or if he's one of those black humans
still mourning after thirty years—
some German Jew
talking about Berlin,

the town that had everything;
some man of love
who dug his own grave and entered there;
some sorrowful husband

refusing to wash, refusing to listen to music
cutting his flesh, rubbing dust in his hair,
throwing in dirt, throwing in dirt, throwing in flowers,
Kissing the shovel good-by, kissing the small shovel.

                                                                (1–32)

Discussing "The Rose Warehouse," again in the 1987 interview with Elizabeth Knight, Stern calls it "a very Jewish poem.
The funeral rite at the end is Jewish." Cutting the flesh is
mourning in extremis. The Jewish custom calls upon mourners to rend only a small but visible piece of their clothing, and
the lapel or necktie is often the item torn. By being literal, the
poem tries to avoid sentimentality, but it is a prayer as well as
a statement of bereavement. "I also incorporate . . . the death
of Jews of Europe, the German Jews in particular. So in the
rhythm and in the ideas and in the tone and the gestures and
the attitude, there's prayer. This poem is a *Kaddish* [the prayer
one recites for the dead], though I didn't say '*Yehai shmai
rabba m'vorach* . . .' [May His great name be blessed for ever
and ever]" (34). Burial and the Holocaust and Jewish
ceremony loom large in "The Rose Warehouse," as does Stern's
concept of poetry as prayer. At a poetry reading in Philadelphia, someone in the audience pointed out to Stern that the
rhythms of this poem had a biblical quality and a linguistic
relationship to the Jewish morning prayer service.

Stern's attunement to the cruel ironies of Jewish history recalls the fate that allowed him to dance before his parents in a small living room in Beechwood Boulevard in Pittsburgh in 1945, "5,000 miles away from the other dancing—in Poland and Germany." Appropriately he titles this poem "The Dancing" (1990):

> In all these rotten shops, in all this broken furniture
> and wrinkled ties and baseball trophies and coffee pots
> I have never seen a post-war Philco
> with the automatic eye
> nor heard Ravel's "Bolero" the way I did
> in 1945 in that tiny living room
> on Beechwood Boulevard, nor danced as I did
> then, my knives all flashing, my hair all streaming,
> my mother red with laughter, my father cupping
> his left hand under his armpit, doing the dance
> of old Ukraine, the sound of his skin half drum,
> half fart, the world at last a meadow,
> the three of us whirling and singing, the three of us
> screaming and falling, as if we were dying,
> as if we could never stop—in 1945—
> in Pittsburgh, beautiful filthy Pittsburgh, home
> of the evil Mellons, 5,000 miles away
> from the other dancing—in Poland and Germany—
> oh god of mercy, oh wild God.
>
> (1–19)

By remembering not only "the evil Mellons" but also that "other dancing," the Stern of the dance of death becomes a political as well as a personal poet, turning his attention back to the historical world, showing how one family's heaven existed alongside another's hell. His work enlarges itself so that the destruction of one kingdom—a private personal world—comes to stand for the destruction of a second kingdom—the larger public world. In these two realms, every paradise is lost. And the repetitive beat of the bolero propelling the dancing is no accident.

Stern tells Moyers (1989) about the concentration camps and the destruction of the Jews and the possibility of dancing on those open graves:

Yes, but "dancing" is a gory word there because in part it was,
forgive me, those Jews dancing in the showers and at the end of
the gallows and as they were shot and as they were tortured. That
was a kind of hideous dancing, Hieronymus Bosch dancing, but it
was also a victorious dancing coming from a Jewish tradition. So it
was partly joyous and partly hideous. I remember my own dancing
in Pittsburgh and I'm also remembering that other dancing.

Then, of course, in the last line I take the turn I do. . . . I didn't
know the poem was going to include the other dancing or that it
was going to take that turn in the last line. These were gifts. Terrible gifts. Sad gifts. Good gifts. I wrote and suddenly, "oh God of
mercy, oh wild God."

I call Him "God of Mercy" and there is irony there because what
mercy was shown? But the wildness . . . is a prayer and it's also a
statement of praise for God. I call Him "wild God" as a way of
almost forgiving Him because He is wild, because He's on another
mission, because He wasn't paying enough attention, "I'll be back
in a minute. I've got to do this wonderful thing. I'm creating a
universe over here."

He's wild and He's unconnected, and He didn't pay enough attention so that horrible thing happened. Of course, that's my metaphor in the poem; I'm not talking about this philosophically or
logically or literally. I was being ironic and not ironic when I called
Him "God of mercy" because He is a God of mercy.

And I was being ironic, but I was mostly praising, when I said, "oh
wild God. . . ." It was an act of forgiveness . I think that's what I
was doing—forgiving God. I should not have the right to forgive
God for others, but for my own self I was partly doing that, and
maybe to a degree for others as well. (388)

Stern denies the claim of those like Adorno who say you cannot write about the Holocaust, and that poetry is no longer
possible after the Holocaust, but he admits, "You can cheapen
it and you can trivialize it." Like Heyen, Stern feels that a bad
poem can do it injustice and most poems are bad poems:

But American Jews—American non-Jews, too—are in a different place because of the Holocaust. What is their debt? What is their duty? Where were they?

We were saving ourselves. We were forgetting. We were not remembering. We were not identifying. . . . It's a complicated story, of course—I feel guilty about—and I'm trying to pay my debt in the ways that I can. (389)

God is both merciful and wild because God remains God, even though the Holocaust happened. God's nature has not changed. Stern's concluding line in "The Dancing" is in accord with the dualistic nature of God as expressed by Ismar Schorsch (1996), the chancellor of the Jewish Theological Seminary, which in a sense puts Stern's theological position in agreement with mainstream Judaic thinking. "God is both transcendent and imminent, incomprehensible and knowable. Ignorance does not deprive me of a sense of relationship. God is a verb and not a noun, an ineffable presence that graces my life with a daily touch of eternity. I have no doubt that Shabbat is a foretaste of the world to come" (83). How very similar this is to Stern's projection of "What is this Sabbath?" Schorsch is most circumspect about being able to detect the hand of God in history. The black hole of the Holocaust has blurred his vision. Theologically he takes refuge in the concept of a self-limiting God. He is numbed by the human capacity to do evil and the divine reluctance to save us from ourselves.

Stern persists in questioning Knight by audaciously asking where the law comes from and is there a God! He continues (42), "Which society do I, as a poet, belong to and what social conventions do I conform to? . . . I insist on the merits of language in evoking reality, truth and justice." The law is a way of finding truth, of expressing faith in something larger than oneself—most certainly a talmudic concept.

"The Jew and the Rooster Are One" (Stern 1995, 45–46), is Stern at his unsettling graphic best. The rooster as synonymous with the Jew tells us how one who once was a force to be reckoned with has been brought low. The sovereign of the barnyard was to issue the morning wake-up call. For the Jew, his manifold contributions to humanity and civilization notwithstanding, the Holocaust constituted the wake-up call that should have awakened all human kind, as he was summoned to ignominious death.

In traditional Jewish homes following an ancient custom, prior to the *Kol Nidre* service on the eve of Yom Kippur, the white rooster served as expiation for one's sins in the hope that the person offering the *Kapporot* (the sacrifice) as atonement would be granted another year of life and peace. One atones by giving the bird to the needy. Only that act as part of repentance gives meaning to the ceremony.

Stern uses the implement of the paintbrush yoked to his wordsmanship to tell the story. He seems to be saying that there is a way to show murderous death that is not degrading, difficult though it may be. The rooster and the Jew stripped bare become objects of art. The rooster cannot contain his sorrow prefiguring the death that was to be his. The shame as well as the pain he feels for his personal suffering is unbearable. He is not killed according to the laws of ritual slaughter and he angrily anticipates his fate:

> No rabbi
> was present, this he knew, and no dead butcher
> had ever been there with his burnished knife
> and his bucket of sand; this was the angry rooster
> (18–21)

His disgrace is magnified because it is so public—taking place as it does in the middle of the living room, in the middle of the house, in the middle of living space:

> and yet at the same time the chair
> as debonair as any, the brown mahogany
> polished, the carving nineteenth century, the velvet
> green, an old velour, as if to match
> the plumes a little, a blue with a green.
> (14–18)

So in many cases was the Jew either snatched from the comfort of his home to the camps or if he resisted, killed in his own space.

The artist as third-person narrator calls upon the reader's imagination to absorb the horror of this picture. As in Chaim

Soutine's portraits of dismembered carcasses, we see in the metaphors for the wanton brutality of our time the closeness of the extremes of ugliness and beauty. Those who should have soared are now bedraggled:

> he still was golden underneath his feathers
> with freckles of blood, for he was a ripped-open Jew,
> and organs all on show, the gizzard, the liver,
> for he was a bleeding Tartar, and he was a Frenchman
> dying on the way to Paris and he was
> tethered to a table, he was slaughtered.
>
> (57–62)

The writer, like the artist, takes in the scene from the other's perspective. Thus, the rooster is golden as Stern, as an American, has the "golden" opportunity to see things as the distant observer and not as the victim. Nonetheless, are we all willing to atone for the Tartar, the Frenchman, the rooster, and the Jew?

In the powerful "Adler" (1990, 177–79), Stern writes with authority of the life of American Jewish immigrants on the Lower East Side of New York and about *King Lear.* When he injects the Holocaust, comparing certain characters and actions in the Shakespearean tragedy adapted for the Yiddish stage, he is careful to qualify his knowledge of that event as second hand. He is therefore freed from including the gruesome images of emaciated/murdered Jews. By concentrating on the life of American Jewish immigrants prior to the war, this honest and profound poem successfully captures the grief and pain particular to the American Jewish experience of the Holocaust.

The poem is first an ode to Jacob Adler, luminary of the Yiddish stage, whose talents were universally recognized and celebrated. "It is said," Stern writes, "that Isadora Duncan came to worship him, / that John Barrymore came to study his acting, / that when he died they carried his coffin around / from theater to theater, that people mourned in the streets, / that he lay in a Windsor tie and a black silk coat" (135–40). At the heart of the poem is Adler's fame beyond the ghetto, suggesting that Yiddish theater and Jewish cultural life in general were highly regarded by the upper echelons of Gentile society.

Congenial relations between Jewish and Anglo-American culture, as established through artistic exchange, contrast sharply with the relationship between Jewish and German culture.

"There is a point where even Yiddish / becomes a tragic tongue and even Adler / can make you weep" (21–23), Stern writes ironically, alluding at once to the historical development in Yiddish theater, which the production of *Lear* signified, as well as to the virtual disappearance of the Yiddish language, along with its Eastern European speakers following World War II. Jewish audiences identified with the universality of Shakespeare's message:

> They sit [the audience] in their chairs for hours
> to hear him curse his God; he looks at the dust
> and asks, what have I done, what have I done,
> for Him to turn on me; that audience murmurs,
> Daughters, daughters, it cries for the sadness
> that came to all of them in America.
>
> (23–28)

In the betrayal of Lear, this audience of immigrants could palpably experience the betrayals they suffered in America as their children abandoned traditional Jewish values and assimilated into the modern, secular, materialistic culture.

Early in the poem, after the Jewish King Lear, as Stern calls Adler, whispers his vision of the future to his daughters, Regan and Goneril "look at him / with hatred reminiscent of the Plains of Auschwitz-Buchenwald—and drive him mad / an inch at a time" (12–15). Stern also notes a connection between Gloucester and one of the "famous pictures" from the Holocaust:

> There is a famous picture
> of a German soldier plucking a beard: I think
> of gentle Gloucester every time I see
> that picture.
>
> (18–21)

As the poem continues, the parallels become more powerful. "I think when they saw him put / a feather over her lips they were relieved / to see her dead" (57–59). Stern continues:

Thank God they died so early, that they were buried
one at a time, each with his own service,
that they were not lined up beside the trucks
or the cattle cars. . . .

(54–57)

I think they [German soldiers] used a broom
on the charred faces
to see if there was a breath—and a match or two
was dropped on the naked bodies.

(69–71)

From these observations he concludes that "for the sake of art," murder was ritualized and carried out with a sense of decorum:

For the sake of art
there always was a German or Ukranian

walking around like a dignified Albany,
or one made sad repentant noises like Kent
and one was philosophical like Edgar,
giving lectures to the burning corpses.

(71–76)

The life-affirming "Yiddish King Lear" offers its audience catharsis, the universal response to tragedy. "When sometimes he comes across the stage / crowned with burdocks and nettles and cuckoo flowers / we forget it is Adler, we are so terrified, we are so touched by pity" (32–35). The Jews leave the theater with renewed energy to face their difficult lives:

I thank God they were able to weep
and wring their hands for Lear, and sweet Cordelia,
that it happened almost forty years
before our hell that there was still time then
to walk out of the theater in the sunlight
and discuss tragedy in the bright sidewalk
and live a while by mercy and innocence
with a king like Adler keeping the tremors alive
in their voices and the tears brimming in their eyes.

(45–53)

For the Adler as Lear, larger than life, was for his audiences "a monster of suffering, so many holes / that he is more like a whistle than a King" (30–31). For today's reader as well, he assumes monumental properties—"a monster of suffering"—representative of the six million Jews, now "so many holes" in the cloth of Jewish life. "Adler" also resounds with historic significance. Near the conclusion, Stern again attempts to transport us to the camps with him that we might bear witness together to the "burning corpses." What had been acting and art, now has become something else, far more permanently terrifying:

> those with gold in their mouths, those with skin
> the color of yellow roses, and those with an arm
> or a hand that dropped affectionately on another,
> and those whose heads were buried
> And those whose black tongues—
>
> as if there were mountains, as if there were cold water
> flowing through the ravines, as if there were wine cups
> Sitting on top of the barrels, as if there were flowers—
> still sang in bitterness, still wept and warbled in sorrow.
>   (77–84)

This poem is rooted in incredible fancy, even though it stems from historical as well as literary reality. By limiting himself to a world he knows well, Stern successfully invokes another world in which he had no direct role, but which nonetheless brought him terrible grief and emotional disturbance, which to this day remains inconceivable to poet, survivor, and reader.

Thus Gerald Stern, product of middle-class American safety far from the troubled regions, comments stridently as well as subtly in his Holocaust poetry and in his poetry on Jewish themes. His works demonstrate that he sees himself as a Jew whose life is pervaded by guilt over his comfort and security while his people were consigned to the gas chambers. His poetry, as well as essays and interviews, expiates this guilt and is cathartic for him. Yes the Holocaust and Judaism not only define who Stern is, but they are also his poetic hallmarks. According to him, history both shapes and informs the present while the poet simultaneously shapes and informs his historical figures and events. Poland, in Stern's poetry, is more than a geographic locale; it is a place of family identity, of nostalgia, and the horrors of recent history. In the same way, he cannot let go of the Holocaust, an inextricable part of his poetic message; it both attracts and repels him.

Gerald Stern is an American original. At times confessional both by nature and by design, his poetry is a declaration of faith. His biblical, classical, historical, and literary references mark him as a poet of the intellect. But he is also a poet of emotion, a romantic with a sense of humor, who lives both inside and outside of history. Sometimes the comic, sometimes a tragic visionary, he cries out against imprisonment and shame, singing of loneliness and rejuvenation in the best Whitmanesque tradition, offering his dreams for social justice and community. His suffering is plural, for all humankind, situated in the venerable philosophy of his ancestors striving for human perfectability for the Edenic dream. And the God whose absence he decries during the Holocaust is Someone he nevertheless forgives.

Fierce memory propels his Jewish/Holocaust poetry. Stern's Judaic particularism drives him to remember, to teach the failures of history. One recalls the overquoted aphorism but nonetheless wise counsel of George Santayana, "Those who cannot remember the past are condemned to repeat it" (1905, 284). In a very beautiful and nostalgic manner, Stern attempts to recover the lost fallen world of the *shtetl.* "By Words Alone" (Ezrahi's book title), he creates the memory with images of soap, death camps, corpses, dental gold, the fantasy of pretended family, the Yiddish theater, American historical personages, Jewish Poland, dancing as death and rebirth, and Jewish ceremonial lore. It is in his singular and unusual interpretations that Stern is separated from other poets who deal with this subject.

Critics such as Pinsker, Hirsch, Knight, Somerville, Monroe, and Hillringhouse praise Stern's spirit, power, candor, wry humor, and anecdotal jauntiness. They laud the triumph over tragedy that pervades his work. Still Chess (1988) is not unconditional in his enthusiasm for Stern's Holocaust poetry. Of Stern's invention of his Jewish/Polish counterpart in "Soap,"

Chess remarks: "This invention allows Stern to do what he's wanted to do all along—'to beg his little brother, if I / should call him that' for forgiveness. After all, Stern confesses it is the counterpart, who 'died instead of me.'" For Chess this just won't wash. He does however consider "Adler" to be the "most powerful, most fully rendered, and most original Holocaust poem" (152–53).

Concerning memory, Stern has said that "it's the poet's job to remember, . . . to keep the past" (quoted in Pinsker, 1990, 186). His Jewish poetic connections, the rhythms and incantatorial quality are quite obviously drawn from his background, the heritage of the Hebrew Bible and his recollections of Hebrew. The result (1984a) is a powerful sense of the eternal present in the quotidian:

> I could go back in a minute to the synagogue in Beechwood
> or the Carnegie Library on the North Side.
> I could turn and shake hands with the tiny man
> sitting beside me and wish him peace.
>
> ("The Shirt Poem," 54–57)

The poems discussed in this chapter mourn unceasingly and yet manage to give survival its due, its right to freshness and joy. The larger discovery in the waning days of an especially brutal century is that historical circumstances have created a climate in which truly to live in the present means to acknowledge and to lament the past, as Stern does so poignantly. To grieve is to give meaning to one's present life. Edward Hirsch (1985) pictures Stern "as an ecstatic Maimonides writing his own idiosyncratic *Guide for the Perplexed* helping us to live in the world as it is, converting our losses, transforming death and sadness into beautiful music" (58). Or as Stern concludes his interview with Hillringhouse (1984):

> Poets are witnesses, living proofs of the uniqueness of the individual soul, of the unforgivable sadness of its perishing, of its immortality. Their poems cry out against all imprisonment. The more living the poet, the more unbearable the death; the greater the poem the more it ransoms. (30)

All of Gerald Stern's Holocaust poems emanate from his understanding of cultural, historical, and mystical Judaism from which he gleans the confession, nostalgia, prayer as poetry, and the ethical obligation to remember. These poems are an anguished response—poems powerful enough to ransom life as well as death.

4

Jerome Rothenberg and the Quest to Assuage Familial Loss: Poetry as an Alternative to Silence

JEROME ROTHENBERG'S OBSESSIVE POETRY OF ANGUISH FIFTY years after the event returns to the past for multiple reasons—the continuing unease and discomfort that reside in the self, and the sense of unpaid debts made manifest by life itself that summons the poet to turn back in time to write about it.

Exorcism and liberation. To free oneself of a nightmare—of history. The psychological term is expurgation, a cleansing not only of what the psyche rejects but also by extension of what the world rejects. That which cannot be tolerated is despised, spat out. Many critics, Julia Kristeva (1982) among them, have written about filth, defilement, abomination—accountings of the unclean, a linguistics of repression. The sometimes obscene poetry of Plath, Heyen, and Stern and the ever-present brutality of Rothenberg, the language of the unsayable, inner utterances, outer utterances—all these might be construed as falling into Kristeva's category of horror. In touching the Holocaust, then, were these poets defiling it, commiting the very acts of barbarism decried by Adorno and Steiner? Does the Holocaust demand instead a detached language of remote ritual?

Holocaust imagery necessarily demands a "special language." The writer's sense that the Holocaust impinges upon the very nature of writing opens up metaphysical, religious, political, and for some, inventive dimensions. In Rothenberg's Holocaust poetry one discerns a three-fold agenda: his answer to Adorno, his compulsion to write for the dead, and his quest through poetry for total identification with his people.

155

Thirteen years after the publication of his book of ancestral poems, *Poland/1931,* Rothenberg visited Poland and Ostrow-Mazowiecka, the small town from which his parents had emigrated in 1920. "I hadn't realized," he observes, "that it was only fifteen miles from Treblinka" (1989). Further:

> The poems that I first began to hear at Treblinka are the clearest message I have ever gotten about why I write poetry. It wasn't the first time that I thought of poetry as the language of the dead but never so powerfully as now. They are an answer also to the proposition by Adorno and others that poetry cannot or should not be written after Auschwitz. Our search since then has been for the origins of poetry, not only as a willful desire to wipe the slate clean but as a recognition of those other voices and the scraps of poems they left behind them in the mud. (4)

In an unpublished lecture, "Poetry and Extremity: Articulations of History: Issues in Holocaust Representation" (1995b), Rothenberg invokes Adorno once again: "that poetry [of the type that Adorno forbade after the Holocaust] he singled out as lyric. Another kind of poetry came to be our central way of speaking: our most human act. It was a poetry that Adorno also recognized, when writing of it some years later: 'Perennial suffering has as much right to expression as a tortured man has to scream; hence it may have been wrong to say that after Auschwitz you could no longer write poems'" (5). Thus while Adorno retracted his original dictum, he did so only conditionally. Rothenberg's poetry encompasses witnessing, commemoration, and admonition.

Along with Rothenberg's earlier theatrical adaptation of Rolf Hochhuth's play, *The Deputy* (1963), *Khurbn and Other Poems* (1989) and "14 Stations" in *Seedings* (1996) represent the culmination of his grappling with the Holocaust. His journey toward the latter works is at once creative, curious, and diverse. Rothenberg comments on his own evolving poetics in *Pre-Faces & Other Writings* (1981): "I see all my work in this regard, as a pre-face to something that comes after. . . . An insistence that the work deny itself the last word, because the consequences of closure & closed mind have been and continue to be horrendous in the world we know" (4). The later works utilize the power of words at their best, whereas Rothenberg's earlier effort represents the chilling, numbing result of silence at its worst, as assent converts to murder. Along his journey to define himself poetically in terms of his ancestors, Rothenberg evolved notions of ethnopoetics, deep image, to apply mystical *Kabbalah,* utilizing *Gematria,* to describe in poetic language apocalyptic messianism, the primitive, and translation (which is in and of itself a secondary representation of an author's work). The term *Gematria* refers to an ancient Jewish numerological method based on the numerical values assigned to Hebrew letters. Each word thus has a numerical value and words of equal value are thought to be linked in meaning. Eventually the technique was adopted for increasingly elaborate purposes. In many of his poems Rothenberg uses *Gematria* "to discover divine angelic names & to uncover correspondences between ideas & images by means of subjective interference" (Rothenberg, quoted by O'Brien, 1994, 28). Intrinsic to Rothenberg, then, are expressions of both rigorously controlled language and its antithesis, the uncontrolled cries of a man personally wounded by the Holocaust.

Ethnopoetics depends on the paradigms and ideals of subterranean and rejected cultures; it is an oral poetry that provides the rhetorical context in which we can read all of Rothenberg's poetry (Gitenstein 1990, 135). Gitenstein contends that Rothenberg's interest in Jewish subjects is as much motivated by his search for an accurate ethnopoetics as it is by a desire to discover his Jewish sources (7). Rothenberg, imaginative collector of ideas and resurrector of lost literatures, coined the term *ethnopoetics* and then proceeded to create the discipline. He sees ethnopoetics as combining vision and conflict, speech and innovation, past and present—as a "redefinition of poetry in terms of cultural specifics, with an emphasis on those alternative traditions to which the West gave names like 'pagan,' 'gentile,' 'tribal,'and 'ethnic'" (Gitenstein, 136).

Himself an integral part of the deep image movement (associated with Diane Wakoski, Louis Simpson, Robert Bly, and James Wright), Rothenberg is a master of open forms, a significant force in counterpoetics and the avant-garde. Counterpoetics shares a great deal with the early movements of imagism and objectivism; the deep image is an image that permeates the form and content of a poem to explain its power. In Rothenberg's words, the deep image is "an exploration of the unconscious region of the mind in such a way that the unconscious is speaking to the unconscious" (Gitenstein, 135).

According to Gitenstein, Rothenberg's ethnopoetics elevates oral, ancient, and pagan traditions. In this spirit he has produced several collections of ethnic or national poetic and sacred texts from cultures not well represented in the mainstream European cultural tradition (136). He has edited *A Seneca Journal* (1978) and *A Big Jewish Book* (1978), imaginative commentaries on Native American and Jewish cultural heritages respectively. Rothenberg's work with Native American poetry directed the focus of his own verse away from the individual unconscious toward the collective unconscious. *A Seneca Journal* chronicles his initiation into Native American culture during an extended stay at the Allegheny Seneca Indian Reservation in the early 1970s. The poems collected here explore similarities between Seneca traditions and rituals and those of his own Polish Jewish heritage. "The therapeutic value of rediscovering other cultures lies," Rothenberg says, "in overcoming a mindless mechanization that has run past any uses it may once have had" (1983a, 142–43). *A Big Jewish Book* is an assemblage—a collage of hundreds of texts dealing with magic, myth, and dream interspersed with hundreds of additional commentaries, notes, and asides that carry the reader along in an uninterrupted discourse. So in his collection we find vials of the animacy, charms, spells, incantations, visions, dreams, and fantasies scrapped by the philosophical upheavals of the European intellectual revolution. For Rothenberg, normative Judaism—rationalist, legalistic, conservative—is the religion of the book—a code rather than a living faith. He is looking for the other side—to rediscover the archaic oral worlds of myth, vision, and revelation, and then to connect them to the poetic revolution of the written word.

In his study of Rothenberg, Sherman Paul (1986), under the umbrella of "primitive," identifies a persistent urge to enlarge our understanding of the dimensions of our own humanity and to relocate areas of human experience and diversity that have been closed off in modern life (vii). Far from being an escape from the present or simply nostalgia for an original simplicity, the "primitive" has direct political implications. The poet who insists on contradictions, on opposing and irreconcilable voices and social and artistic practices that preceded the development of the city-state, "is often at war with the state" (viii).

Although such oppositional use of the primitive owes much to the legacy of romanticism, as Paul notes, it is also a constant presence in the early modernist innovations to which Rothenberg has constantly returned. In terms of poetic forms, his concern for the primitive puts Rothenberg at the experimental edges of modern poetry, rather than in a backward-looking lyrical enclave. Indeed, Rothenberg insists that he is an experimental poet and an avant-gardist and that a serious part of his work has been to suggest an ethnopoetics that tries to encompass a global range of cultures and poetic modes (1997). In stressing the oral and performance, he challenges the very boundaries of the poetic text. In the introduction to his provocative book, Paul glosses the qualities that compelled his engagement with the three poets, David Antin, Jerome Rothenberg, and Gary Snyder. First, the poet must have the ability to "irritate," which Paul defines as carrying "profound consequences"; second, the poet must be "interesting." Throughout this "daybook" journal of readings, scrupulously dated according to Paul's interaction with each poet, the "primitive" of Paul's title acquires a multiple overlay of meanings unique to each poet. The primitive for Rothenberg is often a literal, far-flung cast of ancient cultural exemplars, such as the Seneca, Aztec, Zuni, Kunapipi, and Jews, and includes transcultural spiritual visions of healing and renewal.

For Rothenberg, the primitive inheres both in the specific tribal and in the present shamanistic affinities of those whose steady discipline of language and sacramental experience guides their quest. The primitive directly involves his personal and mythic struggle with the *Kabbalah's* female force of the universe. Many poets turn to *Shekinah* as bride of God or container of all that is feminine in nature. Rothenberg's "She" lists all the meanings of *Shekinah*, all ways of female being, all matriarchs of the Hebrew Bible, all names for her threatening aspect (such as the serpent, Lilith). As bride, *Shekinah* assumes the most powerful and beautiful of roles.

Rothenberg does with Jewish materials what he does with primitive materials—collects fragments and reassembles them. His expertise, in either case, lies in his criteria for selection and his scheme of assembly. The materials must fit together, in a comprehensive way. For the result to be bona fide though, it must include all the items assembled and structured so that new items and their situation can be predicted or, having been found, can be meaningful. The Jewish materials are all bits of Jewish history, their meaning derived from a cosmos driven by the Jewish God and God's interacting with a peculiar people. Of all prior collated systems (from that in which God is materially beneficent, as in his assistance in the conquest of Canaan, to that in which God uses history as a teacher's cane as punishment for recalcitrant behavior), it appears that the two that are operative are in the esoteric line, *Kabbalah* and the tribal cult, which primarily concerns itself with matters of feature distinction. Rothenberg combines two systems of meaning together, comprehensively enough to deal with the movement from Eastern Europe to the new life and facts of Jewish life in America; the mythologized ancestral beginning in Eastern Europe for Rothenberg is continuous with the new life.

Rothenberg offered his first poetic response to the Holocaust in *White Sun, Black Sun* (1960) written after seeing Leni Riefenstahl's *Triumph of the Will* (1939, a Nazi-era propaganda film). The poet reflects on the threat posed by soldiers, the fear engendered by the atomic bomb, the sense of loss, the precariousness and transience of the humanly precious, and the powerlessness one feels in the face of ever-present death. Paul's commentary on Rothenberg's political animus suggests that it is to be found in "seeing Leni Riefenstahl's *Triumph of the Will*" in *White Sun, Black Sun* (74). The poet, as the descendent of European Jews, writes of their persecution during endless wars and pogroms. He is searching for the word that will deliver humankind from the darkness, a position that will find its fullest expression later in his *Khurbn* collection. But in this early poem fact is recounted without images, because Riefenstahl's images projected on the screen belong to phantasmagoria (history as nightmare) and are coextensive with dream. The poem is cinematic, a series of takes. But the film itself is a retake beginning with "Again the curtained armies start out again, again the barriers shudder." That is, we are now past history, and as this inconclusive poem reminds us, history continues, thereby compelling the reader's identification:

> The women rush forward to cover the face of their *Führer*
> Soldiers stalk across Russia with wires white ants drop
>   from the radios nests shoot out of the leaves
> And Hitler stands in a circle of oaks in short pants
> He raises his arms and I see the thin threat of a smile
>   start up from his mustache
> We love and we die in dark rooms
> We are tired we have lived with war and hunger for twenty
>   years and never known what they were
> It is too late to think again of those armies lost in the
>   forest those trees with flayed arms those bodies
>   covered with snow
> Hitler Ist Deutschland and I am the child
>   in the furnace the rotting feet of the
> German soldiers cry out with my pain
>   the tanks roll blindly through Russia
> And the eye of some Jew my mother's
>   brother and son glares without end
>   in the whiteness covering Poland
>
>   (1–19)

"The enormity of that time of terror—when the concentration camp becomes the model of order and efficiency, and good and evil are no longer adequate moral terms—finds its focus in that glaring eye and in the transvaluation of whiteness" (75), an image so stark it defies explanation. That eye awakens guilt as vast as the frozen landscape and juxtaposes it to the bodies covered with snow, but it is too late. Even the ants are white and barely perceptible. That icy waste figures the absence of love. This line ends but does not close the poem, for there is an endlessness to the vision of white death. We are asked to visualize the political and poetic burden of Rothenberg's work.

The poetic response to Riefenstahl's film was written early in Rothenberg's poetic career, when he was twenty-eight and had already served in the United States Army in Germany. We find in this poem his abiding sense of the internationality of the energies of poetry in the face of the narrowness of warring states. The death and destruction of European Jewry and the accompanying silence were to haunt him throughout his later poetic career as selective translation on this subject became an important venue of expression for him. Rothenberg recalls that a friend who read the poem on the Riefenstahl film suggested that "he turn to and not away from his Jewish identity" (Paul 1986, 76). Why? Was his essential autobiography as well as the essential myth of our time to be found there? This "Jewish poem," as Rothenberg now considers the Reifenstahl poem, already presupposes *Poland/1931*.

For Rothenberg, translation would provide a way to extend poetics. His theory of translation, which emphasizes the circumstances surrounding a poem's presentation including ritual, music, and pictograph, demonstrates his belief that poetry is an expression of the collective consciousness of a culture. In a 1963 interview with David Ossman, Rothenberg explains why he translates:

> First, there's the same pleasure that one gets out of writing poetry in general. But it's a somewhat different process. You have a poem in another language, which takes the place of an immediate inspiration out of a life experience. In a way, I do look at it as being the same kind of life experience, as I would say too that all poets "translate" things and experiences into words, to apprehend them in a sense no longer foreign but accessible as something of one's own. (28, 29)

Ossman continues to probe:

> There seem to be more and more poets who find translation not an academic labor, but a very important part of their craft. Do you agree? (29)

Rothenberg:

> I think we're entering into a major period of translation, as long as it's the poet who does the translation, and as long as the effort with living poetry is to re-create poems in one's own language. There is a value in the literal translation, but I think the primary concern

has to be, as with one's own work, the creation of poems—not a slavishness to the cultural boundaries of another person's language. There are things which simply won't stand up when presented literally, without re-creation, because we think differently, because we have a different world about us. Part of this difference has to come through in the translations. It's not just a substitute. . . . Sometimes poetry gets found in translation. (30)

Rothenberg (1995) acknowledges the influence of Paul Celan, who embodies for him the very best in Holocaust poetry. In fact, Rothenberg was among the earliest poets to translate Celan into English. He discusses his Paris meeting with Celan in an interview with Barry Alpert in which Celan called Rothenberg's Judaism into question:

Celan was crazy on the question of being Jewish. . . . Some possibility had been raised . . . about my doing a book of Celan's work, and he kept questioning me on that, challenging my credentials to work on his poetry. . . . [T]he challenge to the credentials was a specifically Jewish challenge: was I Jewish enough to do them? (1975, 115)

The impact of their meeting and Rothenberg's admiration for Celan's poetry led him to write a memorial in which he reviews the commonalities of their relationship, simple shared pleasures, invoking Yiddish phrases, concluding with a loving benediction of Celan's blessedness *gebentsht* (Rothenberg 1980, 44).

Rothenberg's inclusion of Celan's "Zurich, zum Storchen" in his lecture "Poetry & Extremity" (1995) is important, and suggests how Rothenberg perceives God. It is a statement about Judaism with which he concurs. God appears as the final and ultimate arbiter in the human pursuit to define our place in the universe, but we do not have the key to unlock all knowledge. The reference to the Holocaust, so pervasive in Celan's poetry, is oblique in terms of God's angry word:

> The talk was of too much,
> too little. Of Thou
> and Thou again, of
> the dimming through light, of

Jewishness, of
Your God

of
that,
on the day of an ascension, the
cathedral stood on the other side, it passed
over the water with some gold

The talk was of your God, I spoke
against Him, I
let the heart that I had,
hope:
for
His highest, His death rattled, His
angry word—

Your eye looked at me, looked away,
your mouth
spoke to your eye, I heard:
We
simply do not know, you know,
We
simply do not know,
what
counts.

                                        (1–27)

Rothenberg's translation presents yet another confrontation with the Holocaust as naked experience is metamorphosed into the language of memory. The poetry draws its authority from the tradition of scriptural "lamentations." Celan's work demonstrates how difficult and how painful it is to write in a language into which one has been born. An American poet has observed how Celan executed the language in which he wrote and that his verses enact the gradual dying of language.

The irrevocable fate of his people and humanity's attendant silence crowded Rothenberg's consciousness. That, along with his theories about the power of translation, motivated him to offer his view of Rolf Hochhuth's *The Deputy*. His work on *The Deputy*, although it may have misinterpreted another artist's play, partially contributed to his later original and creatively stunning poetry on the Holocaust. The story line is heartbreaking: the Germans occupied Rome in September 1943. Until then, Roman Jews had been relatively safe, but at 5:30 A.M. on 16 October, gunshots rang out over the ghetto, home at the time to four thousand Jews. The streets leading out of the quarter were blocked. S.S. officers expelled residents from their homes and in a few hours arrested more than twelve hundred people. The Jews were incarcerated in the Italian Military College, which stood only two hundred yards from Vatican City. But the Vatican raised no public voice on behalf of the Jews. Indeed, a new study, *Hitler's Pope: The Secret History of Pius XII* by John Cornwell (1999) points the finger at Pope Pius XII for failing to heed the urgent pleas from the world to condemn the mass murder he clearly knew about. This book corroborates the fact that Hochhuth's play was highly controversial in its time, an enigma of moral history that will not die.

Two days following the story the prisoners were put into trucks, taken to the railroad station, and loaded into boxcars. Once again no word of protest. The Jews were simply gone. Five days later, the following entry appears in the meticulously kept log at Auschwitz: "Transport, Jews from Rome. After the selection 149 men registered with numbers 158451–158639 and 47 women registered with numbers 66172–66218 have been admitted to the detention camp. The rest have been gassed." These are the events at the heart of *The Deputy*, which quotes the German ambassador as saying that "the incident took place, as it were, under the Pope's window" (Carroll 1997, 56).

Hochhuth's drama asserted that since the Pope, Christ's Vicar on Earth, His "deputy," was silent even as a roundup took place at the foot of Vatican Hill, Hitler could reasonably count on church silence everywhere. And in the ensuing weeks, the Nazis arrested many Jews in other Italian cities. Approximately eight thousand, more than fifteen percent of Italian Jewry, died in the death camps.

Even if one does not accept *The Deputy* as a completely historical account, one must bow to it as parable. Real persons are loosely disguised. The power of this play derives from Hochhuth's ability to bring to bear the full weight of mass

suffering caused by the Nazi Antichrist, even as he still acknowledges the possibility of individual option and responsibility. Not only does Hochhuth incorporate documentary material in the fictive space, but he appends a sixty-page essay on
the historicity of the events portrayed and the aesthetic principles that can be admitted into such a dense historical
moment.

At the beginning of the first scene, a young SS officer, Kurt
Gerstein, forces his way into the Papal Legation in Berlin to
attempt to bring home to the pope's representatives the full
horror of the mass extermination in Poland. Gerstein makes
an irresistible impression on the young Jesuit Riccardo Fontana. At Gerstein's apartment, Fontana helps in the escape of
a Jew whom Gerstein has been harboring. Fontana narrowly
misses betraying Gerstein to the already suspicious camp
doctor from Auschwitz who had visited the apartment just
before him, carrying specimens of the brains of Jewish children. The doctor exhibits almost mythic fascination with pure
evil.

Throughout the rest of the play, Gerstein and Fontana, in
situations of great danger, try to save individuals, but above
all try desperately to get the Roman Catholic Church to condemn the mass killings in the death camps. The moment of
truth comes when the Germans round up Jews under the
pope's very eyes. But the attempts fail, and most of the princi-
pals meet once again for the last time in the glow and stench of
the human pyres at Auschwitz.

John Simon in *The Nation* faults Rothenberg's adaptation
for cutting out all scenes of utter horror, Jewish collaboration,
Protestant indifference, and Catholic inadequacy other than
the pope's. To name but a few of the glaring omissions from
the original Hochhuth text, there is no mention of Himmler's
modeling the SS on the Society of Jesus, the Holy See acting as
bankers for the Italian Royal House while also doing business with Mussolini, the pope's concern with liquidating the
church's Hungarian assets before the Russians march in, the
callousness of the German bishops and their active support of
the Nazis. Almost anything beyond a decorous suggestion of
Jewish suffering and papal indifference is cut. Similarly ex-
cised are discussions of philosophy, theology, history, lit-

erature—or even just politically complex passages (1964, 272).

Simon criticizes Rothenberg for his vulgar depiction of the Jew Jacobson as a violent proletarian type continually complaining about his fleas. "They're killing me, the bastards. Look my navel is raw from them!" "Pee stains on my underwear. What a mess!" Some of the doctor's lines make no sense: "You spread their legs apart and read a textbook: list confessions in the curls of hair." Poor Gerstein is obliged to chant incessant litanies—Rothenberg's poetic device—and to repeat over and over in two separate scenes, "My name is Gerstein!" and "No matter!" When a young Italian girl is questioned by a Nazi about her fiancé, the Hochhuth version has her reveal that he died fighting in Africa. Here, however, he is made merely a prisoner of war and Rothenberg lets the girl scream, "He's blonder than you are! His hair is blond all over his body. It shines in the light." Vulgarisms used to describe a befouled world in this dramatic adaptation are more fully and brutally utilized in Rothenberg's later Holocaust poetry, notably "Vienna Blood," "Abulafia's Circles" (*Vienna Blood & Other Poems*, 1980), and *Khurbn* (1989).

Having seen the Rothenberg adaptation on Broadway, I recall clichés of the Hollywood Nazi movies of the late forties: the jagged line of prisoners, rags carefully arranged, moving stagily behind barbed wires, threatened by guards; the immaculate Nazis, cracking whips against their boots and curling their lips contemptuously at their victims; the idealistic martyr-heroes, striking lofty postures, whipping up the emotions and spewing righteous rhetoric.

Nevertheless the play, whatever its aesthetic and interpretive shortcomings, is a document of power and persuasion. We need drama of discriminating moral intelligence and courage. In this era when the "death of tragedy" has become a literary commonplace, *The Deputy* stands as a valid tragedy: not great but good, thought provoking, and anything but commonplace—the beginnings of the young Rothenberg's inquiry into the Holocaust. In commenting on Rothenberg's translation/adaptation, Hochhuth describes the difficulty confronting any author who chooses to write on the Holocaust: "Because he is faced with such a plethora of raw material, as well as with such difficulties in collating it, the writer must hold fast to his freedom, which alone empowers him to give form to the matter" (1963, 288).

In the late 1960s Rothenberg turned to himself as subject, as Jew in the era of the Holocaust, as member of a victimized "tribe." This conception of himself as "other" closed a gap between his critical interests and his own writing. From this introspection came *Poland/1931* (1969), a fusion of surrealism and his experiments in performance pieces. Rothenberg delights in reading his own poetry, especially *Poland/1931*. He sings songs, does sound poetry, uses vocables more extensively than words, and brings in the riches of his wide ranging mind. (Rothenberg comments on listening to the Mazel Tov Klezmer Band play and sing a wordless traditional melody, "Now that's sound poetry" [Roche, 20]). *Poland/1931* treats the Poland of his parents' youth, the site of Nazi persecution, a Poland of ancestry and traditions called up through chanting. This volume earned Rothenberg the label of oral poet.

The book's title refers both to Rothenberg's patrimonial homeland and to the date of his birth in the United States. Prefaced by a quotation from Edward Dahlberg ("And I said, 'O defiled flock, take a harp, and chant to the ancient relics, lest understanding perish'"), *Poland/1931* is a series of poems that explores the uniqueness of the Jewish experience, with particular attention to ghetto life in Europe and the Jewish immigrant in America. Rothenberg himself called *Poland/1931* "an attempt to write ancestral poetry":

> What I've been trying to do in various ways is to create through these poems an analogue, a presentation of the Eastern European Jewish world from which I had been cut off by birth, place and circumstance, and to which I have gone back towards an exploration of the reality in general, through the terms of a collective unconscious, to the particular terms of a particular people of which I have some understanding, although it is something I carry entirely in my mind. I do use aids to that understanding, to supplement the imagination and memory with whatever becomes available to me. (Packard 1971, unpaginated)

In summoning images from his past, Rothenberg strives to avoid the all-too-common maudlin nostalgia. To this end he employs the Bible,Yiddish literature, numerology (*Gematria*), primitive verse, oral legends, the *Zohar,* and other Jewish mystical commentaries. He creates a "grab bag," a "miscellany of the mind" that, as Kevin Power writes, "tackles the problem of establishing a coherent cultural identity in a reality defined essentially by tension and contradiction" (1975, 143). Although *Poland/1931* is a search for identity, it does not lapse into autobiography because Rothenberg feels that the history of an individual is not as interesting as the history of a people:

> I've never been particularly interested in myself as a subject for poetry—autobiography—It doesn't interest me to go through the process of the autobiographical poem. I've never gone through that process, and I think simply that there are other things in the world that are more interesting than my personal psychological development. I just don't see my own life as much of a subject for poetry. Poetry is many things. Poetry may be autobiographical but to say that a poet must be restricted to things out of his personal experience, things from his psyche, seems to me to put limits on poetry—puts limits on any writer or artist to define his art in those terms. (Packard 1971)

To what extent should the writer's self and personal history be present in his works? We have seen Stern, too, was concerned with this issue. Rothenberg is more ambivalent in his response to Barry Alpert (1975): "Were you able to suppress autobiography in the final version of *Poland/1931?* Or what function will autobiographical material play later on?" (115, 116).

Rothenberg had addressed the point some years earlier:

> *Poland/1931* is the self in terms of ethnos; a kind of participation mystique in something very old. It's all extremely specific to what I am, but it's not what you think of as autobiography. I think what happens in the poems after Poland is that I begin to open myself up to a further dimension: of writing out of the particular place at which I find myself at a particular time. I'm trying to reconstruct for myself a world to which I am both closely connected—and therefore do not totally deny autobiography in some sense—and from which I am at great distance, with no possibility of returning. Therefore something to be reconstructed by the imagination. I work partly out of reminiscences remembered from my family,

partly from old Yiddish novels, partly from letters, histories, pictures, images coming out of pictures, old family postcards, other
pictures of Jewish Poland, photographs by men like Roman Vish-
niac and others. (Packard 1971)

Eric Mottram writes that the poet, in Rothenberg's view,
works between the requirements of the political state (noting
Rothenberg's antigovernment stand vis-à-vis Vietnam), and
the pressures of autobiographical self (1975, 235). His mild
protests to the contrary, Rothenberg's autobiographical self is
very palpable in *Poland/1931,* as it is in all of his Holocaust
poetry. His personal past is also included in the poems in the
form of voices, memories, and fantasies that create a vision of
shtetl life and describe the trauma of cultural assimilation.
Poland/1931 chronicles the effort to recover his Jewish
inheritance. Rothenberg's past—a background similar to
Stern's—consists of snatches of conversation that suffused
the air of a Brooklyn ghetto where his parents struggled to set
their lives in order and of the impressions and stories about a
country he has never seen. It is a childhood where Tarzan and
Torah coexist, where *brit milah* (ritual circumcision) meets re-
volver, where Shabbat becomes Sunday. Both worlds find
their place within Rothenberg—the rooted, traditional way of
life and the circumstances of its newly adopted home. And so
Poland/1931 documents the struggle, the compromises, the
gains and losses of this clash between a closed life of orthodoxy and the loosely defined society of America. This first-
generation child is, of course, an active agent in this process of
transferring *shtetl* life to the New World with all the resulting
trauma. The echoes of the former life ring insistently. Rothenberg gives us a sense of history that may be perceived to fall
short of the Holocaust, of that which was not to be spoken. It
was there but without the naming.
     Through incantation and lists of images, Rothenberg's "The
Wedding," in *Poland/1931,* brings this archetypal subject to
life:

     my mind is stuffed with tablecloths
     & with rings but my mind
     is dreaming of poland stuffed with poland
     brought in the imagination

to a black wedding
a naked bridegroom hovering above
his naked bride mad poland
how terrible thy jews at weddings
thy synagogues with camphor smells & almonds
thy thermos bottles thy electric fogs
thy braided armpits
thy underwear alive with roots of poland
poland poland poland poland poland
how thy bells wrapped in their flowers toll
how they do offer up their tongues to kiss the moon
old moon old mother stuck in thy sky thyself
an old bell with no tongue a lost udder
o poland thy beer is ever made of rotting bread
thy silks are linens merely thy tradesmen
dance at weddings where fanatic grooms
still dream of bridesmaids still are screaming
past their red moustaches poland
we have lain awake in thy soft arms forever
thy feathers have been balm to us
thy pillows capture us like sickly wombs & guard us
let us sail through thy fierce weddings poland
let us tread thy markets where thy sausages grow ripe & full
let us bite thy peppercorns let thy oxen's dung be sugar to
    thy dying jews
o poland o sweet resourceful restless poland
o poland of the saints unbuttoned poland repeating endlessly
    the triple names of mary
poland poland poland poland poland
have we not tired of thee poland no for thy cheeses
shall never tire us nor the honey of thy goats
thy grooms shall work ferociously upon their looming brides
shall bring forth executioners
shall stand like kings inside thy doorways
shall throw their arms around thy lintels poland
& begin to crow

                                                    (1–40)

Rothenberg's voice shifts fluidly through multiple identities, including the archaic "thy" of a guest at the old Polish weddings. The repetitions combine the incantatory language of rituals with the stirring tempos of a modern lamentation over a violent history. The imagery projects a kaleidoscope of impressions, memories, associations, and racial caricatures, but a wry surrealistic humor threads through the language, such as we find in Marc Chagall's artistic renderings and reveries over his Russian roots. Both of them look to the fable as a source of imagery; they live in a world peopled with figures from Y. L. Peretz or Sholom Aleichem. But neither is telling mere tales—both bring a sense of reality to their imaginative worlds. Chagall writes: "I am against the terms fantasy and symbolism in themselves. All our interior world is reality and that perhaps more so than our apparent world. To call everything that appears illogical, 'fantasy,' fairytale, or chimera—would be practically to admit not understanding nature (quoted in Power, 1975a, 687). Over and over again, *Poland/ 1931* conjures up the freely associated, but finally homogeneous, world of Chagall's *Fiddler.* We find the same obsessive recurrences, the same magical incantation of beings and objects. Both Rothenberg and Chagall fuse separate events into one image, as the concluding lines of "The Wedding" testify. The surge is not simply of impressions, but of roots, identities, locations, and roles. Rothenberg and Chagall have created their own space-time continuum. Their collages are organic; they spring to life as they fuse disparate fragments of memory. In Rothenberg's world, just as in Chagall's, a man can sit on a roof while a cow stares blankly at him in her easy flight across the village; or while a bride falls from the sky in her wedding dress a man can be temporarily separated from his head.

Poland is essential for Rothenberg, a place in which he feels at home. In an unpublished lecture, he states that in "The Wedding," "with its executioners procreated by the Polish Jewish bride and groom, you can sense the Holocaust if you choose. 'The Wedding' was the start of my entry into the history of the Jews: an exploration that I hope has not yet ended" (1994b, 7). His reference to the Holocaust in this poem is covert, without indicating why: "The indirect focus of the Holocaust is something else—both for myself and others" (Rothenberg 1997).

Rothenberg (1994b) notes that the Holocaust is more in evidence in another poem, "The Student's Testimony," in which his analysis in "Poetry & Extremity" is that of "a war and of a man hidden in a cellar while above him the stars draw letters across a ruined sky" (1995, 2) The eternal sky has been blotted and darkened by the *aleph-bet,* the Hebrew Alphabet, symbol of the eternal Jewish student. The imagery of death is nonetheless pervasive. One is at once reminded of the martyrology tradition, an inextricable part of the liturgy of Yom Kippur, the Day of Atonement. During the Roman occupation of Judea in C.E. 70, when the study of the Torah was forbidden, Rabbi Hanina ben Tradyon chose to violate this decree and teach the law. After his capture and during his prolonged and agonizing death, he proclaimed to his students that though the parchment was burning the letters were flying free against the sky (Babylonian Talmud, Avodah Zarah, 18A, 92).

From the coda, which appears as a separately numbered addendum in "The Student's Testimony":

> once in a lifetime man
> may meet a hostile spirit once
> he may be imprisoned for his
> dreams and pay for them
> lightning is like oil the motor
> once it starts keeps
> running
> such was their wisdom though we had
> no use for it
> only later seeing it
> reborn
> in Joplin on a billboard
> his own shadow
> was more than he could bear the war
> came and he ran from it
> back in the cellar drinking
> too much he grew thin
> the great encounter ended it
> in flames the candelabrum rose did it become
> a heart
> that broke into sparks and letters
> a shower of ruined cities from which
> my demon
> vanished fled from the light when I was born.
>
> (1–24)

Prior to this coda that concludes the poem, the student's memories take him back in time. The destiny of the scholar is manifest:

> what grease
> what aromas from the bookshelves
> what smells of jews ripe for the sabbath.
>   (22–24)

The synagogue as a gathering place is warmly recalled:

> I would sing
> and we would share the backroom of
> the synagogue guzzling
> the gentile's beer and
> snapping paper clips
> against the rabbi's silks.
>   (11–16)

This selection is taken from the section "The Book of Testimony," a book of representative Jewish characters, of beards and males; a book exclusively concerned with Poland, with the Orthodox world represented in the photograph of a woman helping Rothenberg put on *tefillin* (phylacteries). Traditional women do not do this: the daily morning prayer of an Orthodox male Jew begins with thanks to God for having not made him a woman. Prefigured here is the defilement that constitutes the theme of this section. Women are not obligated to perform the 613 commandments incumbent upon the male and must engage in a ritual cleansing (*mikveh*) before resuming marital relations after menstruation. There are five testimonies from individual speakers, including the student and the ritual slaughterer. The lines step down from right to left, a curiously artificial style that the eye resists. But for Rothenberg it suggests the right-to-left reading of Hebrew, and he uses it elsewhere for his translations of early Hebrew texts. In his hands the technique remains fluid—lines often divide within themselves and run over, syncopating the narratives in a manner befitting the mad, fantastic, visionary, confused world presented here—a visionary world that Polish Jewry needs.

We enter that world by experiencing defilement. The book offers blood, sweat, sensual hunger, and sexual license. Rothenberg enjoys sexually suggestive images, for him a sign of healthy humanity. Thus, even when sexuality possesses the student in the form of a demon, it stirs him to imaginative flights. "The Slaughterer's Testimony" and "The Student's Testimony" reach a visionary pitch in which the profane employs sacred imagery. The coda that concludes the latter poem ends on a note of restored spirituality, with the candelabrum of light and the holy sparks emanating from the Hebrew letters in kabbalistic fashion.

Jews of Rothenberg's poetry are nearly coterminous with their God in mystical fashion: they are God's paradoxical army warring against chaos. Hence they are still in evidence in places where they no longer live. They have been to places they never went. They are always in possession of the same chaotic problems. They have been driven out of Poland yet will never leave. Thus Rothenberg skillfully juxtaposes absence and presence.

Rothenberg explores the question of Polish identity via the use of the Polish surname and its quick conversion to the Jewish name. Lodz, named in the poem, was also once a thriving Jewish center of learning and figures as a place where Jews once lived. And the trains bespeak the madness of the times. What endures is the poetic and creative impulse to write poems. Light will be there for all time to come. And this is the essence of "The Connoisseur of the Jews":

> if there were locomotives to ride home on
> & no jews
> there would still be jews & locomotives
> just as there are jews & oranges
> & jews & jars
> there would still be someone to write the jewish poem
> others to write their mothers' names in light—
> just as others, born angry
> have the moon's face burned onto their arms
> & don't complain
> my love, my lady, be a connoisseur of jews
> the fur across your lap
> was shedding

on the sheet were hairs
the first jew to come to you is mad
the train pulls into lodz
he calls you
by your polish name
then he tells the other passengers a story
there are jews & there are alphabets
he tells them
but there are also jewish alphabets
just as there are jewish locomotives
& jewish hair
& just as there are some with jewish fingers
such men are jews
just as other men are not jews
snot mad
don't call you by your polish name
or ride the train to lodz
if there are men who ride the train to lodz
there are still jews
just as there are still oranges
& jars
there is still someone to write the jewish poem
others to write their mothers' names in light

(1–36)

The poems of *Poland/1931*, ethnic rather than political, emphasize the energy of the tightly defined system of Judaism more than the oppressed condition of the Jew. The Polish Jew is a cellular unit who is defined most starkly in terms of his opposition to the surrounding culture, both dependent on it and separate from it. He is at once a genetic plunge and a tribal projection. The journey into the poet's roots locates certain propositions that act as admissions of loss and as measures of change, underlining the need for continuities.

Not unlike a character out of Beckett, Rothenberg carries around bundles of newspapers, letting them accumulate as commentaries on his life. In *Poland/1931* he opens up the bundles and lets his imagination make its way through the faded photos, smells, and sacred texts. He offers what is insistently present, not meanings or interpretations, but events, things, and actions:

Take a newspaper
Take a pair of scissors
Select an article from the paper roughly equal in length
to the poem you wish to write
Cut out the article
Carefully cut out each of the words in the article
& put them in a bag
Shake it gently
Then pull out the cut-up words one by one, keeping them
in the same order as you draw them out of the bag
Write them down carefully
The poem will look like you

(1–12)

So much for Rothenberg's disclaimer of autobiographical substance! As he explores the meaning of being a Jewish poet, amulets, smells, bodies, prohibitions, the family, dreams, and defense fill the text. "The Fish" relocates ancestral past into myth created in the present, about a world that has been forcibly caused to disappear:

poland
has no eyes
& so we live without associations
in the past we live
nourishing incredible polands
lazy and alive remembering
our mothers' pictures in the grass.
(2–8)

The family is associated with a cluster of meanings, definitions of a way of life, redefinitions of the tribe. And at the center of the tribe is the poet. "The Mothers" represents the mysteries of creation and continuity:

all is secret sing the mothers
all is innocent
& draws a white circle
behind their eyes
the circle starts to swell moistens
& leaves a trail of fat
how beautiful she says
(pt. 2, ll. 8–14)

And "The Fathers," similarly, pulls together memories, motives, desires, and confusions. They have fought for survival;
they will fight again:

> some broke through a wall others
> fatter with a smell of fish
> around their lips threatened & choked
> eager lovely forgetful violent
> they waited at the dock
> someone told them it was nearly daylight
> others didn't know & others
> spoke of night as though they lived in it
> in love with colors some were tolerant
> of sleep but nervous at remembrance
> some were kings others knew kings
> & dreamed about the weather
> when it rained our fathers left their cities
> as we were always being told.
>
> (pt. 3, ll. 1–14)

Thus even as Rothenberg articulates the acute loss of family,
he tries to reaffirm its potentiality. "The Mothers" and "The
Fathers" prefigure ultimate loss as detailed in *Khurbn.*

The *Kabbalah,* Judaism's mystical approach to the divine,
was intended as a defense of God, to be penetrated only with
great effort. Consequently Rothenberg's treatment of numbers, the alphabet, esoterica, and amulets—integral parts of
Kabbalah—are protective thrusts against evil. Amulets were
quite common in Eastern Europe up until World War II. They
were, for example, worn in pregnancy to prevent miscarriage
and often placed above the head or under the pillow of a
woman in labor to ward off Lilith, Adam's rebellious first wife,
who thereafter assumed an independent individuality of her
own. Amulets resonate with Rothenberg's text. The amulet
directed against Lilith contains names that turn up in "A Book
of Histories." Ancient amulets serve to concentrate the power
of word, image, or story and closely link Rothenberg's sub-
mergence into his Jewish roots with his interest in "primitive"
verse. But as should be obvious to all, there was no protective
amulet against the ultimate devastation of the Holocaust.

Like amulets, symbolism is also an integral element in Rothenberg's work. His references to specific Hebrew characters

introduce us to a language capable of conveying limitless meaning. The individual characters renew and proliferate meanings that activate the tradition. Rothenberg implies that language is a divine manifestation and belongs to the person who has been granted this power. "His Name" (the Divine), says Rothenberg, "shapes 22 verbs" ("Amulet," 71). It is therefore a complete power that comprises the twenty-two letters of the *aleph-bet* and gives to each one of them the force of an active verb. *Aleph*, in the mystical tradition, means both unthinkable life-death and unthinkable, immense energy. The poet's use of the Hebrew *aleph-bet*, his oral projection of the letters into the context of his society, symbolizes his culture's particular understanding. He has the power to push forward and define the limits of its thinking. The poem as a spoken entity becomes an assertion of existence itself, a temporal projection of the timeless energy of *aleph*. The letters are forever juxtaposed to bodily annihilation as we observed in the coda of "The Student's Testimony." The alphabet poems that follow are additional examples of Rothenberg's devotion to the power of the Hebrew language, found in *Vienna Blood & Other Poems*.

> Aleph Poem
> in peace the aleph
> rises: on bishop's hat
> the aleph rests
>
> aleph & a day
> are friendly
>
> as the masked man stumbles
> to the street
> a wind pipe bursts
> words & letters pour out
> on the pavement
>
> alephs sit beside a truck
> sound before a sound
> is spoken: aleph
>
> the tear inside a tear
>
> (1–15)

And the power of *Kabbalah:*

> (A dream)
> the Alphabet came to me
> in a dream
> he said
> "I am alphabet
> "take your light from me
> & I thought
> "you are numbers first before you are sound
> "you are the finger's progression & you end in the fist
> "a solid mass against the world
> but the Alphabet was dark
> like my hand writing these words
> he rose
> not as light at first though issuing from light
> but fear a double headed body
> with the pen a blacker line at center
> "A" began it but in Hebrew not a vowel
> a choked sound it was the larynx stopped the midrash said
>   contained all sound
> sound of Alphabet initial to all speech
> as one or zero
> called it WORK of CREATION in my dream
> a creature more than solid more than space or distance
> & he said
> "all numbers & all sounds
> "converge here
> but I knew it said
> that I would count my way
> into the vision
> groomed thus with numbers & with sound
> the distances to every side of us
> as in a poem

(1–32)

The letters as part of the whole, nevertheless unintelligible, are a part of the kabbalistic system, here seen as part of Rothenberg's apocalyptic vision. The sound of *aleph* becomes the symbol of the mystical reticence about analysis. The Hebrew letters provide the foundation of creation in the dream; they are the basis for all numbers and all sound. Like the metrics of poetry, the letters in the *Kabbalah* guide the vision. Rothen-

berg sees the poet and his craft as similar to the Kabbalist and
his study. Poetics assume cosmic significance and promise
salvation.

Rothenberg exploits the symbolism and power of numbers—largely tribal—in a similar vein. The number seven has
its own labyrinthine set of roots and significances, bringing
each member of the tribe into the poem. Seven refers to the
seven openings in the face, the seven righteous men who act
as mediating influences between God and man, the seven
archers who emerged from primeval chaos, the seven-
branched candelabrum, the "seven clouds of Glory which accompanied and protected Israel during their sojourn in the
desert" (quoted by David Wolfe-Blank in *Meta-Parshiot,* 2) and
many additional symbolic and arithmetical meanings. Such a
breadth of significances inevitably produces fresh reverberations and borrowings from other cultures. His interest in numerology and *Kabbalah* has led Rothenberg (1995a) to translate this poem by Naftali Bacharach, a Kabbalist who lived in
the first half of the seventeenth century:

A Poem For the Sefirot as Wheel of Light follows with its ten
verses:

(The rim)
& going round
the ten
sephirot
of
the ball
& orbit
of the world
of first space

· · · · · ·

(the spokes)
1.
crown
light from light
extreme light
2.
wisdom
splendor from splendor
hidden light

3.
   understanding
   sparkle from sparkle
   sparkling light
4.
   greatness.
   splendor from splendor
   pure light
5.
   power
   light from splendor
   of light pure
6.
   beauty
   sparkle from light
   light shining
7.
   victory
   light from sparkle
   light refined
8.
   majesty
   splendor from sparkle
   light bright
9.
   foundation
   sparkle from splendor
   purer light
   pure pure
10.
   kingdom
   most precious precious
   shining lights.

                    (1–41)

Traditional religious mappings (diagrams, amulets, symbols) have often combined words and images in ways that resemble Rothenberg's later experiments with visual, concrete, and deep image poetry. In Jewish mysticism the *sefirot,* or emanations of God in the perceived world, have been depicted by a range of such visual and verbal images—lights, powers, crowns, qualities, mirrors, sources—and their configurations imagined as a tree, a man, a chariot, a series of concentric circles or reflected lights. The names of the *sefirot* are drawn from the attributes of God in 1 Chron. 29:11. Their presentation as a revolving wheel of light around a point in space (a vacuum left by God's withdrawal) is suggested by and seems unique to Bacharach. We know from the literature of witness that numerology and *Kabbalah* sustained many men intellectually in the concentration camps.

Assembling a Jewish poetics or isolating a series of tensions unique to the Jewish people, Rothenberg (1994b) condenses his personal sense of the tradition as follows:

> 1. A sense of exile both as cosmic principle (exile of God from God), and as the Jewish fate, experienced as the alienation of group and individual, so that the myth, whether orthodox or gnostic, is never only symbol but history, experience, as well;
> 2. from which there comes a distancing from nature and from God (infinite, inaccessible), but countered in turn by a poesis older than the Jews, still based on namings, on an imaging of faces, bodies, powers, a working out of possibilities (but principally the female side of God—*Shekinah*—as Herself in exile) evaded by orthodoxy, now returning (via artists and poets) to astound us;
> 3. or, projected into language (in Edmond Jabes's phrase) of being "exiled in the word"—a conflict, as I read it, with a text, a web of letters, which can capture, can captivate, can force the mind toward abstract pattern or, conversely, toward the framing, raising, of an endless, truly Jewish "book of questions";
> 4. and, finally the Jews identified as mental rebels, who refuse consensus, thus become—even when bound to their own Law, or in the face of "Holocaust," the model for the Great Refusal to the lie of Church and State. (5)

In this manner Rothenberg can deal with tragic failure and its antithesis, tragic hope, both of which are inextricably tied to his Holocaust poetry. He can evoke those who in the face of impending doom, as in the Warsaw Ghetto uprising, used every and any means to alter their fate.

Thus we have the genre of the apocalypse that is associated with the exile. Associated as it is with all other times of upheaval experienced by the Jewish people, this genre is especially apt for contemporary Jewish poetry as a strong indicator of the terrors of the Holocaust. In Rothenberg's "The Bride," in *Poland/1931*, the feminine principle of God, *Shekinah*, offers solace to the exiled Jews of Poland who suffered pogroms and rapes:

> thy tits will I squeeze upon for wisdom
> of a milk that drop like letters
> sacred alphabet soup we lap up. . . .
>
> (10–12)

Shekinah, protecter of all Jews in exile, is the final cosmic equalizer of men and the singer of the song of angels. She represents the release of the Jew from Europe's persecution. And the sacred *aleph-bet* offers a comfort as well.

In *Vienna Blood & Other Poems* (1980) Rothenberg synthesizes work from the 1970s that stands apart from *Poland/1931* and *A Seneca Journal (1978),* yet continues the melding of past and present begun in those books. To provide some sense of context Rothenberg appends brief comments to many of the major sections of the book—as might be done orally at a poetry reading.

To the signature poem "Vienna Blood" Rothenberg adds the following comment:

> In August 1977 I spent a week outside Vienna. . . . The setting was an old castle—Burg Wartenstein—in a ruined tower where I read & chanted poems: an atmosphere charged by Victor Turner ideas of "communitas" & "liminality" & by a sense of ghostly European histories, the shadow of Hitler's home town (Linz) nearby. . . .Conversations with one Herman Hakel—a Jewish Survivor—raised further phantoms & that colored the rest of the Vienna visit & even the next week spent in still vigorous Paris. Vienna stuck in my mind along with that title out of Johann Strauss's *Wienerblut.* (23)

He describes Vienna:

> like carnival
> for street & house
> our action holds the place
> between the women
> guard the door
> no longer
> they rush into the squares

& find
Vienna in the night
a jewless
hauptstadt city without
rime or grace
                    (1–12)

This poem is dedicated to Herman Hakel and continues:

the others have survived
alone who stand
—friend Hakel—
muted cattle dumb
& lost
the darkness is their own
now   there is no one
can do again the thing
we did   the victim
dies
the mothers cannot
heal this birth
disorder of the town
where Hitler walked
he saw (sweet shadow) looming
the devil Jew
my grandfather
this one could be
who scared him
shitless to Linz
                    (13–32)

Combined are the images of the transport cattle cars as well
as the stereotypic Jew. Analogous to cattle in the darkness,
the lone survivors are mute and lost in the blackness of their
release. In section two, "The Danube Waltz," he discusses
Vienna as *judenrein:*

where is thy river
& thy woods
so old like Jews
forever gone
we walk too among ghosts
the sound of poetry

—ka ka—
the only music left us.
                    (18–25)

Again, Rothenberg (1995b) reiterates his theme that the language of poetry helps us to touch life. Ka ka, he tells us, is the raw material of the soul, the corporeal breath of shit, the opium of eternal survival. The odor of the eternal ass of death is the stifled energy of a soul whom the world refused to let live (6). And the excremental images reappear not only in his *Khurbn* poetry but also in his commentary on his Eastern European journey. In 1987–88, while traveling from Germany to Poland, Rothenberg wrote:

> Crossing the line I felt myself moving into a world still in ruins—an empty world—a world of ghosts. At the border, waiting, we sat in our car beside a line of trucks filled with cattle on their way to slaughter. Bellowing. The sounds were heavy—lost and painful. The air stunk of excrement, became itself an animal. I walked into a latrine to relieve myself, to piss, and was overwhelmed by the accumulated human smells. And I remembered the books of witness I had read before, the visions of a death by excrement so often written there. I felt myself (this man, this animal) in a condition of unrest as never before—and in a condition of poetry. (1995, 6)

In this same lecture Rothenberg quotes Robert Creeley, an American poet who, he alleges, has saved the "lyric voice" for us:

Ever since Hitler
or well before that
fact of human appetite
addressed with brutal
indifference others
killed or tortured or ate
the same bodies they
themselves had we ourselves
had plunged into density
of selves all seeming stinking
one no possible way
out of it smiled or cried
or tore at it & died

apparently dead at last
Just no other way out.

                    (1–15)

Rothenberg selected this poem because of Creeley's recognition of the existence of poetry to which the term "Holocaust poetry" might be meaningfully applied; that is, not necessarily poetry about the Holocaust per se, but rather poetry that characterizes what it is to be a maker of poems after Auschwitz. Poetry after Auschwitz is poetry touched, transformed, altered down to its roots (its language), and the extent of this transformation tests its value as poetry. This is the measure by which Rothenberg's work must be judged. He rejects regularity and clarity as a reflection of nature or of God. Instead, reality is revealed in the twisted, rotting dead at Auschwitz. This poetry after Auschwitz then is a poetry *in extremis*—a poetry at the margins of language—of thought and feeling.

The complex and eclectic three-section tour de force "Abulafia's Circles," included in *Vienna Blood, & Other Poems* is one of the most imaginative contemporary American renditions of Jewish sources, a poem written for performance, as well as a ritual presentation of all of Rothenberg's own ideas about poetry's overwhelming spectrum of possibilities. There is incantation and cataloging, historical perspective and narrative devices, surrealist and realist imagery, ritual, song, and analytical discussion.

This poem is a meditation on Jewish messianism with apocalyptic overtones. Beginning with one of the most bizarre yet spiritualized versions of Messiah in Jewish history, it focuses upon *Kabbalah* and celebrates the life of Abraham Abulafia, the thirteenth-century mystic and master of linguistic manipulation. For the medieval Jew, the mystery of the universe inhered in Hebrew language and its letters. A Hebrew letter in both its phonetic and mathematical significance was therefore a principle of existence, and to understand the Hebrew language was to understand cosmology and ontology. Thus *Abulafian Kabbalah* prescribed a pattern of meditation on certain letters of the alphabet (those that made up what was called the seventy-two-letter name of God) in order to reveal the mystical truths hidden in the Hebrew alphabet.

Rothenberg begins with the philosophical and mystical principle as found in Abulafia, but he also recognizes its various mutations in contemporary Western experience: in the art of Hannah Weiner, in the lives of Mafia thugs, in the actions of a Charlie Chaplin character, in the rejection of Hitler's murders, and in the sexually charged relationship of men and women. Most importantly, Rothenberg's Abulafia is symbolic of almost anarchic creativity, and the poet contrasts Abulafian power with the repressive and destructive power of Adolph Hitler:

> o Hitler I messiah Abulafia
> am bound to you
> in history
> where vowel calls to vowel
> our paths have crossed
> you kill I bring them
> back to life
> God's double nature shines thru' us
>   (pt. 1, ll. 191–98)

Hitler wishes to destroy the forces of creativity and evolution in the contemporary world. Hitler says "I curse out Dada / freaks who scrub not" (166, 167). Society identifies these creative freaks with Rothenberg himself, as Hitler calls Rothenberg the "false Jew" and says to him "dirty you are / needing soap" (158, 159).

> Abulafia who travels
> fast down the jew street
> turns the corner
> where Hitler turned
> I see him
> I dream of Hitler now
> myself o false Jew
> "man of enterprise
> (he mocks me)
> dirty you are
> "needing soap
> "These people are so dirty
> (pheh)
> I Hitler Shitler
> "Smelling so smartly of wagnerian highs

.   .   .   .

"I am pure
"like Viennese confections
"no Slav I but the fairest Deutscher
"confronting here
"visage of this monster
"he who counts
"wrong making 2 plus 2
"be five
thus spoken only thus
the power of his eye
his sour lip
clears out Vienna in
An eye wink
empty

(pt. 1, ll. 149–81)

The reference to showers and soap inferentially calls forth the image of the Nazis making soap out of human ash and human fat of those they considered to be subhuman. And "wagnerian highs" alludes to Richard Wagner, the arch anti-Semite whose hateful pronouncements were used by the Nazis to justify their anti-Jewish actions. Wagner spewed his anti-Jewish invective in *Das Judentum in der Musik* [Judaism in Music]. (Did Wagner's behavior serve as an example? Did his anti-Jewish statements influence the ideology of the anti-Semitic movement or, at the very least, did his conduct as an individual anticipate later, broader social developments?) Many of the spokesmen for anti-Semitism, especially Adolph Hitler, believed they had found in Wagner the prototype for their views. The image of Wagner has been fixed as the symbol of mortal enmity toward the Jews—a development reflected in the resistance of broad sectors of the Israeli public to the performance of Wagner's music in their country (Katz 1986, 2). The "fairest Deutscher" is an attack on the *Ostjuden*—the Jews of Slavic origin seen by the Nazis to be the contaminating agents of the pure Aryan culture. With one facial gesture Hitler emptied Vienna of its Jewish inhabitants.

To summarize the remaining portions of the poem: the second section, "The Secret Dream of Jacob Frank," ostensibly relates the life of a self-proclaimed messiah of the eighteenth century. The passionate sexuality and strange habits of this messianic movement are described and paralleled with other messianic impulses. Frank's attraction to the Catholic worship of Mary is connected to his questionable relationship with his daughter, whom he called his *Shekinah*. The final section of *Vienna Blood*, "The Holy Words of Tristan Tzara," turns from leaders in the religious or spiritual realm to the leader/revolutionary in the artistic world. Rothenberg sees the iconoclastic nature of dada and its leader as messianic and transformative in the very same fashion as *Abulafia's Kabbalah*. Rothenberg's choice of Tzara and dadaism is striking in that the unit of meaning is to be found in the letter and not in the word. Tzara aimed at the articulation of the primitive sources of communication so evident in Tom Stoppard's *Travestie* (1975), where language often becomes absurd and nonsensical. Are these figures representative of Rothenberg's self-proclaimed avant-gardism?

> dada
> dada ice
> dada piano
> dada flowers
> dada tears
> dada pendulum
> dada vanilla
> dada don quixote
> dada humid
> (pt. 3, ll. 19–27)

Rothenberg prefigures in this poem a kind of dadaist sense of post-Holocaust language collapsing in on itself. Nihilistic in character and needing to be reconstructed by all who wish to make language serve new purposes, dadaism was inevitably self destroying in its assault on the very sources of its own origin (*Encyclopedia Britannica*1969, s.v. "dadaism"). Finally, "Abulafia's Circles" beginning with "the master of the book or lights" (line 1) and concluding with "exuding light" (part 3, last line) becomes a treatise on poetic inspiration and an argument in favor of the poet's prophetic powers. The poem closes as the poet, the new leader of the new poetics, leaps onto the saddle of a horse and heads off after Tzara who really is Frank who really is Abulafia who really is the messiah (Gitenstein 1986, 137).

Rothenberg, in reexamining history, has to create a poetics of identity for himself. He must revise himself. In light of his personal history his *Khurbn* poems inevitably had to confront the death camps. The camps ultimately become our bodies not only filled with wrath, guilt, and the potential for unmaking creation but also with the potential for transforming and creating. Rothenberg eschews the term "Holocaust," for in his view it misconstrues the fate of those in the death camps. What did occur was total ruination, devastation, or *khurbn*, the Yiddish term from the Hebrew *churban*, which refers to the destruction of the Temple in Jerusalem first in 586 B.C.E. and then again in C.E. 70. For Rothenberg the very word *khurbn* conjures up childhood memories of his grandmother weeping for her family, too early dead, memories that still cause tightening in his throat and chest. Responding to the root definition of "Holocaust" as sacrifice by fire, Rothenberg says:

> A totality of fire, that is, in human terms, a genocide. The fire I believe is true, the sacrifice a euphemism for the terror. Or if we think of sacrifice, the question next comes up: a sacrifice to what? to whom? And the answers come rushing back, like questions to God? To Adolph Hitler? To make atonement for inherent sin? Or Jewish sin? To set the circumstances for a Jewish state? And it seemed to me then and now that the word itself was false, that the questions that it raised were false, that the answers that it seemed to force only increased the sense of pain and madness. *Khurbn* was the word I knew for it: disaster pure and simple, with no false ennoblement. Nothing left to say beyond the word. No sacrifice to ponder. (And no meaning). (1995a, 5)

On one level *Khurbn* sets out to reclaim poetry from Adorno's dismissive dictum. To this end Rothenberg chooses language that sometimes rises to a searing fury but also descends into violence itself. It is therefore not a very satisfying answer to barbarity, even if quite powerful. On a more personal level, at the end of the introduction, Rothenberg tells the story of his only uncle whose death during the Holocaust was recorded: upon learning that his wife and children had been murdered at Treblinka, his uncle "drank himself blind in a deserted cellar & blew his brains out" (3).

Rothenberg uses free verse to avoid any resemblance to the kind of poetry Adorno rejected—overly civilized, eloquent verses that falsify the nature of the world after Auschwitz. *Khurbn* (of chapbook length) reflects Rothenberg's view of the world as a shattered object. He wants to attach poetry to its modernist base as well as to its ancient, wild origins, thereby resettling it on the margins—that turf where poetry can once again be dangerous. Rothenberg's personal poetic "I" moves smoothly in and out of this work, as postbiblical seer, a descendant of victims, and always as a Jew severed from an essential and engaged part of his past, the culture preceding the Holocaust. The voice is always wild with grief and rage. Rothenberg assaults the senses. Where it deals in fierce elegy, the *Kaddish* of *Khurbn* achieves a disquieting inelegance, often miring itself in its own revulsion. The poetry exhausts and spends both its reader and itself, on fire from its own passionate anger.

Rothenberg hears the voices silenced in the Holocaust; they compel him to write poetry. His notion of poetry as the language of the dead in Western civilization harks back to the myth of Orpheus in hell. In the Judeo-Christian tradition language—the word—precedes both life and death. The introductory poem, "In the Dark Word Khurbn," does not break for breath between the title, in capital letters and the first line. Containing no punctuation and no other capital letters among Rothenberg's stylistic signatures (the others being the lack of complete quotation marks, repetitive phrases, the use of & throughout, and an inconsistency about capitalizing proper nouns), all the lines work as a single sentence, spoken between the staccato breaths of a speaker heaving for relief.

This absence of the living, this vacuum in which the dead are free to speak, constitutes a creative nucleus out of which *Khurbn* cries. The poem begins in silence, in darkness:

> IN THE DARK WORD KHURBN
> all their lights went out
>
> their words were silences
> memories

> drifting along the horse roads
> into malkiner street
>
> a disaster in the mother's tongue
> her words emptied
> by speaking
>
> returning to a single word
> the child word
> spoken red-eyed on
> the frozen pond
>
> was how they spoke it
> how I would take it from your voice
> & cradle it
>
> that ancient & dark word
> those who spoke it in the old days
> now held their tongues
>
> (1–19)

The allusive language leaves the reader dependent on personal knowledge about the subject's history. The poet here is distinctly the speaker; indeed, Rothenberg has identified these poems as the result of a journey he undertook to his family's birthplace. The poetic "I" demands that the reader assume a persona to which he has little access. Unlike *Vienna Blood & Other Poems, Khurbn* has no commentaries. The "frozen pond" and "malkiner street" offer no cities of refuge, no sensatory or historical background. This poem, like the history it suggests, is dislocated and dislocating, leaving the reader with only an obscure sense of doom.

However, it is also oddly based. The opening echoes of the Gospel of John: "In the beginning was the Word, and the Word was made flesh and dwelt among us" (1:1,14), an arresting and subtle demarcation of the Final Solution as Jewish territory. Here, the word ceases to be flesh, and John's Gospel is reversed, both reclaiming the "New" Testament and unnerving the reader to recall that both the conversion and banishment of the Jews has always been the harsh side of Christianity's design. The dark word of the *Khurbn* is juxtaposed to John's Gospel in another way. John is the apostle who describes

Christ in terms of light and the world before Christ as dark. This, too, although beyond Rothenberg's religious orientation, may be behind the poet's introductory poem's claiming of the darkness in the world of *Khurbn.*

The poem's opening also both echoes and reinvents the creation of light in Genesis, naming the darkness by a word, by fiat, "God divided light from darkness. . . . And darkness He called night" (1:4, 5). The second stanza heightens the reinvention by silencing the people to whom the *Khurbn* happens, seizing from them even the word itself. The poem may give voice to the word, Rothenberg may inscribe the word, and as the speaker of the poem, may even nurture the word, handling it with parental protectiveness. But the people upon whom the malignant calamity was visited are speechless.

Many other poems are titled in Yiddish, the language of the dead. Most denote specific localities and base the reader in a time-warped Poland where past and present are filtered through the lines and texts of classic Judaic theology. Yiddish folklore is there and then gone. In . . . "Passing Chelmno on the Main Road Driving Past It," real ghosts come from the destroyed Lidice, although it is not clear whether the speaker really sees them, intuits them, or merely believes them to be there:

> In May
> along the road to Warsaw
> little ghosts
> of Lidice.
>
> (1–4)

This sentence has no verb. The lines are enjambed, unable to invent or play with meaning. And so we are offered nothing but apparitions. The ghosts are apparently little, perhaps seen from a distance, like the little bathers in a later line or perhaps like mere children. Are the ghosts evanescent as is the scene? But ghosts have a deep memory for the sins that make a peaceful rest impossible. That's why they linger: to remind us that all is not well. The language would seem to be intentionally imprecise, leaving the reader to move by as quickly as the poem does.

The broken lines make the poem a road physically long and narrow. The second sentence is as unattached as the first:

> A row of peasants
> cutting up the earth
>
> on bended
> knees.
>
> (5–8)

Are these real peasants? Are they the ghosts of peasants? Are they dissecting the earth as they rise from it? The phrase "on bended knees" signifies prayer: does cutting up the earth then constitute a prayer? Are "knees" so important that they have a line for themselves? In biblical times the bent knee was a welcoming sign of hospitality. There could be a linguistic connection between the Hebrew *birkayim* (knees) and its derivative, a blessing, hence a prayer. While the single word does not function as a hinge to double meaning between the line before it and the line that follows, it does take one convincingly into the next lines in which

> A man spiffs up
> a roadside shrine,
>
> leaving a bunch
> of tacky flowers.
>
> (9–12)

There is ample evidence that the Polish Catholic peasants, in their religious fervor, were easily manipulated by the Nazis— believing as they did, and in many cases still do, that the Jews are forever to be maligned and persecuted for having sought to crucify Christ. The charge of deicide is slow to die. The speaker's contempt seems unmotivated, unexplained, unjustified. It points to something problematic with many of the poems in this sequence. They are didactic in that they direct the reader's thinking. Hence, the man on the side of the road does not tend a shrine; he "spiffs" it up, a verb that denotes flaunting, and he does so with flowers that are "tacky."

The penultimate stanza notes "Little figures / bathing in the Warta" (13–14), not only reverberating the "little" ghosts of the second stanza, but also reemphasizing the diminution of the entire poem. The ultimate stanza, "Little thought / to what was there" (15–16), blames life for continuing: the river for flowing, the bathers for bathing, the peasants for laboring on their knees, the man for watching the shrine with the ugly flowers. And thus the poem concludes. That Chelmno has existed beyond its nefarious history is not an indictment of Chelmno, as the poem suggests that it ought to be. The poem itself acknowledges by its very title that it is a fleeting thought by its use of the word "passing" in two different forms. There is no pretense to complexity or depth.

Perhaps the poem means to comment on the extent to which the ghosts of Lidice have become diminished, something that tourists imagine they see in passing. The tasteless shrine may be a mirror image of the insignificant shrine such a quick glance seems to want to make of Chelmno. The poem is possibly an indictment of the trivializing of places such as Chelmno—places to be gazed at, trembled over, but quickly traversed. And possibly totally ignored. The poem evades meaning, which may be appropriate in the face of the Holocaust, where meaning is elusive and always risks being trivialized. In evading meaning, the poem opens itself to an ambiguous response and various interpretations.

"Dos Osleydikn" (The Emptying), appears early in this poetic sequence. It takes the feeling of emptiness and futility that *Khurbn* has aroused and gives it a staying power. In our time *Khurbn* has become total destruction, secular and spiritual, of individual lives as well as of the temples and most certainly of the decimation of six million Jews. Destruction is complete and "those who spoke it in the old days now held their tongues" ("In the Dark Word, Khurbn," 16–17). "Dos Osleydikn" describes the small, innocuous *judenrein* villages in Poland—Ostrova, Miadowa, Ostrolenka, and Vyzhkov. The shadows of the *mezuzah* (literally "doorpost," a small parchment on which are inscribed the first two paragraphs of the *Shema*, the ultimate Judaic proclamation of monotheism, found in Deut. 6:4–9;11:13–21) with God's name (*Shaddai*) on its cover offer mute testimony to the former presence and present absence of Jews in these towns. The purpose of the *mezuzah* is to sanctify the home by offering this constant re-

minder of God's omnipresence. Rothenberg deals with the un-
adorned fact without theological commentary:

> the shadow of an empty name still on their doors
> shadai & shadow shattering the mother tongue
> the mother's tongue but empty
> the way the streets are empty where we walk
> (7–10)

And Yiddish was the "mother tongue," dead and empty. This
holding or withholding involves an utter emptying out of language, resisting the "rage for beauty" and "the artistry of
death" ("Nokh Aushvits," 31). This very emptying is at once the
emptying out of lives ravaged, destroyed in the Holocaust, and
an emptying into language those absences, those silences that
inhabit both the streets and the poem, brimming with emptiness (Featherston 1998,135). The complete void of the commonalities of Jewish life in these *shtetls* is stunning: "the
empty sorrel soup, the empty bakery, the empty yellow
wooden houses" (5, 6)—the Poland that was lost to its Jewish
inhabitants. The places depicted were ordinary towns where
ordinary Jewish life was destroyed. And here lies the power of
this modest poem. Rothenberg calls the former residents
"honey people," a play perhaps on their ancestral origins, in
the land of milk and honey. Or an allusion to the main ingre-
dient in the traditional holiday cakes. And the emptiness of
death is mirrored in the trains as they move inexorably east-
ward down a hole:

> only the cattle bellow in and
> like jews the dew-eyed wanderers
> still present still the flies
> cover their eyeballs
> the trains drive eastward, falling
> down a hole (a holocaust) of empty houses
> (23–28)

The houses still standing have been emptied of their owners
and therefore represent another kind of holocaust. What remains are the ghosts with which Rothenberg wrestles
throughout *Khurbn:*

> the road led brightly to treblinka
>
> . . . .
>
> past which their ghosts walk
> their ghosts refuse to walk
> tomorrow in empty fields of poland
> still cold against their feet
> an empty pump black water drips from
> will form a hill of ice
> the porters will dissolve with burning sticks
> they will find a babe's face at the bottom
> Invisible & frozen imprinted in the rock
>
> (41, 46–54)

Empty, empty, all is empty. The palpable emptiness is all-enveloping.

In this collection, stories, histories, and fragments are revisited, just as they were in the poetry of Plath, Heyen, and Stern: children turn their devastated, anguished faces open-mouthed to their parents and the reader, deportees end their own lives in boxcars, entire villages disappear, soon-to-be corpses neatly pile the already dead. These are not trivial pictures. All bear emphatic repetition. However, in this collection these images are accompanied by a commentary that directs the reader's feelings or reminds the reader that his/her feelings are inadequate. For example, in the poem "Dibbukim" (Dibbiks), the poet laments "if only our eyes were wild enough / our hearts to know their terror" (13). Rothenberg himself is *dibbik* possessed and the poems of *Khurbn* are his effort at exorcism. And when in "Der Gilgul" (The Possessed) the poem informs us that the earth is

> growing fat with
> the slime of corpses green & pink
>
> that ooze like treacle, turn
> into a kind of tallow
>
> that are black
> at evening that absorb
>
> all light
>
> (pt. 3, ll. 1–7)

The reader is left disgusted by the corpses themselves, not by the murderous circumstances that made them corpses. Preceding the poem quoted above, Rothenberg lapses into prose and writes dispassionately:

> Each night another one would hang himself. Airless boxcars. Kaddish. "What will they do with us?" The brown & black spots on their bellies. So many clothes. The field was littered. Ten thousand corpses in one place. Arranged in layers. I am moving down the field from right to left—reversing myself at every step. The ground approaches. Money. And still his greatest fear was that he would lose his shoes. (pt. 2, ll. 1–7)

The movement follows the way Hebrew is read and thus becomes a linguistic as well as a spiritual *Kaddish*. Often the book wanders into a nearly sensationalist rehearsal of the obscenities of the Holocaust, as in the prose rendering of "Di Magilas fun Auschvitz" [The Scrolls of Auschwitz)], when a man dreams:

> Three thousand naked women cry in pain. It is impossible to count them but the dreamer does. Their bodies will be used for kindling, their blood for fuel. No one will cry or turn away, but sometimes the world will force a tear out of his eye, & his tongue & teeth will follow, flying from his mouth. "Ah," the young girl will say, her legs twisted behind her back. "The tear of a live Jew will go with me to my death." (27–28)

In this passage, with its focus of death, *Khurbn* is not about the Holocaust. It approaches obscenity and dwells on the raw emotions of rage, grief, and disgust that seem part and parcel of a project designed to deny Adorno's dictum.

Khurbn holds fast to the heritage of *Yiddishkeit*, the Jewish culture of Eastern Europe, profaned, violated, and eviscerated by the Final Solution. Yiddish titles, Yiddish words, and Yiddish folk traditions illuminate and locate the poems. *Khurbn* is also propelled by poetry itself, the making of poetry and being part of a poetic movement. Following the prose introduction, in which Rothenberg almost dares Adorno to understand what writing about the Holocaust really means, comes the poetic introduction where Rothenberg makes it abundantly clear that *Khurbn* is the haunting obsession of the work.

The first two poems concern themselves solely with what was destroyed, with Chelmno and the barrenness of the ghettos and villages. The third poem opens like the introductory poem, with its first line completely capitalized and serving as its title. It deals with the panic and terror of being "HIDDEN IN WOODS BAGGED / like an Indian," and the "cry (darkest in / the pauses)" which "cannot be heard" (1–5). The one hiding is a man whose children have been torn from him, and his mind races from image to invocation through the thirty-two lines of the poem in attempting to find a foothold. The loss of tongue or speech in the face of calamity is of course biblical. The frozen chattering teeth reinforce a sense of coldness and blueness that pervades Rothenberg's Holocaust poetry. He fails or succeeds, but all he is left with at the end of the poem is the conviction that "the cry you can hear / is no cry" (33–34). "Cry" appears in the poem multiple times, a significant repetition (though a Rothenberg stylized hallmark) for so short a piece. Its repetition gathers neither meaning nor rhythm and in the middle of the poem is identified needlessly as "a father's cry" (16). But it does return the focus of the whole poem to the speaking of words:

> HIDDEN IN WOODS BAGGED
> like an Indian
>
> a cry (darkest in
> the pauses)
>
> cannot be heard But inward
> he discerns it
>
> what his life had been
> & several trusting in him
>
> (children
>
> or the dead) life's burden
> I cannot escape it any longer
>
> in a vodka sleep (the cry
> cutting still deeper

into his bones) Bright spots
a Zohar of possibilities

a father's cry

(oh mother hold me) how I have lost
my tongue

my hand chewed down
to the bone must bellow

like a heifer
& crawling through their blood

my children severed from me
(their souls

stuck in my mouth) teeth
frozen

the room turns to ice

in moonlight
it flies through the woods

a cry a spirit
his death turns loose

with no roots
runs deeper the cry you can hear

is no cry

(1–34)

Khurbn's dense, almost brutal physicality, the dialectic of created language and the tortured body, is fully evident in "Dos Geshray" (The Scream):

this man whose body
is a crab's
his gut turned outward
the pink flesh of his children
hanging from him

that his knees slide up against
there is no holocaust
for these but khurbn only
the word still spoken by the dead
who say my khurbn
& my children's khurbn
it is the only word that the poem allows
because it is their own
the word as prelude to the scream
it enters
through the asshole
circles along the gut
into the throat
& breaks out
in a cry a scream
it is his scream that shakes me
weeping in oshvientsim
& that allows the poem to come
                                        (40–62)

Oshvientsim is the original Polish place-name for what the Germans later designated as Auschwitz. Serving as epigraph underneath the title is the quotation in Yiddish from Job 16:18.

Erd, zolst nit tsudekn mayn blut
un zol nit kayn ort zayn far mayn geshray

[Oh Earth, cover not thou my blood
and let my cry have no resting place]

The poem begins with the muffled screams of the Jew locked in the metaphorical prison—the survivor unable to speak about his experience—and suggests that uttering the word *khurbn* is a "prelude to the scream" (53). Treblinka's field, as described by Rothenberg, contains "the absence of the living [which] seemed to create a vacuum in which the dead—the *dibbiks* who had died before—were free to speak" (3). The *dibbik* of Rothenberg's uncle enters this poem. The poem is haunted; it has sought the sources of suffering in the human body to exorcize them and then to make them knowable. Even as personal memories and family history inform portions of this work, then, these memories are part of the public record and must be remembered as part of the public legacy. To give public ownership to his work, Rothenberg selects the most intimate space; his poem delves into the body and traces the course of physical as well as spiritual suffering. And thus the body becomes the site of suffering—Treblinka as one vast body in Rothenberg's personal geography.

"Dos Geshray" traces the haunting of the poet's body and then transfers the haunting to our bodies. The primary image of the poem is obscene in releasing repressed visions. The obscene as *pharmikon* acts as antidote to the obscene use of reason and imagination that produced the death camps. Foul shit is clean in comparison to them. The scream hovers between the poet and the *dibbuk* who inhabits him. However it is not the poet's scream. The poet does not speak over the voice of the dead, for this scream has no sound. Similar to shoes, hair, teeth, and the stones of Treblinka, the poem is a thing, acknowledging through its writing the existence of the *dibbuk* that reinhabits the living through language. Responding to the poem witnesses the poet's agony and, for lack of a better word, inhaunting, and forces one beyond voyeurism to the only possible salvation: to share the agony and, as with Greek tragedy, to experience total catharsis (Parmet 1994, 79).

Is not Rothenberg cognizant of the old Jewish superstition that to speak of evil is to invoke it? So great is the power of language that one must approach the question of profound evil with fear, trembling, and great awe, so as to propitiate the dark spirits and not arouse them. Perhaps this unconsciously is Adorno's and Steiner's real fear. It has been said that the Holocaust happened because God turned his back on humankind for an instant. Such an assumption extends to language itself, as if it is implicated. Is it true that to write/speak of defilement is to be defiled? Certainly Rothenberg enters "Dos Geshray" by brutally defiling language. The question, again, is whether speaking/writing it validates it as art, as art often tends to validate its subject, or whether this writing/speaking trivializes the subject such that its sinister power emerges beyond the words. But neither can we remember, imagine, or regret without words. For the Holocaust after all was largely initiated and perpetrated by language—secret plans formulated, commands written, orders barked. Language preceded the silence of death.

Alvin Rosenfeld refers to a statement by Edmond Jabes that raises a question that must stand at the beginning of all post-Holocaust writing: "At the origin, there is language, but what about the end point: Is language still there?" (1980, 11). In "Dos Geshray" Rothenberg pushes language to its limits, and after "Dos Geshray," nearly every poem mentions poetry. While a poem is arguably external to that which it moves toward, to be silent is to ensure that there is nothing beyond the silence that overtakes the centers of both experience and language. For the victims of the camps, there was no outside, no voice from the world community:

> no holocaust because no sacrifice
> no sacrifice to give the lie
> of meaning & no meaning after auschwitz
> there is only poetry   no hope
> no other language left to heal
> no language   & no faces
> because no faces left   no names
> no sudden recognitions on the street
> only the dead still swarming   only Khurbn
> ("Dibbukim" [Dibbiks], 52–60)

If poetry is that which redeems, undoes, or rewrites history, then following Adorno, no poetry after Auschwitz. If poetry is that which would offer meaning and hope, faces and names to what has no meaning, no hope, no faces, no names, again means no poetry after Auschwitz. Poetry as mastery of the total is totalitarianism, a "delusion of the absolute" that would give:

> a parody of telos   of completion
> in the monstrous mind of the masters those
> who give themselves authority
> over the rest of life   who dole
> out life & death
> ("The Domain of the Total Closes Around Them," 3–6)

Protracted and uncontrollably rapturous, this poem is also concerned with the dichotomy between the artistry of the

Nazis ("artists of the new hell" [8]) and the exultation that greeted the birth of the state of Israel after the Holocaust as a new kind of artistic expression ("yours is the world of art writ large joined to life until the boundaries split apart" [42]). It focuses as well on the speaker's personal loss of family and culture. Its conclusion returns to the question of writing poetry after Auschwitz: "o god of caves (the stricken fathers cry) if you are light / then there can be no metaphor" (pt. 5, ll. 25–26). In section 5, we find the sole reference to God in the entire *Khurbn* collection:

> the grandfather who would have carried god with him
> into the pit   would he have cursed as I will for him?
>
> Or for that uncle who died, surely, with a malediction on his
>   tongue
> screamed it until the tongue dissolved the bullet achieved its
>   mark bit deeper
>
> into a world of fact (alas) the mind that cries cried out
> the god is real he whom the dead bear with them
>
> who bear witness to the death of metaphor & cry:
> "do not forget us! Help us! Think of us!"
>
> he is a man called yoshka is a name we share that grandfather
>   & I
> name that the jews called jesus that they screamed out of the
>   slime
>
> the world is god's then   & its ugliness   follows from his
>   (pt. 5, ll. 1–15)

Was the grandfather to curse God and die as Job's wife enjoined him to do early on in the course of his afflictions (Job 2:9)? Or is one of God's roles to be silent witness to calamity? The poet does not castigate God for the ugliness of the world, nor does he deny God's existence. Still, man's cry resounds to the heavens about the nature of such a God.

Is it the business of language to heal? Can poetry alone be assigned the work of healing and of offering hope? Or is Rothenberg naive or desperate?

The excremental interpretation offered earlier—whose characteristics might encompass madness, primary matter, our self-created clay, the human elemental, expulsion, otherness, the irreducible to the profane, but always a transformation that reduces—becomes the only way for Rothenberg either to share the wrenching hurt or to forge an autonomous space for reacting to the incomprehensible. Thus Rothenberg boldly addresses the cloacal world of the camps where the victims are reminded in inescapable physical terms of their utter helplessness at controlling even their own bodily functions. Human excrement and its description are part and parcel of that dehumanized society. The Auschwitz universe was made of shit: the *anus mundi* wallowed in excremental filfth:

> this is extremity
>
> these images of shit, too raw
> for feeling,
> that drips onto their faces
>
> women squatting on long planks
> to shit "like birds
> perched on a telegraph wire"
>   ("Those Who Are Beautiful &
>   Those Who Are Not," 8–14)

> no
> not a moment's grace nor beauty to obstruct
> whatever the age demanded or the poem
> shit poured on wall & floor
> . . . .
> shitting
> globules of fat & shit
> that trickle down the pit in which the victim—
> the girl without a tongue—stares up
> & reads her final heartbreak
> ("Nokh Auschvits" [After Auschwitz], 7–10, 49–53)

> a dead man in a Rabbi's clothes
> who squats outside the mortuary house
> who guards their privies who is called

> master of shit
>> ("Dibbukim" [Dibbiks], 61–64])

let his excretions pour out
> across the room
Let it flood the bottoms of the women's cages let it drip through
> the cracks into the faces of the women down below
>> ("Di Toyte Kloles" [The Maledictions], 32–35)

One can be haunted in many ways, but to be haunted by the *dibbiks* of Treblinka or of this particular century is to recognize that we live in a topsy-turvy world where the tables have turned, where what is valorized is not creating but unmaking, guised as creation:

> THOSE WHO ARE BEAUTIFUL & THOSE WHO
> ARE NOT
>
> change places to relive
> a death by excrement
>
> victims thrown into the pit & drowning
> in their ordure
> suffocating in the body's dross
>
> this is extremity
>
> these images of shit, too raw
> for feeling,
> that drips onto their faces
>
> women squatting on long planks
> to shit "like birds
> perched on a telegraph wire"
>
> who daub each other
>
> have no language for the horror
> left to speak, the stink
> has so much caked their throats,
>
> they who would live with shit
> & scrape it
> from drinking cups

this is extremity this place

is where desire ends
where the warm flux inside the corpse
changes to stone

(21–24)

This is the image of fixity, locating a kind of life, a still life. One might be tempted to dismiss the poem in its entirety as sensationalism—but we must bear in mind the demand to maintain a familiar rhetoric, the coercion of decorum, and hence to be politically correct. Such a demand silences and maintains a silence around what is difficult if not impossible to put into words. The political reasons to silence the body's pain are obvious. The language of pain is so limited, as Elaine Scarry illustrates in *The Body in Pain* (1985), and becomes a way of disciplining the culture to accept the social manifestations of pain, such as hunger, the passive neglect of the disabled, war, and torture. Were we not to silence pain, we would ostensibly be paralyzed (hence another form of pain metaphorically asserts itself, demanding attention). But, to silence pain is to deny our perception of history and to prevent our understanding, however tenuous, of the condition of others, of otherness. As Scarry points out in her brilliant and difficult book, no one actually feels the pain of another—we live in certainty about our own pain, in doubt about the reality of another's. There is nothing natural about empathy, that rope bridge of language suspended across the abyss that separates us from the skins of others. She further reminds us that torture seeks to destroy the language and the world of its victims. However as John Donne ("Devotions Upon Emergent Occasions," 344) wrote, "No man is an island entire of itself."

Rothenberg asks in the poem what the composition of beauty is and whether ugliness disables language. He concludes that the two polarities, beauty and ugliness, exchange places in extreme situations. The extremism of the poem is emphasized by the opposing forces of the images—human beings swimming in shit and robbed of language is an extreme image and therefore interchangeable with something positive. A problem with this binary opposition is that while many survivors have found it impossible to tell their story, and have been silenced, many others have spoken—fluently, precisely, and voluminously. The specter of a poet removing language from the victims is strange, especially when he does so to make a case for poetry. The poet's obligation, as Rothenberg's "Dibbukim" cited in another context passionately demonstrates, is the revelation of the secrets of pain, the painfulness of our histories, the revolting stench:

> over a field of rags half-rotted shoes
> & tableclothed old thermos bottles rings
> lost tribes in empty synagogues
> at night their voices
> carrying across the fields
> to rot your kasha your barley
> stricken beneath their acid rains
> no holocaust because no sacrifice
> no sacrifice to give the lie
> of meaning & no meaning after auschwitz
> there is only poetry no hope
> no other language left to heal
> no language & no faces
> because no faces left no names
> no sudden recognitions on the street
> only the dead still swarming only khurbn
> a dead man in a rabbi's clothes
> who squats outside the mortuary house
> who guards their privies who is called
> master of shit an old alarm clock
> hung around his neck who holds
> a wreath of leaves under his nose
> from eden "to drive out
> the stinking odor of this world"
>
> (45–68)

It is this persistence of graphic images, words, history, and place that dwell within the living:

> the poetry is there too
> it is in the scraps of language
> by which the century is read to us the streets the dogs
> the faces fading out the eyes receding

> they are the dead & want so much to speak
> that all the writing in the world will not contain them
>> ("Der Vidershtand" [The Resistance] 58–63]

As it was the forces of totality that countenanced the Holocaust, it is language as "the domain of the total" that Holocaust poetry must resist, simultaneously also resisting the domain of total silence.

"Nokh Auschvitz (After Auschwitz)" engages Adorno directly:

> the poem is ugly & they make it uglier
> wherein the power resides
> that duncan did—or didn't understand
> when listening that evening to the other poet read
> he said "that was pure ugliness" & oh it was
> it was & it made my heart skip a beat
> because the poem wouldn't allow it no
> not a moment's grace not beauty to obstruct
> whatever the age demanded or the poem
> shit poured on wall & floor
> sex shredded genitals torn loose by dog claws
> & the ugliness that you were to suffer
> later that they had suffered
> not as dante dreamed it but in the funnel
>> (1–14)

"Duncan" is Rothenberg's friend, the poet Robert Duncan, to whom *Khurbn* is dedicated: "(For Robert Duncan, comrade [d. 1988]. . . . Now be the angel of my poem.)" "Whatever the age demanded" is reminiscent of one of modernism's dominant figures, Ezra Pound, quoted from his "Mauberley." The third reference to a poet, Dante, appears in line fourteen. George Steiner has suggested that the Holocaust is the Christian idea of hell made real and that Dante is actually the most knowledgeable guide to the camps. Robert Pinsky, poet laureate of the United States, responds: "In magnitude, in challenge to the imagination, in degree of horror, in terrifying questions it raises, that's an appropriate analogy. But we must never forget the defect of the analogy. Souls are assigned in the Inferno according to a system of justice; souls were assigned in the camps according to a system of injustice" (quoted by Robert Leiter 1997, ix).

Lines 15–25 recite a litany of horrors, including a father jumping into a muddy pool of bones containing the remains of his child. In lines 26–31, before the poem returns to its list of horrors, the father says

> how he must fight
> his rage for beauty must make a poem
> so ugly it can drive out the other voices
> like artaud's squawk the poem addressed
> to ugliness must resist
> even the artistry of death.
>
> (26–31)

Artaud, in joining the other literary figures, connects the poem to the tradition of Western antipoetry and to the specific continuum within that tradition of poetry and drama that explores darkness and absurdity. Moreover, references to Artaud and Pound link Rothenberg's work to modernism in general and to modernism's embrace of ugliness most especially. Despite Pound's flagrant anti-Semitism, Rothenberg credits him with a profound influence on his poetry. Referring to Duncan, a member of his own poetic circle, Rothenberg also deals with the question of how new poetry, one that responds to both Auschwitz and Adorno, will be received. One might ask what the mention of Olson or Duncan or Artaud has to do with getting into the guts and gore of a killing ground. What is written in blood has no need for invocations to male muses of the American poetry scene. Or could this reference be a response to the critique of ugliness, as these artists too affirm the ugly?

In "Nokh Aushvitz (After Auschwitz)" the victims of the horror are not fully actualized characters; they are artlessly dehumanized targets of savagry, even meat: "jews / it is not good it is your own sad meat / that hangs there poor & bagged like animals" (34–36). This strophe is more occupied with the nature of the violence done to Jewish bodies than with the Jewish bodies to whom it was perpetrated. When at the conclusion of the poem, which has concentrated solely on violence done to male bodies, a girl appears in the bottom of a gore-filled pit "without a tongue" and "stares up / & reads her final heartbreak" (52–53), the reader has difficulty accessing this girl, the pathos of her heartbreak. Why suddenly a girl in this poem so steeped in male references? Does her heartbreak seem more delicate, more heartbreaking than that of a tortured man? Or is the girl witness, though tongueless, to a particular tragedy as well as to an anonymous one?

"Di Toyte Kloles" (The Maledictions, 33) is a list poem of thirty-nine savagely intense curses. The literal meaning of *toyte,* deadly, sets the tone. Some of the curses resound with biblical rhetoric: "Let him [the dead man] say that every man is a murderer & that he is a murderer like all the rest" (8–9). Some are bitterly lifelike: "Let the holes in his body drop open let his excretions pour out across the room" (32). Some are metaphorical: "Let 10,000 bodies be gathered in one place until they vanish let the earth & sky vanish with them & then return" (49–50). This poem is fierce as the long list gathers momentum. Much of the imagery found in *Khurbn*—excrement, blood, screaming women, dismembered men, the skeletons of children—reappears here, cursed and cursing as the poem gains impetus, erupting near the end in a Yiddish passage, resurrecting the dead language from its own grave:

> My face & half my body have vanished & am I still alive?
> But the movement of my soul through space & time brings me
>   inside you
> The immeasurable part of a language is what we speak he says
>   who am I? *Dayn mamas bruder farshvunden in dem khurbn*
>   *un muz in mayn eygenem losn loz mikh es redn*
>   *durkh dir dos vort khurbn*
> *Mayne oygen zaynen blind fun mayn khurbn ikh bin yetst a*
> *peyger*
>
>   (65—73)
>
>
> [Your mother's brother disappeared in the Khurbn and I must
>   speak in my own
> Language speak through you the word Khurbn
> My eyes are blind from my Khurbn I am now a dead one.]
>   (Author's translation of italics)

This appears amidst the hortatory maledictions, interrupting itself to comment on language as a means of self-definition.

Rothenberg invokes *mamma loshn,* the speech of the dead now totally orphaned, to reinforce the thoroughness of the destruction and the reality that the "mother tongue" is one with it. To speak of all-encompassing death one must use its own language.

And then the final curses:

> Let the light be lost & voices cry forever in the dark & let
>   them know no joy in it
> Let murderers multiply & torturers let fields rot & forests shrink
>   let children dig up bones under the market square
> Let fools wield power let saints & martyrs root up in a money
>   field of blood
> Let madness be the highest virtue let rage choke all who will
>   not rage
> Let children murder children let bombs rain down let houses
>   fall
> Let ghosts & dibbiks overwhelm the living
> Let the invisible overwhelm the visible until nothing more is
>   sccn or heard
>
> (75–87)

As with other strophes, this poem concludes without a period. It appears to have simply stopped where it was, overcome by its own vehemence. This unclosed ending, however, implies too that the curses could go on forever, that there is no end to the maledictions the Holocaust could rain down on all of us, to destroy everyone, not just Jews. Rothenberg in his introduction reminds us that he wants to make poetry speak for the dead: "Let the dead man call out in you because he is a dead man" (1). Is this what he imagines the dead of the *khurbn* would wish? Is this what "survivor guilt" imagines the dead wish to be?

The curses are a raw and bleeding commemorative candle. They are a *Ner Tamid,* the eternal light placed before the Ark where the scrolls of the Law are kept for the millions of candles extinguished all over Europe. But even in the midst of all these invectives, the poem attends to the writing of poetry. It commands the reader:

> Let the dead man call out to you because he is a dead man
> Lct him look at your hands in the light that

> filters through the table where he sits
> Let him tell you what he thinks & let your
> throat gag on his voice
> Let his words be the poem & the poem be what you
> wouldn't say yourself.

(1–7)

The curse allows the dead to speak through (presumably) both the poet and the reader. That not being enough, the listener-reader-poet is enjoined to allow the dead man's words to gag him, and therefore to force him to vomit. Is the listener to spew up what he/she hears? Is this then the only way to "speak" those words because they are words you "wouldn't say yourself"? Rothenberg makes a grandiose supposition—that a poet might speak for the dead, that the dead might speak through a poet, that a poet might replace the voice of a poet. Nonetheless this poem provides the reader with an unusual combination of ferocity, black but arabesque language, and the dark vision we have come to associate with Rothenberg's treatment of big subjects.

Playfully and almost abruptly in the Yiddish tradition of humorous curses he gives us:

> Let a worm the size of a small corner of the table come out where
> you're sitting
> Let it be covered with red mucus falling from his nose (but
> only you will see it).

(28–31)

Because Rothenberg writes large-purposed words and rarely opts for the political message, *Khurbn* is far more than a poem about this loathsome episode in human history. In the tradition of Pound and Olson, political concerns and aesthetic concerns are for Rothenberg the same or at least are interacting realities, as in these lines from "Der Vidershtand" (The Resistance):

> began with this in Olson's words it was
> the pre/face so much fat for soap
> superphosphate for soil fillings & shops for sale
> such fragmentation delivered by whatever means

the scrolls of auschwitz buried now brought to light
again

(1–6)

So much fat for soap and so much superphosphate for soil are the precisely measured deadly components of Auschwitz. The scrolls of the place document these realities. Who witnesses? And how? Are not all images, all words, a poverty, a failure to tell, to show, to explain?

"Peroration For A Lost Town," with which *Khurbn* concludes, faces the loss of the town where the speaker's family lived, asking first what to say to the town, then evoking images of the town both alive and dead, and finally at the end of the first section of the strophe summoning the town itself to answer. This obviously futile command would usually be understood as such in the context of this poem. Rothenberg has previously asserted the capacity to speak for the dead—the curse of being the mouth for the dead—against Adorno's accusation that writing poetry at all after Auschwitz is barbaric.

The second section (part 2), a prose poem sets the stage. It begins, "I have come here looking for the bone of my grandfather (I said) Daylight had intervened. The town was no more empty as we walked its length" (38). The speaker walks through the town, opening himself up to the voices of the dead. He encounters a very old man, a sepulchral figure who has come in search of the bones of his child. A question is asked: "Then he asked—or was it I who asked him?" (38). Time then collapses on itself, alternating layers of past and present, and the history of the village is heard through the mouth of the speaker in total disarray. Standing by is a family of six-fingered people, similar to the bride in Eugene Ionesco's absurdist play *The Submission,* and people with pink and red names: "vanished vanished in the earth, they said. The red names & the flower names. The pink names" (38).

There can be no peroration, no recapitulation, for a town leveled by the Holocaust or a poem that would address it. The peroration therefore becomes a series of rhetorical questions: "were there once Jews here?" (paragraph 2). It is uncertain, in the quest for lineage, for origins, for answers, who asked: "he asked—/ or was it I who asked or asked for him?" (paragraph

2). It is "they, the townspeople, who answer—not with history, for "if there was a history they couldn't find it," but with a fiction:

> (There was a people once, they said, we called the old believers. A people with black beards & eyes like shriveled raisins. Out of the earth they came & lived among us. When they walked their bodies bent like yours & scraped the ground. They had six fingers on each hand. Their old men had the touch of women when we rubbed against them. One day they dug a hole and went back into the earth. They live there to this day.)
> . . .The village pump you spoke about still stands back of the city hall (they told us) The rest was all a dream. (part 2, paragraph 3)

The "village pump" (which also appears in "Dos Osleydikn") seems an innocuous enough image, but it is also a "thing that testifies," literally and figuratively commingling the dead under the earth with the living who walk over the earth But at the vanishing point of the comprehension of the magnitude of such a genocide, history and fiction blur: the people who came from the earth have gone back into the earth but not according to the natural order of things.

And what of the meaning of red and pink? Are the names pink and red because they are covered in grave markers with fresh, partially sanitized blood? Because they represent communist and socialist families? Do they recall the labelings prevalent in the McCarthy era of the fifties? Pink and red because some are more butchered than others? Rothenberg summons the images of nightmare and surrealism, almost as if the dead were the unconscious with whom the artist seeks contact. This strophe is reminiscent of Celan's "Death Fugue," pulling itself toward an irrationality whose connection to the Holocaust is all the more potent because it is savagely fierce, untamed, and grotesque.

However, the last lines of the strophe grant that all of this is senseless and return to the fixed present. "You" in this context is Rothenberg's uncle who had lived in the village of Ostrow-Mazowiecka in Poland. "They" are the villagers. The dream fails in having the old man, the uncle, speak through the poet. The voices are dream-voices, ravaged by the terror of their anguish and their illogical deaths. The world wants to make sense but is irrational. Or is the "rest" that was all a dream actually the *Khurbn* that the voices cry? The confusion here is doubtless intended, as the poem scorns facile conclusions and rejects closure at the end of every strophe. Our acquiescence to accept *Khurbn's* argument about the possibility of poetry after Auschwitz relies upon some understanding of what this volume and its words do, and where they locate themselves in relation to both history and poetry. Poetry after Auschwitz must speak for the dead: Rothenberg's avowed aim. If becoming the mouth of the dead means that the poet must speak of shit and blood, torture and dismemberment, then so be it:

> Is it true that Jews come sometimes in the night & spoil the cows' milk? Some of us have seen them in the meadows—beyond the pond. Long gowns they wear & have no faces. Their women have sharpened breasts with long black hairs around the nipples. At night they weep. (Heads forced in the bowls until their heads ran with excrement.) No one is certain if they still exist. (paragraph 2)

But if what comes out when the poet speaks is a dream, then what is the dream, what is the poem, what is the *Khurbn,* what is the poet, and how can poetry that admits its own insubstantiality save poetry? is not the confrontation of such reality in the realm of the surreal? There are no answers to these questions in the third and final strophe of the poem:

> (by gematria)
>
> a wheel
> dyed red
>
> an apparition
> set apart
>
> out of the furnace
> (pt. 3, ll. 1–6)

The apparition, then, has been obtained by numerology. So much understanding depends on these final lines of this long poem, but in the end the poem retreats from commitment and leaves us with only a vision taken from the furnace and set apart. Perhaps it is that reclaiming of a vision, or ghost of a vision, that is all the totality of what speaking of *khurbn* can ultimately accomplish. Poetry it seems can do little against the brutal cruelty of Auschwitz. The closing of a strophe is designated a peroration, a rhetorical construct, which suggests that the piece is, after all, only a speech. Is it possible that the specter of the dead has been set as clearly apart from the furnace (the *khurbn*) as the lines are separated from each other in the poem? The wheel that has been divined by numerology has been dyed red. It is a revolving wheel. If its revolving has colored it red, then it has been revolving in the red stuff, the obscene elements of the Holocaust—blood and fire. And the wheel has also *died* bloody, so that it has ceased to revolve. Something has changed, charged with the power of numbers or a number, clearly Six Million. And the Six Million have become a single apparition the poem isolates from the furnace. The poem itself has emanated finally, from "out of the furnace."

Gematria beckons to Rothenberg in his "14 Stations," written to accompany Arie Galles's monumental charcoal drawings based on World War II aerial views of the principal Nazi extermination camps—each with an attendant railroad station—known to have been the sites of Holocaust. As Galles worked from documentary photographs to establish some pretense at distance, thereby striving for objectivity, Rothenberg too sought objectivity in *Gematria* as a way of determining the words and phrases of his poems. "The counts were made off the Hebrew and/or Yiddish spellings of the camp names, then keyed to the numerical values of words and word combinations in the first five books of the Hebrew Bible. It is my hope that this small degree of objective chance will not so much mask feeling or meaning as allow them to emerge" (Rothenberg 1996, 100). The title of this set of poems is obviously fraught with one of the ultimate images of suffering, the stations of the cross, the agonizing walk of Jesus on the way to Calvary, "14 Stations": Auschwitz-Birkenau, Belzec, Bergen-Belsen, Gross-Rosen, Dachau, Chelmno, Treblinka, Mauthausen, Maidanek, Sobibor, Ravensbruck are a powerful and sad meditation on tragedy without the galloping fury of *Khurbn*. They move one to quiet introspection and reflection.

Fierce, effective, irritating, gory, violent, there is notably in the final strophe and opening in the prose poem of "Di Magilas Fun Aushvitz" [The Scrolls of Aushwitz] rich, anguished imagery recalling the loathing of the Brothers Grimm. How non-benign their writing seems, most especially for children in a post-Auschwitz world:

> He had vanished & reappeared in a room no bigger than a giant's hand. Asleep in it. His arms & legs were rusted, his eyes swam in his head like mercury. He was twice forgotten. A stranger to his memory of who he was.

> When a man moves up & down across the field, the earth moves with him. The condition described as double thunder—reprinted by the ones called souls, the hopeless dead. It is most likely they who move, the rest is an illusion. The stranger in the giant's hand knows who they are. (paragraphs 1–2)

Revulsion, abhorrence, and frenzy propel the poem with its complex questions and complex aims. In the end, however, those questions and aims dominate to the extent that they resolve into an inconclusive conversation about poetry. "It was all a dream," an "apparition ." The reader is left suspended: one cannot hold an apparition, and an apparition cannot answer questions. In *Khurbn* Rothenberg challenges Adorno's assertion that writing poetry after Auschwitz is barbaric: is not an apparition better than nothing at all? Or are we settling for the minimum once again?

Rothenberg's poems, in trying to redefine the boundaries for poetry after Auschwitz and to reclaim it from Adorno, resort to a frantic voice that insists that there is absolutely nothing that it cannot say, no place that it cannot force the reader's gaze. Rothenberg takes his reader deep into the maelstrom, to bear more of its darkness, and perhaps to sensitize them to the pain of others.

Thus poetry offers possibly the sole opportunity for us to hear the voices of the dead. Accounts of what has transpired are offered in this autonomous space of dialogues. Poetry is part of the social construction afforded by language, its modality part of the method of silencing. As such, poetry is both the poison and the antidote—the poison of our century, but also, in its ability to create the space in which we become haunted by others, an antidote. "It is the condition of our lives for forty years now . . . that poetry is the speech of ghosts" ("The Scrolls of Auschwitz," in *Khurbn* paragraph 8, 28). Rothenberg initiates healing by bringing us into intimate contact with a pain that only the poem can provide. For it allows our own indwelling, our own endless returns. And it posits an ethics of voice demanding change.

Such a declaration is somewhat incongruous in a poetic sequence claiming to be written in the language of the dead, but in many ways Rothenberg remains truer to his project's use of words in other than their literal sense. It is appropriate, for instance, that *Khurbn* and Rothenberg's other Holocaust poetry should lack the overt patterns or structures that a retrospective consciousness might impose. Instead we find poem after poem repeating in one way or another the common nouns of extermination—blood, ditch, forest, hair, pit, scream, train, or shifting from observations of present landscapes to hallucinatory images of suffering and death. Claude Lanzmann's 1985 documentary film, *Shoah*, serves as an analogue, with its avoidance of chronology, its repetitions, and its images of silent fields and forests, the ghosts of Eastern European Jewry juxtaposed to accounts of what happened there. Events of *Khurbn* transcend the factual and move into the mythological. For many this history has become the material of documentaries, fictive movies, novels, and poems more than it has remained a historical reality. *Khurbn* and Rothenberg's oeuvre of Holocaust poetry, while jagged and fragmented, reflecting the nature of the subject at hand, restore mystery to the past and make the past present. A problem for the poet in the face of such an ugly subject is the beauty of his language. Therefore, the phrases have a crudeness, a rightness that gives his images the power to shock. Rothenberg also is one of those rare free-verse poets, according to Nathan Whiting, who actually does allow the form to come from meaning, and this ability saves him. The monument takes on its own shape. Each room has its own character: some few are very lovely, full of air and vision; some are dense with the images of horror; others are like stones on the ground at Treblinka "a cry (darkest in / the pauses)." Thus Rothenberg uses the greatest attribute of the lyric, *beauty*, to express emotion in the hardest area, that of catastrophic destruction. Where the ugliness is so extreme, goes the truism, one can find beauty. This poet succeeds because he allows the lyric to go to whatever length it needs, to take whatever shape it requires. This method is not a dead end, then, but a useful direction, which Rothenberg has taken not to its limits but to a crossroads (1989, 89).

Rothenberg's poetic response to the gas chambers is reflected in his stunning blue tonality—dark, almost purple in some places, fading into cloudlike shades in others. He knew that the bluish-gray pellets of the Zyklon B gas left a blue residue formed by the deposit of countless poison-soaked breaths. Each blue therefore was not just a life lost, a voice muted, but a manner of death—personal in repugnance and agony. For Rothenberg this direct confrontation with history was with people he could have loved and embraced but can now only reach through the medium of words. Is it any wonder that abyss and loss haunt this poetry, which aims at nothing less than totalization of the entire picture? Instead of subordinating either emotion or intellect, it fuses them both in an attempt to empower the dead and to reconstruct the scraps of poems they left behind in the mud.

It would be a disservice to Rothenberg not to mention that he, like Stern and Heyen, also has a close connection to Walt Whitman that, according to Gitenstein (1986), is "quite deliberate." In fact, Rothenberg reminds us of this in his "Pre-Face" to *The New and Collected Poems: 1970–1985:*

> Everything & everyone around here are welcome to come into the poem—in particular what has been hidden for so long that the poem has almost to create it (or to seem to do so) to make it visible again. This is the open invitation of our poetry since Whitman. Wecome to it in whatever ways we can. (viii)

Rothenberg, poet of the barbaric and the abhorrent, is bound to recall Whitman's insistence that things usually rejected as improper have their rightful place in the world and thus belong in poetry. Furthermore, as Whitman wrote *Leaves of Grass* over a thirty-six-year period, Rothenberg's *Poland/ 1931* is an ever-evolving collection that first began to appear more than twenty years ago. Additionally, Rothenberg's sense of his own poetic mode parallels Whitman's "Camerado, this is no book/who touches this touches a man." The very personal nature, the impulse to redeem and translate voices long despised and rejected, the emphasis on sexuality and bodily function, the panoramic vision—all are present in both poets.

And Rothenberg (1994b) refers to Whitman again:

> A *Big Jewish Book* was for me a way to explore or to recover all the possibilities of what a Jewish poem was or still might be—and to do it from where I was, as Whitman had written of his own explorations in "Song of Myself," without cheek, with original energy. . . . I spoke of the work in a larger sense as part of the process of recovery in our time, of the long forbidden voices invoked by Whitman over a century ago. (4)

Rothenberg's poems are profoundly Jewish; however, they must be seen as his exploration of ancestral roots as a means of mapping his own understanding of himself as a poet and a man. He knows from his historical tradition what it means to be lost, obscure, and forgotten; he knows that he must be attentive to the differences and peculiarities of being a man alone (part of a people alone). He knows that writing of the events that truly matter to him are part of his eternal *Kaddish*. The narratives therefore create a landscape as well as tell a story. But it is no coincidence that Rothenberg spent a major part of his career following a passion for the poetry of primitive cultures, all of which reflect cultural concerns and much of which reflects these concerns in religious form. He always sounds Jewish—beautifully, fully, historically, deeply poetically Jewish: the religious chant is never far from his voice. Poets in primitive societies had to summon a whole mythological culture to create an identity, and this Rothenberg has done most successfully. He takes almost a pagan delight in invoking the ugly, the sinful. Rothenberg's sensuality reminds one of an infant playing with shit (or an adult in the last stages of senility) and liking the texture, being untroubled by the odor and unperturbed by the notion that this is noxious waste.

Rothenberg appropriated his enjoyment of the unspeakable from primitive poetries. Later it reechoes in the poverty and persecution that invests so much of Jewish history with imagery and reality that sanitized, hygiene-obsessed Americans find repulsive. Rothenberg's Holocaust poetry is not for the fainthearted. One thing is certain: it is impossible to read *Khurbn* through in one sitting. The other poems in this volume, although shorter in length, pack much of the same power.

Khurbn exemplifies how the poet might act as witness. The poet, seeking to let reality reveal itself, attempts to remove himself from the stance of interpreter, translator, and judge and calls instead for the testimony to speak. In *Khurbn*, then, the dead speak through the poet and show that imagination is not merely and solely the antithesis of reality but a way of comprehending reality when facts and documents fail us.

Biblical Jacob wrestles with an angel. Jerome Rothenberg wrestles with ghosts, and who among us who has lost family to the black hole of Europe does not? Each house of Israel contains a mourner. The very name *Yisrael—Israel—*means to strive, to struggle with the Lord. And the struggle to express the inexpressible is what is at stake in Rothenberg's poetry. The word genocide touches upon all of our ghosts. *Khurbn* and Rothenberg's Holocaust poetry expose us to what most would like to ignore, forget, revise, or relegate to some special category as aberrant human behavior. Is violent language anywhere near the violence of the silence of the inhabitants of the European countryside or of eighty-seven death camps? Is overstatement or understatement, or any statement, a solution to the ultimate solution?

Of course, nothing is resolved or can be resolved. Every poet must come to terms with his/her own *dibbiks*, voices from the past that claim and possess him/her. The dead rely upon the living to represent them; forgetting really would be the Final Solution. Jerome Rothenberg, whose bare bones are revealed by his unique process of emptying out, gives us a poetry that teems with life in those spaces, albeit a life of fear, trembling, and wildness replete with the terrors of an unfathomable particularized history.

5

Conclusion: Finding the Words

This poetry aims to remember, smash, amplify or offer an eternal *Kaddish* for the individual and collective stillness left by the Holocaust. It is inextricably tied to an uncommonly intricate chain of accountabilities—to the history of the Final Solution, which it must neither distort nor diffuse; to the victims whose experience it retells; and to the readers, who must remain with the poem and empathize with it, no matter how penetrating its examination. Poet and reader are arbiters of whether this poetry fulfills these duties right-mindedly and tastefully. The poems discussed by Sylvia Plath, William Heyen, Gerald Stern, and Jerome Rothenberg depict a range of form, voice and approach, style, generation, and personal background. Evolving out of a calamitous history, these poems attain the desired result or are found wanting to the extent that they enact an intimate relationship between moral posture and aesthetic strictness. This must be a relationship between one kind of good and another, between the good that beauty always provided and a beauty derived from the poem's ability to do both educational and moral tasks. The poems finally should both *do* and *be* good.

Since one of the prime functions of Holocaust art is to awaken people, this examination has affirmed the significance of paying attention to the poems as poems, of observing the extent to which their aesthetic characteristics fulfill ethical purposes.

Of paramount concern are what the poems affect, how they affect it, how the poet negotiates the material, what the poem exacts from the reader, and what the poem gives the reader by amplifying the capability to respond and to learn, concurrently rewarding this partnership with the joy of observing the poem reveal itself. The reader must ask how well the poem does both its moral and historical job. It should reignite the reader's remembrance of the Holocaust, present information, make the event sharper and more specific. It should lure the reader away from easy pieties, creating a more intricate and vivid response of anguish, rage, revulsion, empathy, and above all, uneasiness. Where the poem presses toward this uneasiness, it should provide the reader with the stimulation of words and the minimal consolation of withstanding silence and forgetting in return for an inclination to share the poet's insight.

Hovering over any discussion of the purpose, propriety, and feasibility of poetry after Auschwitz is the shadow of Adorno's radical suggestion that an art form should or could disappear in response to the enormity of this cataclysmic event. In Berel Lang's collection of essays (1988), seven of the nineteen essayists and Lang himself direct attention to Adorno's dictum. Certainly questions about the capability of any art form to comment on or record the Holocaust were, and are, unavoidable. The Holocaust was and remains both a discontinuous moment in human history—a place and time that compels everything else to stop and search for understanding—and a painfully wrenching part of the continuity of Western culture's assault on Jews, political dissidents, homosexuals, and gypsies. Adorno's dictum also offers a suitable and commanding point of departure or debate.

Following close on the heels of Adorno is George Steiner, who proposes silence as the only decent response to the Holocaust, even while turning against the silence he himself advocated by writing both fiction and nonfiction about it. He opts for the broadest interpretation of Adorno:

> What kind of rationality, what kind of ordered logic of the human, social and psychological circumstance, what processes of rational analysis and causal explanation are available to language after the cancer of reason, the travesty of meaningfulness, enacted in the Shoah? It is doubts of this order that have generated my own (provisional) feeling that silence is the only, though in its way suicidal, option that to speak or write intelligibly . . . about Auschwitz is to misconceive totally the nature of that event and to mis-

construe totally the necessary constraints of humanity within language. (156)

This statement is specious at best, and it is clear from Steiner's own writings that he does not really countenance this position himself. For Holocaust art is not only possible but also capable of meeting a high artistic standard, and therefore cannot be reconciled with the claim that to write intelligently about the Holocaust is to misconceive it. What is particularly compelling about Holocaust poetry, however, is the close connection between flawed poetry and ethical failure. The poetry that settles for cliché, that makes emotion easy or simple, that refamiliarizes this genre rather than defamiliarizing it is not good poetry. Triteness makes Holocaust poetry safe, makes it acceptable to feel bad or sad about the Holocaust. But Holocaust art ought to be dangerous and challenging. It should make us uncomfortable, annoy us, intimidate us by being good art.

Further, Steiner equates Adorno's statement about poetry with eloquence. He sees Auschwitz as an uncrossable crevasse in the slowly erupting volcano of Western philosophical progress continuing with

Where the language is still humane, in the root sense of that word, it is being spoken by survivors, remembrancers and ghosts. Its cooling ash is of dead fire. Eloquence after Auschwitz would be a kind of obscenity (this is the meaning of Theodor Adorno's so often misunderstood call for "no poetry after Auschwitz"). (156)

The Holocaust poems chosen for this discussion are warnings, ritualistic, epics, mournful, inspirational, questionings, lamentations, and even purgatives. Heyen, Stern, and Rothenberg share an intensity of purpose: to establish a partnership with the victim. Plath's conflict with her father makes any kind of a statement about her identifying with the victims disingenuous, for her all-consuming struggle is of a far lower magnitude than the Nazi atrocity. However, all of this Holocaust poetry taken collectively aims to change its readers through its reflection on this formidable event.

The work of American poets writing about the Holocaust has

been greatly overshadowed by the plethora of poetry by European writers and overwhelmed by judgmental dissertations concerning the amount of American prose on the subject. From an American perspective, the poets examined here offer convincing evidence that the Holocaust was not a German matter, a European matter, or even a Jewish matter, but a universal human matter—a stark reality fit for poetry, even necessary and vital to poetry, perhaps even crying out for poetry.

Yet even uneasiness needs to be questioned, since it can never be adequate to the event; it is potentially accompanied by a quality of self-righteous sufficiency. The pain elicited by Holocaust art entails an acquiescence on the part of the viewer/reader to experience that poem. To engage the substance of the Holocaust repeatedly, whether as an artist or a historian, insists upon some pulling power beyond obligation to the extremity of the subject matter, and a response that might be called satisfaction. Reader-response theory, whose adherents claim that the meanings of a text are the "production" or "creation" of the individual reader, is applicable here (Abrams 1993, 269). It takes a reader to pick up the black marks on the page and make real the text's potential. Something unanticipated, that was not brought to the reading in the first instance, must happen for the reader. The strange and hurtful part of this complicated arrangement may be the defamiliarizing process, so oddly similar to the effect of torture on the victim's concept of ordinary objects. Whereas in the normal course of events repetition and necessity combine, to numb perception and response and familiarity batters people in alienating waves of white noise. Art, if successful, penetrates this protective amniotic fluid and leaves its audience agonizingly exposed and life's margins sharply honed and attentive.

The momentous questions raised by Adorno and Steiner, despite their literal statements, are not those of silence versus writing. They are, rather, of appropriate writing and useful voicing—of the ethics and morals of writing and the Holocaust, of imagination and the Holocaust, and of the limits of writing and the Holocaust. And we must repeatedly raise the question of response and responsibility to a history so extreme and so wrong it should change at the very least everything following it. For Adorno, and to a limited degree Steiner, if we read and write poetry after Auschwitz, we act as if Auschwitz did not interrupt or turn the flow of human history, and the *Auschwitz-Weltanschauung* is thereby triumphant. Yet if we turn away from poetry, then we have permitted Auschwitz to take yet another good away from us, thereby portraying the *Auschwitz-Weltanschauung* as triumphant.

Living in a condition of consciousness concerning the ways the past intrudes into the present is one kind of awareness. It is even a sort of resistance, both of the abominations of the past and of those possible in the future. Because so many of the conditions and assumptions that produced the Holocaust have not changed, resistance is still crucial, albeit still inadequate. Holocaust poems provide another kind of resistance as well, by naming the dead and thereby affirming obliterated lives. Employing poetry to name the dead reindividualizes the victims and insists upon their having existed. Ultimately, this is a resistance to the Final Solution, a refusal to let it be final. The subject is not beautiful, nor can it be made beautiful, but the act of resistance has intrinsic beauty, and this must be conceded to a poem as well.

Hannah Arendt once commented at Columbia University, following the publication of her book *Eichmann in Jerusalem,* "We must wait for the poets." Poetry, this seems to imply, might have some distinctive role in ordering and arranging the world after Auschwitz. Lawrence Langer (1975), who obsesses over the intrusions and deceptions involved in the clash between the facts of the Shoah and literary work, still prefers poetry to prose, implying very clearly that there are things poems can give that even survivor testimony cannot (30). Even so, he worries about how to inscribe the event in either historical or literary narratives that attempts to reduce to some semblance of order or pattern the spontaneous defilement implicit in such deeds (1998, 105).

What qualities might poetry bring to the commemoration and contemplative study of the Holocaust? Poetry is, in a variety of ways and degrees, part of the ritual system of Western culture, its roots in antiquity notwithstanding. The manner in which poetry handles emotion is most crucial in its relation-

ship to the Holocaust. Good poems, aesthetically and emotionally compelling poems, move us from the bottomless pit of
numbers with which the reader is unable to identify—crushed
as they are—to the particular—a single child, one day, one
voice, one death, one situation, even one generation. Good
poems have the same effect as the photograph of the child with
the yellow *Magen David* (Star of David) emblazoned on his
jacket, his hands raised in surrender, when the Nazis came to
deport and transport his town to the concentration camps. We
know with some certainty the motivation for this act. In a
normal situation we can imagine the youngster dressing himself for the day, eating his breakfast and going off to school. We
turn from envisioning the child in the gas chamber itself, but
the vision—for all that we sigh deeply—is etched in our minds
and hearts. That boy in that photograph not only makes the
Holocaust near and current, but he also positions its realities
out of the museum, the documentary, and the textbook.

This kind of apprehension is especially important as a
mode, if not of comprehension, at least of rendering the Holocaust thinkable, and more importantly, possible to experience. Our imagination makes it conceivable to recall that the
Holocaust is a matter not of six million indistinct deaths but
rather of six million single, palpable deaths enacted as part of
one diabolical intention. One suitcase, one exhausted child,
one shoe, one pair of eyeglasses, one heroism, one act of loving
kindness, one ancestor is at once more than we can really
grasp or emotionally absorb at one time. Since it borders on
absurdity to talk about seeing and feeling the Holocaust in its
totality, the best anyone can hope for is a melange of partial
seeings and incomplete feelings that will amount to an extended knowledge.

Knowledge is not enough to fathom this event. Emotion has
to be a critical and inextricable component of this knowledge.
Ignoring or denying emotions concerning the Final Solution is
to deny knowledge. But disbelief, anger, sorrow, and repugnance are feelings most people evade; they batter any reader or
listener confronting fragments of the Holocaust. And people
tend to try to move beyond those wounding emotions as
quickly as they can, in search of healing (Edmundson 1997,
34). Rhetoricians and tyrants routinely manipulate these emo-

tions to brainwash their constituencies, first by shattering already wounded cultural identities and then by offering false solace to populations too weakened and too hungry to question any source of comfort. Nationalism, collective pride, exhilaration, and a sense of destiny all proffer the sense of reintegration and of rightness. Hitler in his infinite wisdom utilized a large variety of modes to cajole and control an eager audience, seeing to it that the visual arts, film, music, twilight spectacle, and printed materials all contributed to exploiting emotions in the German populace. But the absence of emotion in public discourse can be just as exploitative and as dangerous.

Teaching people to see everything in terms of numbers, programs, facts, and systems can lead to the same kinds of desensitization and misdirection, the same impotent questioning provided by the mammoth orchestration of a people's emotions. Those who object to the making of literature and art from the history of the Holocaust argue that the arts and their direct relationship to the emotions will simplify, cheapen, or muddle the memory of Auschwitz. Fortunately they represent a minority viewpoint. The artistically gripping work of Leni Riefenstahl (its stunning and motivational impact on Rothenberg previously discussed) is perhaps the best known example of the ways in which aesthetically brilliant work can serve a morally repugnant propagandistic agenda—in this case the glorification of Nazism. It also mirrors an anxiety-ridden adherence to an Enlightenment belief among intellectuals that emotionless objectivity is the only secure route to truth, progress, and human growth. Where in this complicated connectedness of emotions to ethics does poetry fit? And where does Holocaust poetry fit in particular?

Where the Holocaust is involved—not to mention Hiroshima, Bosnia, Rwanda, and Kosovo—the only valid use for facts is in this power to make us feel the invasion of lives and bodies, to empathize with the victims' angst, and thereby to remind ourselves these people suffer as we might. But poetry, because it shakes us, excites us, stirs us, is among the genres that has the potential to redirect us, if not to a moral perfection than perhaps toward moral growth, but most certainly away from a barbarism in which we allow ourselves safety, separateness, and uniqueness.

Kenneth Burke, critic and linguist, has articulated sociological categories for literature:

> strategies for selecting enemies and allies, for socializing louses
> for warding off the evil eye, for purification, propitiation and de-
> sanctification, consolation and vengeance, admonition and ex-
> hortation, implicit commands or instructions of one sort or an-
> other. Art forms like "tragedy" or "comedy" or "satire" would be
> treated as equipment for living, that size up situations in various
> ways and in keeping with correspondingly various attitudes. The
> typical ingredients of such forms would be sought. Their relation
> to typical situations would be stressed. Their comparative values
> would be considered, with the intention of formulating a "strategy
> of strategies," the "overall" strategy obtained by inspection of the
> lot. (1989, 304)

Burke's list is operative as a fractional catalog of the "something" that happens in the work of each of the four poets
discussed, although the situations these poems explore are
not certainly conventional. Plath's demon is within herself,
her poems, a personal expiative. Heyen seeks consolation and
attempts to ward off the demon of complacency and indifference. Rothenberg takes aim at more than one demon—
smug self-satisfaction is one, Adorno's dictum is another, and
comfort is a third—while also looking for some kind of vengeance on a complex world. It would be a stretch to place
Stern's poems in this catalog, however; they appear to be more
interested in demystification and desanctification, working
more at becoming allies (in place and person) than at choosing
them, assuming the identities of victims instead of watching
them.

The connection between aesthetic rigor, aesthetic quality,
and ethical precepts is complex in the poetry of witness in
general and in Holocaust poetry in particular. May one speak
of an aesthetics of atrocity? To pose the question so boldly is to
appear either uninformed or already committed to a response.
Whether framed explicitly or simply assumed, this question
underwrites and sometimes overdetermines any critical discussion of poetry that focuses on the experiences and reactions of victims and former victims of Nazi atrocity (Horowitz
1997, 15). Paradoxically, it is the very power of the aesthetic

modes for approaching the inaccessible and inarticulable that evokes disquiet. To the extent that literary narrative substitutes language for world or symbol-making for bare chronology, it uneasily evokes the mechanism that facilitated the Final Solution (19).

The poetry of witness bears the traces of extremity within it and is as such evidence of what occurred. This poetry presents the reader with an engaging problem. We are most familiar with rather easy categories: "personal" and "political"—the former evoking lyrics of love and emotional loss, the latter indicating a public partnership that is considered divisive even when necessary. The distinction between the personal and the political gives the political too much and too little scope; at the same time it renders the personal too important and not important enough. If we give up the dimension of the personal, we risk relinquishing one of the most powerful sites of resistance. Perhaps, writes Carolyn Forche (1993), we need a middle ground between the two: the "social." For the social is a place of resistance and struggle, where books are published, poems read, and protest disseminated. It is the sphere in which the claims against the political are made in the name of justice. By placing poetry in the social space we are called from the other side of a situation of extremity and cannot use simplistic notions of accuracy or truth to life as evaluating mechanisms. Poetry will have to be judged by its affect and not by one's ability to verify its truth. In many cases, the poem might be our only evidence, a sole trace that an event has occurred (30, 31).

To discuss a poem as the sole trace of an event, to see it in purely evidentiary terms, is perhaps to believe in our own figures of speech too vigorously. If, as Walter Benjamin indicates, a poem is *itself* an event, a trauma that changes both a common language and an individual psyche, it is a special kind of event, a special kind of trauma. And one, to read or listen, must be willing to accept the trauma. So if a poem is an event, it has to belong to a different order of being from the trauma that marked its language in the first place (Forshe, 1993, 33).

The poetry of witness frequently resorts to paradox and difficult equivocation, to the invocation of what is *not* there as if it *were,* in order to bring forth the real. That it must defy common sense to speak of the common indicates that traditional modes of thought, the purview of common sense, no longer *make* sense (40). In the Auschwitz world poetry seeks truth through direction as well as indirection in wounded words, as we have seen. Holocaust poems must offer readers substantive witness even before answering to any accepted aesthetic standards. But they must also respect a set of aesthetic standards capable of crystallizing and sharpening witnessing. Holocaust poetry does not have to be clear—although successful American Holocaust poetry tends to be—but it must be sharp; the poem must attach itself to the reader's gut, because that is the place where the Burkean "something" has to happen. In order to do that, the poem needs to have submitted to some kind of order, discipline, or structure. In Holocaust poetry intentional fallacy cannot speak to or for the muddled metarealities of the late-twentieth-century mind. If the author denies intention and requires no intention from the reader, then who is to be accountable for the "something" that happens? Similarly, the poet must be hyperconscious of objectives; and demonstrating the author's right-mindedness, or conferring right-mindedness to the reader, should not figure among them. Nor should Holocaust poetry be palliative: some of it might help a reader be better, but all of it should help a reader know better.

The function of the traditional lyric "I" in poetry has not been shattered by Auschwitz or any of the century's other all-engulfing mass atrocities, but it has been metamorphosed. It still suits the discontinuous moment—the epiphanies, flashbacks, shocks, and momentary sublimities that interrupt our delusions of linear consciousness. Both in the poetry of witness and in other poetries, its subjectivity remains a bridge from aloneness to isolation. But in the poetry of witness, the conventional, autobiographical "I" can be an ambiguous presence, leading the poem away from dispassionate witness and toward a proclamation of the poet's righteousness, sensitivity, and sermonic discourse, the poet's ability to distance the poem from its own content.

The task of the witness poem is that what has been taught is untrue; it does not claim to teach so much as to unteach. It is neither a fable nor a narrative; "I" graphically tells not a whole story, but a backdrop. In that sense it is reportage as much as poetry. Its "I" voice is there as a speaker; it says that this moment has transpired because the "I" has seen it. Wiesel (1967) particularizes the concept of witness. In his eyes all Jews living today—and not only those who came out of the camps and the decimated Jewish communities of Europe— are survivors in the sense that they are all witnesses. "We are all survivors. We are all witnesses. We all embody the intense destiny of our people—a destiny which resists being divided into sections and selected periods. Each Jew represents all Jews and is Jewish history. . . . Each of us is therefore responsible for the past and future of Israel, because each of us carries within himself the vision of Sinai and the flames of the *Khurbn*" (47). Wiesel commented some years later in a lecture at Temple Beth El, Beth Hillel, Wynnewood: "I believe in words. The best witnesses are those who leave us their words. Remember those words. What we have lived and endured matters. Somehow it all matters" (1997).

The poems examined here are successful as witness and as poetry when they succeed in abiding by this lyric decorum in which the "I"-as-poet sublimates itself to the "I"-as-witness, regardless of whether that "I" and that eye is the poet's. Plath, Heyen, Stern, and Rothenberg manage to stare into the hollow ground, acknowledge their place, and remain competent to move on. Their poetry is achingly visceral. And this is some kind of comfort. As with the consolations offered by reading poetry that witnesses to the evil to which we are heir (notably in Heyen), its consolations are inevitably murky, difficult, and frigid.

It may well be that the most important function of Adorno's pronouncement is to remind those who inhabit the post-Holocaust world that its consequences extend beyond the immediate history and all that connect with it. Even lyric poetry, among the highest of cultural expressions, is intimidated by Auschwitz, not with annihilation, but with something equally reprehensible—barbarism. Not only might there be no more lyric poetry, but poetry itself might become a weapon of barbarism, as demonstrated by Rothenberg. As a statement of cultural extremity Adorno's dictum is explicit and fervent.

In undertaking to temper barbarism and to focus on the primacy of human relationships, Irving Halperin has compiled a list of quasi commandments for Holocaust readers and writers:

> THOU SHALT NOT BE THE EXECUTIONER
> THOU SHALT NOT BE SILENT
> THOU SHALT NOT BE THE SPECTATOR
> THOU SHALT NOT BE THE "DOG"
> THOU SHALT NOT LOOK TOO LONG INTO THE FIRE
> THOU SHALT CONTINUE TO INTERROGATE.
>
> (1970, 123)

Halperin's first commandment bids us to recognize that the proper place for both reader and writer of Holocaust literature is with the victims. The word "executioner" is expanded to mean that one must never inflict individualized suffering on others; we are admonished that we all have within us latent impulses for evil. Heyen is very strong on this issue. Halperin's second commandment speaks for the necessity of telling, of witnessing, of crying out loud. He is concerned that readers and writers alike not allow themselves to be like the Poles and Germans and others whose crime (among many) consisted in watching, but not seeing, or seeing and implicitly consenting by silence and indifference. Thus suffering is not to be a mere abstraction. The "ultimate evil" in Sartrean terms "is to make abstract that which is concrete"—the concrete of the Holocaust is the anguish of pitifully harassed frightened people. The next commandment requires that the reader not behave like the executioners' dogs who treated human beings like cattle to be rounded up. We must not become less than human. The fifth commandment speaks to the need to stay sane and sighted. Staring too long into the fire can be blinding; even the responsible work of reading and writing Holocaust material must have some relief. One must experience the parts of the world that are not Auschwitz and must live with zeal. The last commandment insists on an active relationship with both the literature and the history of the Holocaust. It also raises the issue of evaluation and aesthetics; it is imperative that we ask questions of the poem, about the poem, as well as about the poem's relationship with history and grievous torment. We must be amenable to writing and reading about a universe beyond poetry even as we depend upon the poem to take us there. The pieces of paper with which we engage are our weapons for resisting barbarism.

Because the poetry of witness marks a resistance to false attempts at unification, it can take many forms. It is at once impassioned or ironic. It speaks in the language of the common man or in an esoteric language of paradox or literary privilege. It can curse as did Rothenberg and it can bless; it can blaspheme or it can ignore the holy. Its protest might rest on a heady peroration to an audience as present in Rothenberg. It can be partisan in the best of senses—"the party of humanity" in which the partisanship of humanity is a rejection of unwarranted pain inflicted on some humans by others' illegitimate domination (Forche 1993, 46).

The poetry examined here has attempted in many instances to mitigate suffering by giving expression—at times controlled, at times uncontrolled—to the tragedy. Generally, brevity serves this genre well, by conferring a minimal order and form on chaos and horror. This poetry can inform as well as move us to sadness, as despondency is grounded in the awareness of the finality of the Holocaust. Wiesel views the Holocaust as a sacred subject akin to the revelation at Sinai. "One should take off one's shoes," he observes "when entering its domain, one should tremble each time one pronounces the word" (quoted by Berger 1982, 166). Surely the comparison of Auschwitz to the defining moment in Jewish history invites poetic response. Thus the poetry of Plath, Heyen, Stern, and Rothenberg is an effort to extract the moral and emotional options from the extreme conditions of the Holocaust and to explore implications for post-Holocaust humankind. History imagined also presents an experience totally outside the realm of the author's, but with the passage of time and accumulation of documentation, it acquires authenticity. The purpose of words is not just to redeem the past, but also elaborate upon it by explaining, talking, reasoning, scolding, complaining, recreating, and repairing. Milosz once wrote, "Language is the only homecoming" (quoted in Eichler 1987, 38): again, silence is the enemy. We must keep talking—this poetry is "in the pity," in Wilfred Owen's terms, as well as in the anger, the bitterness, and the amazement.

Plath, Heyen, Stern, and Rothenberg speak of absence, of a God whose creation includes death camps and modern physics, of a world to which no adequate response is possible. Stern and Rothenberg seek solace in the mystical defense of God as found in *Kabbalah*. Is Wiesel's comment on the nature of the Divine plausible, "the silence of God is God? . . If God chooses not to answer, He must have His reasons. God is God and His will is independent from ours—as is His reasoning" (1979, 132). Eliezer Berkovits, eminent theologian (1973), too, challenges some of the post-Holocaust theological formulations that contest the nature of God (how could God have remained silent and permitted such atrocities?) And question the possibility of human faith (can faith in God after Auschwitz be tenable?). These, he says, are clearly valid and compelling, but they dodge the most fundamental issue inherent in these questions: what is "the essence of faith within the system of Judaism?" Convinced, however, that the answer to this question can be gained only through "empathic contact" with the faith of Jews who experienced the Holocaust, Berkovits explores the theological issue against the backdrop of religious tenacity.

Unlike Berkovits, however, our poets do not enter into theological analysis of the faith of the Jews who endured the Holocaust, or of their covenantal relationship with God, which exacted specified norms of behavior. Rather than superimposing a conceptually derived definition of religion and faith on the people themselves, these poets approach God tentatively. For Plath, God is dark, unapproachable, and interpreted through the lens of Christianity. Heyen's disillusionment with God, made manifest by His blueness that the poet equates with death, is voiced through his discourse on the perished children. For him, God, while not dead, is ominously mute. Of the four, Stern is the most cavalier in his theistic and anthropomorphic comments about the wildness and capriciousness of God. And Rothenberg, in his *Poland/1931* sequence, avoids the theological issue, focusing instead on the pursuit of a religious ethos: the "doing" of the commandments. Collectively these poets do speak of evil incarnate, and of hopelessness, as well as of possibilities for human redemption.

For Celan, poetic role model to our poets, the apparent absence of God leads us back to His presence, his absence is the mark of His presence. Divine absence in the age of atrocity takes two forms—the threat of the abyss and the void the other, the death camps signified by the horror of Auschwitz. This paradox, the insistence of God's existence in the face of His apparent disappearance, is derived from *Kabbalah,* which impacted greatly on Stern and Rothenberg in a vastly different light, where the world in its imperfection is created by God's recession. According to this mystical view, God draws a curtain of darkness down before Himself to allow light to appear as darkness, which is the essential thwart for illumination.

Conspicuous by its absence amid the rich array of images is any poetic rendering of physical passion and yearning of one human being for another in the concentration camp universe. We must consider the possibility that those (poets) who were not there are unable to imagine "love" in such circumstances. For this most natural and human of perspectives, we must look to Tadeusz Borowski's (1983) "Auschwitz Sun," from which "other planet" comes a poem of incredible tenderness and elegiac lyricism. Borowski, a political prisoner in Auschwitz and Dachau, managed to survive and write his terrifying and wonderful prose account, *This Way for the Gas, Ladies and Gentlemen* (1967). Holocaust writing as a whole presents a variety of possible imaginative interpretations of historical events that also suggests alternative ways of existing in a world that has countenanced Auschwitz. For Borowski and for his protagonists, the *univers concentrationnaire* is the sole reality. There can be no post-Holocaust existence; hence suicide is the only logical answer to survival beyond liberation. In 1951, at the age of twenty-nine, having outlived the Nazi gas chambers, Borowski chose to gas himself. Looking out from his compound of death and stench, he wrote of the person he loved, a most palpable and poignant statement of desire. The vulgarity of the place is submerged as he reveals his tenderly romantic and transcendental self. Only the title "Auschwitz Sun" provides us with the ominous, oxymoronic clue of the place—does the sun shine in Auschwitz? As Borowski carries us off with:

> the far green of fields lightly
> lifted by birds into the clouds . . .
>   I remember
> your smile slippery
> as a shade the color of the wind
> that shakes a leaf on the verge
> of sun and shadow, but continually
> changes and remains. So are you
> today for me: through the aquamarine
> of the sky, through green and a wind
> shaking a leaf.
> (trans. Bross 1981, 19–20)

The emotional focus of lyric poetry is conventionally the poet's emotional consciousness tied to a tenderly responsive conscience. The confusion of that conscience about the poet's experience and reactions is a dominant feature in the poetry of Plath, Heyen, Stern, and Rothenberg. The poet-spokesman is replaced by the poet-confessor. In this way, general or communal confession takes on the task of creating post-Auschwitz rituals. Of the works discussed in this study, Heyen's poems come closest to offering themselves as ritual. On the one hand, they appear to be a sort of German-American-Gentile *Kaddish* for the loss of the poet's unconflicted sense of identity; on the other hand, they are an act of contrition for the sins of the blood brothers. Heyen does not respond with silence.

The images of her skin as a Nazi lampshade of ashes, a cake of soap, a gold filling summons premonitions of Plath's own death. Moreover, she came to regard herself as "an imaginary Jew from the concentration camp of the mind" (Alvarez 1972, 19). Thus, the fantasy of her Prussian-born father as Nazi and herself as Jewish victim was meant to represent the problematic father-daughter relationship; the kitchen oven emblematic of the of the crematoria and the fat of the Sunday lamb recalled the fat of the Jews; the speaker's "heart" is entered like a "holocaust," which is manifestation of the process by which she arrived at the identification.

George Steiner, through his discussion of a poet who symbolically chose silence by suicide in her kitchen oven, is invaluable in focusing our thinking:

> The question of whether the poet should speak or be silent, of
> whether language is in a condition to accommodate his/her own
> needs is a real one. "No poetry after Auschwitz," said Adorno, and
> Sylvia Plath enacted the underlying meaning of his statement in a
> manner both histrionic and profoundly sincere. (Langer 1975,
> quoting Steiner, 19)

Using Plath's death as an example, Steiner persists, asking
whether our civilization "by virtue of the inhumanity it has
carried out and condoned" has "forfeited its claims to that
indispensable luxury which we call literature? Not forever, not
everywhere but simply in this time and place" (Steiner 1967,
53). Steiner, however, is not without contradiction, for he had
asserted that in "Daddy" Plath had written "one of the very few
poems I know of in any language to come near the last horror"
(1987, 301). Langer continues:

> But this would make Adorno's aphorism . . . itself a histrionic
> verbal gesture, unless we take it to signify that, after the unutter-
> able horrors represented by Auschwitz no one should wish to, no
> one should be encouraged or permitted to evoke with the mere
> instrument of language, the indescribably torment of the victims,
> or the insane "rationality" which led up to it. (1975, 20)

The critic pleads for silence. But had he been heeded, how
many imaginative voices would have been stifled? Steiner continues, however:

> Was there latent in Sylvia Plath's sensibility, as in that of many of
> us who remember only by fiat or imagination, a fearful envy, a dim
> resentment at not having been there, of having missed the ren-
> dezvous with hell? Perhaps it is only those who had no part in the
> events (of the Holocaust) who *can* focus on them rationally and
> imaginatively: to those who experienced the thin, it has lost the
> hard edges of possibility, it has stepped outside the real. (301)

Whether writers who did *not* experience the concentrationary
universe could re-create its atmosphere is open to question.

And the aesthetics of the poetry is the determining factor. Sylvia Plath's Holocaust poetry, as well as that of Heyen, Stern, and Rothenberg, suggests this critical possibility that it can be done albeit only to a limited degree. But silence is not an option.

Stern's work is closely and carefully circumscribed by Judaic ritual. The *Kaddish,* for example, is integral to his Holocaust poetry. He does not invent new ritual but emphasizes what exists, including the confessional. Like Rothenberg, he is emotionally tied to Yiddish as the most suitable medium of lament for a world that is no more. And Stern is more concerned with the aesthetics of poetry than with issues of silence—is the writing good?

Rothenberg's Holocaust poetry, while functioning as a commemorative elegy for his own destroyed European family, is anxious to establish the validity of poetry more broadly as a viable cultural endeavor after Adorno. The problem with Rothenberg's direct confrontation with Adorno's dictum, addressed explicitly in the introduction to *Khurbn,* is that Adorno's pronouncement is not so much a proscription of poetry per se as it is a statement of the impossibility of making art out of language after language itself became a victim. But poetry needs no defense, and therefore Rothenberg's effort at rescuing poetry after Auschwitz from Adorno seems contrived. His statement that this is the goal of *Khurbn* almost waylays the poems, no matter how significant Adorno's problematic dictum is for literature in general after Auschwitz. Rothenberg is, however, at one with his literary colleagues in felling the need to address Adorno. Thus in this process of reclaiming poetry, Rothenberg achieves some measure of ritual grief and catharsis, but to a degree undercuts his own work by allowing reclamation to override ritual.

All four poets have made poems that *do* something that resists the Holocaust, that both affirms that history and takes a stand against it. Their poetry amply demonstrates the affinity between beauty and the obscene ugliness. Plath homeopathically appropriates Holocaust symbols to exorcize the demons of her own personally dysfunctional life. Heyen's poems propose the capacity of the individual voice to speak for an individual conscience through poetry, even as they confront a tremendous multiplicity of perspectives and narrative responses. Stern expiates the private guilt of missing the Holocaust by envisaging and transposing himself into the victims. Rothenberg uses poetry to reignite the love of poetry Auschwitz extinguished along with so much else and so many others. All four poets articulate a collective consciousness echoing historical truths from a position of hindsight. And in them, Sir Philip Sidney's eloquent statement in *The Defence of Poesy.* The significant role of poetry in recapitulating history is borne out:

> Let learned Greece in any of his manifold sciences be able to show me one book before Musaeus, Homer, and Hesiod, all three nothing else but poets. Nay, let any history be brought that can say any writers were there before them, if they were not men of the same skill. . . . Who having been the first of that country that made pens deliverers of their knowledge to the posterity, may justly challenge to be called their fathers in learning. . . . And even historiographers (although their lips sound of things done, and verity be written on their foreheads) have been glad to borrow both fashion and, perchance, weight of the poets. (213, 214)

And where the historical matter is total devastation, the versions of history reflected in poetry reveal each artist's struggle between continuity and discontinuity with the cultural and private past. (Narrative, symbolic or distant in time from the brutalizing facts, is often a function of an effort to build and maintain bridges.) The poetry considered here is obviously not a polite poetry—the subject matter mandates inelegance. Poetic rhythms are fast and powerful: there are moments when the current sucks you under and you are grasping for air. This Holocaust poetry is dense and crowded with moving thought. Diverse though Plath, Heyen, Stern, and Rothenberg are in style and approach, they all follow a time-honored tradition that destruction, however devastating and consuming, must be the basis for fathoming and for rebuilding. Blue reverberates in each of their works; darkness is the inescapable, all-pervasive condition.

The question of identity in Jewish terms constituted a major quest for Stern and Rothenberg, while humanistic yet personal relationships have been articulated by Plath and Heyen through their unusual approach to the Holocaust. The four poets share an assessment that Western culture has refused to acknowledge accountability for the savaging of the Jews. Each perceives himself to be a mourner. Yet none of the poets attempts to design a formula to prevent future holocausts. The particularized Jewish suffering is wedded to the universal suffering of all humankind. Gerald Stern, in the forward to *Ghosts of the Holocaust* (1989), wonders at the ability—his and everyone else's—to live the quotidian life after Auschwitz:

> And I can't believe that I went on with my own life the way I did, that I entertained long hair and flowers and poesy, that I learned French, that I taught Hopkins and Keats and sat in chairs memorizing them, that I agonized over my own petty failures. How is it that I didn't give up this sweet life and go from city to city raging, explaining, blaspheming and demanding? How is it that I didn't become a murderer, or at the very least a suicide? How is it that Jews in America and Argentina and France can go on with their ordinary lives, preparing for professions, memorizing a little script for the Bar Mitzvah? And how is it that Germans can return to normalcy, and how is it that the Christians can go on preparing themselves so exquisitely for paradise, as if they had not forgotten something, and how is it that the state and people of Israel can proceed with politics as usual in the face of the Covenants, and oppression, and even bigotry in the face of Jewish history. (15)

Even as the systems that once sustained the spirit have defaulted, art is still called upon to salvage the voices of the dead and the dying. The poem is summoned to replace the disrupted ceremonies of mourning, to give dignity and form to ignominious, unmarked death. The poetic mythmakers extend the boundaries of the concentration camp to encompass all of existence. Their works move beyond memory to create a perspective that hopes to lead out of the abyss. However, it is not that we will either forget or reclaim those years because of these poems; it is not that the poems will even make the past bearable.

> Cemeteries confine death itself. But where the enormity and senselessness of death defy confinement, the wandering souls of the unburied permeate the entire universe, and may reappear anywhere at anytime. They infuse the words of the poet with a

restlessness that finds no resolution in any art form, that can never fully engage or relinquish history. Chaim Nachman Bialik [late Poet Laureate of Israel] observed that the speech of the poet is born of the "magnitude of his fear of remaining even one moment . . . unmediated nothingness" of a speechless encounter with reality. (Ezrahi, 219)

In the final analysis, the poetry of the Holocaust demands a giant act of creation, inducing form and order into a universe unformed and void, where the messengers from the dead are trumpets blowing through the darkness hovering over the face of the deep and piercing the billowing clouds issuing from the chimneys breathing smoke over the earth. For the sake of our own future, as much as any moral imperative to commemorate the victims, we must struggle to absorb the *Shoah*, the *Khurbn*, the Holocaust, understand it, learn from it. As this study and the poems here suggest, "we must do so with language, against language, and beyond language" (Horowitz 1997, 226).

Glossary

Alef-bet. The Hebrew alphabet.

Anschluss. German: joining together. On 12 March 1938 Hitler annexed Austria to Germany.

Brit milah. Hebrew: covenant of circumcision between God and the Israelites. The Jewish ceremony of circumcision when the eight-day-old male is given his Hebrew name.

Dibbik. Hebrew: attachment. The disembodied spirit of a dead person that finds no rest because of sins committed during life and that seeks a haven in the body of a living person. The belief that a dibbik can be exorcized by religious rite became widespread from the seventeenth century onward and found expression in popular legends and literature. Dibbik is Rothenberg's spelling, which is also found as dybbuk.

Gebentsht. Yiddish: blessed.

Gematria. Aramaic: calculation. The calculation of the numerical value of Hebrew words. Each Hebrew letter receives a numerical value according to its position in the Hebrew alphabet. Thus the first letter *aleph* equals one and the final letter *tof* equals four hundred. Correspondences between words of equal numerical value (and likewise between the concepts represented by the words) can then be discovered, and hidden links in the world may be revealed. Under the influence of letter-mysticism which played an important part in esoteric tradition, Gematria became a major feature of *Kabbalistic* exposition, as well as of magical practice.

Haggadah. Hebrew: a telling. The story of Passover read and retold during the seder (Hebrew: order), a ceremonial meal that opens the Passover festival.

245

Hassidism. From the Hebrew Hassidim: pious ones. A mystical religious movement originating in southern Poland and Ukraine in the eighteenth century. The Hassidim sought a fervent, ecstatic communion with God in their worship.

Kabbalah. Hebrew: that which is received. Mystical system and doctrine developed in thirteenth-century France and Spain. Two texts are crucial to this movement, the Zohar, (book of splendor), and the Sefer Yetzirah (book of creation).

Kaddish. Hebrew: sanctify. One of the most basic Jewish prayers extolling the divine, recited by mourners to honor the dead, though it lacks any mention of death.

Kaporot. Hebrew: atonement. Ritual of repentance performed on behalf of a particular person, in which a white rooster for a male or a white hen for a female is slaughtered according to a customary order. The bird is later given to the poor for food. This ceremony takes place on the day before Yom Kippur, and its meaning is derived from the act of giving to the needy as money may be substituted for the fowl.

Klezmorim. From the Hebrew *klei zemer:* instruments of song. Bands of itinerent Jewish musicians in Eastern Europe before World War II, who performed their specific form of folk music at weddings.

Kol Nidre. Hebrew: all vows. The formulaic prayer, recited before sunset, with which the evening service of Yom Kippur begins.

Kosher. Hebrew: fit for use. The word used to describe foods or ritual acts that are correct, faultless, and permitted within the framework of Jewish law. The legalistic term for kosher is *kashrut.*

Magen David. Hebrew: shield of David. The star-shaped emblem of the state of Israel, consisting of two superimposed equilateral triangles, forming a hexagon. During the Nazi era it was the yellow badge of shame Jews were required to wear.

Mamma Loshn. Yiddish: mother tongue. The Yiddish language, with special implication concerning its role as the source of creative emotional discourse.

Messiah. Hebrew: annointed one. In the tradition the Messiah, chosen by God, is a descendant of King David, who will bring God's message and peace to the world.

Mezuzah. Hebrew: doorpost. Metal or ceramic box nailed to the doorpost of a Jewish home containing a parchment inscribed with the Shema, the quintessential prayer of affirmation of monotheism.

Midrash. Hebrew: inquire or investigate. The discovery of meanings other than the literal in the Bible, interprets scripture in order to extract its full implication and meaning.

Mikveh. Hebrew: gathering. A bath for the ritual immersion of persons or utensils that have contacted ritual impurities. It is used in the conversion of a person to Judaism and after menstruation for married women.

Minyan. Hebrew: counting. In traditional Judaism the quorum of ten males required to conduct liturgical worship purposes.

Mishnah. Hebrew: teaching. The earliest portion of the Talmud, compiled by Rabbi Judah ha-Nasi about c.e. 200. It contains the Oral Law transmitted through the generations.

Mitzvah. Hebrew: commandment. To do a mitzvah is to do what God asks of us; to do a good or kind deed.

Ner Tamid. Hebrew: eternal lamp. A lamp prescribed in Exodus 27: 20—21and Leviticus 24:2 as an essential appointment of the sanctuary in the wilderness and later on in the holy temple. Burning constantly as a symbol of God's watchfulness and His providence over his people, it is placed before the holy ark in a modern synagogue.

Olah. Hebrew. that which is brought up. A sacrifice that was burnt completely and therefore considered to be of particular holiness. It was slaughtered on the north side of the altar when the Temple stood in Jerusalem. The word *Holocaust* is derived from this term.

Sayings or Ethics of the Fathers. The best known treatise of the Mishnah, ethical maxims attributed to sixty-five teachers, covering a period of about two centuries B.C.E. and two centuries C.E.

Sefirot. Hebrew: numbers. In the Kabbalistic scheme, the ten stages of the inner divine world through which God descends—from the innermost recesses of His hiddenness down to His manifestations in the emanations of the godhead, the Shekinah.

Seraphim. Hebrew and Greek: angels of the highest order. Heavenly beings associated with angelology, mentioned in the apocryphal book of Enoch and in Numbers 21:6.

Shekinah. Hebrew: in-dwelling or resting. Refers most often to God's presence in the world. In Kabbalah, the tenth sphere seen by the mystics as the feminine aspect of God.

Shoah. Hebrew: wasteness and desolation. The prefered term for the decimation of six million European Jews. Jewish scholars feel that Holocaust has lost much of its significance through overuse and wrongful application. The term appears in the Hebrew Bible in Zephaniah 1:15 and in Job 30:3.

Shokhet. Hebrew: animal slaughterer. A Jewish male trained and rabbinically ordained to perform ritual slaughter in accord with Jewish law.

Shtetl. German: little town. A village inhabited primarily by Jews in Eastern Europe prior to World War II.

Siddur. Hebrew: order. The Hebrew prayer book, containing the entire liturgy used in the synagogue and home.

Talmud. Hebrew: teaching. A unique literary work, the result and record of study and discussions over a period of eight hundred years by Jewish scholars working in the acadamies of Babylonia and Palestine. Its spiritual roots are the Hebrew Bible, Jewish law, and interpretations that crystallized during the second temple period.

Tanakh. Hebrew: the acronym and usual name fot the Hebrew Bible, derived from the initial letters of its three divisions: Torah for Pentateuch, Neviim for Prophets, and Ketuvim for Hagiographa.

Tashlikh. Hebrew: you shall cast. The ritual in which on the first day of Rosh Hashannah (the Jewish new year) (or on the second day if the first falls on a Sabbath), traditional Jews after the afternoon service visit a river, the seashore, or some other body of water and recite verses from scripture that seek repentance and the forgiveness of sins.

Tefillin. Hebrew: phylacteries. Two black leather boxes containing passages from Exodus and Deuteronomy. They are bound by black strips on the left hand and on the head, and are worn by males for morning services on all days of the year except Sabbaths and special scriptural holy days.

Temple. In ancient Israel, the central building for the worship of God, located on Mount Moriah in Jerusalem. The Western Wall built by Herod is the last remaining section of this hallowed temple and is revered by Jews to this very day.

Tohu-vavohu. Hebrew: unformed and void. Genesis 1:2. Refers particularly to the condition of things before Creation.

Torah. Hebrew: teaching or direction. Refers specifically to the Five Books of Moses as distinct from the rest of the Hebrew Bible, which includes the Prophets and Writings. In its broadest sense, Torah encompasses the entire Bible and the oral law.

Yiddische mensch. Yiddish: a Jewish person who epitomizes all the attributes of righteous living, one who lives the mitzvot.

Yiddishkeit. Yiddish: the quality of Jewishness, culture, religion, behavior, the essence of Judaism encompassing its moral and ethical codes.

Yom Kippur. Hebrew: day of atonement. The most solemn day in the Hebrew calendar, on which Jews engage in a twenty-four-hour fast and seek absolution for their sinful behavior during the past year.

Zohar. Hebrew: splendor. A *Kabbalistic* text comprising several literary units by different authors. Since the fourteenth century, the *Kabbalists* have recognized the Zohar as the most important work of mystical teaching and commentary on parts of the Hebrew Bible.

Bibliography

Abrams, M. H. *A Glossary of Literary Terms*. 6th ed. Fort Worth, Texas: Harcourt, Brace, Jovanovich, 1993.

Adorno, T.W. "Engagement." *Noten Zur Literatur,* edited by T. W. Adorno. Vol. 3. Frankfurt am Main: Suhrkamp Verlag, 1965, 109–135.

Alexander, Edward. "Isaac Bashevis Singer: Rebel and Traditionalist," *Congress Monthly* 58, no. 6 (1991): 8–10.

———. *The Resonance of Dust: Essays on Holocaust Literature and Jewish Fate.* Columbus: Ohio State University Press, 1979.

Allen-Shore, Lena. *Forty Years after Darkness.* Philadelphia: Association of Jewish Holocaust Survivors, 1985.

Alpert, Barry. ed. *Vort Twenty-First Century Previews: David Antin- Jerome Rothenberg.* Silver Spring, Md: Vort Works Ink, 1975.

Alter, Robert. *Defenses of the Imagination: Jewish Writers and Modern Historical Crisis.* Philadelphia: Jewish Publication Society, 1977.

———. "Malamud as a Jewish Writer," *Commentary* 42, no. 3 (1966): 74.

———. "A Poet of the Holocaust," *Commentary* 56, no. 5 (November 1973): 57–63.

Alvarez, Alfred. *Beyond All This Fiddle: Essays 1955–1967.* New York: Random House, 1969.

———. "The Literature of the Holocaust," *Commentary* 38, no. 5 (November 1964): 65–69.

———. *The Savage God: A Study of Suicide.* New York: Random House, 1972.

Arendt, Hannah. *Eichmann in Jerusalem: A Report on the Banality of Evil.* New York: Viking, 1963.

Bacharach, Naftali. "A Poem for the Sefirot as Wheel of Light," in *Poems for the Millenium,* ed. and trans. by Jerome Rothenberg and Harris Lenowitz. Berkeley: University of California Press, 1995.

Balakian, Peter. Review of "The Red Coal," by Gerald Stern. *The American Book Review* 5, no. 2 (January/February 1983): 21.

Barnard, Caroline King. *Sylvia Plath.* Boston: Twayne Publishers, 1978.

Beckett, Samuel. *Waiting for Godot.* New York: Grove Weidenfeld, 1982.

Bellow, Saul. *Mr. Sammler's Planet.* New York: Viking, 1970.

———. "Some Notes on Recent American Fiction." *Encounter* 20, no. 122 (1963): 22–29.

Berger, Alan L. "Academia and the Holocaust," *Judaism* 31, no. 2 (spring 1982): 166–76.

Berkovits, Eliezar. *Faith after the Holocaust*. New York: Ktav, 1973.

Blaydes, Sophie. "Metaphors of Life and Death in the Poetry of Denise Levertov and Sylvia Plath." *Dalhousie Review* 57, no. 3 (1977): 494–506.

Borowski, Tadeusz. "Auschwitz Sun." Translated and annotated by Addison Bross. *The Webster Review* 6, no. 1 (spring 1981): 19–20.

———. *This Way for the Gas, Ladies and Gentlemen*. New York: Viking, 1967.

Braham, Randolph L. "Ashes and Hope: The Holocaust in Second Generation American Literature." In *Reflections of the Holocaust in Art and Literature*, edited by Randolph L. Braham. New York: Columbia University Press, 1990.

Burke, Kenneth. *Language and Symbolic Action*. Berkeley: Universeity of California Press, 1966.

———. *On Symbols and Society*. Chicago: University of Chicago Press, 1989.

Butscher, Edward. *Sylvia Plath: Methods and Madness*. New York: Seabury Press, 1976.

Camus, Albert. *The Stranger*. Translated by Stewart Gilbert. New York: Alfred A. Knopf, 1946.

———. *Mythe de Sisyphe*. Paris: Galimard, 1964.

Carroll, James. "The Silence." *The New Yorker* 23. no. 7 (April 7, 1997): 52–68.

Carruth, Hayden. "The Swastika Poems," *Manassas Review* 1 (summer/fall 1978): 97–98.

Celan, Paul. *Gedichte I*. Frankfurt: Suhrkamp, 1978.

Chapman, Abraham, ed. *Jewish American Literature: An Anthology of Fiction, Poetry, Autobiography and Criticism*. New York: New American Library, 1974.

Chess, Richard. "Stern's Holocaust." *Poetry East* (fall 1988): 150–59.

Christensen, Paul. "Some Bearings on Ethnopoetics." *Parnassas Poetry in Review* 15, no. 1 (1989): 125–62.

Clare, George. *Last Waltz in Vienna: The Rise and Destruction of a Family, 1842–1942*. New York: Holt, Rinehart, and Winston, 1982.

Clewell, David. "In Blue Light," *Chowder Review*, no. 5 (October/November 1978): 159–62.

Cohn, Robert, A. A review of *Falling From Heaven: Holocaust Poems of a Jew and a Gentile* by Louis Daniel Brodsky and William Heyen. *St. Louis Jewish Lights* (31 March 1991): 12a.

Cornwell, John. *Hitler's Pope: The Secret History of Pius XII*. New York: Viking, 1999.

Donat, Alexander. *The Holocaust Kingdom: A Memoir*. New York: Holt, Reinhardt and Winston, 1965.

Donne, John. "Devotions XVII" in *Devotions Upon Emergent Occasions*. In *The Oxford Authors*, edited by John Carey. Oxford: Oxford University Press, 1990.

Edmundson, Mack. "Save Sigmund Freud." *New York Times Magazine,* 13 July 1997, 33–36.

Eichler, Jeremy. Untitled commentary. *Jerusalem Report,* 24 July 1987, 38.

Eliot, T. S. *"The Waste Land."* New York: Liveright Press, 1930.

——. *The Complete Poems and Plays.* New York: Harcourt, Brace & World, Inc., 1971.

Elkin, Michael. "Arthur Miller: Life of a Theatrical Salesman." *Jewish Exponent,* 25 February 1996, 3X.

Encyclopedia Britannica. Hundreth Year Edition, s.v. *"Dadism."* Chicago: William Benton, Publisher, 1969

Encyclopedia Judaica. Vol. 8, s.v. "Kabbalah." Jerusalem: Keter Publishing House, 1972.

Encyclopedia Judaica. Vol. 10, s.v. "Kabbalah." Jerusalem: Keter Publishing House, 1977.

Epstein, I. *Babylonian Talmud.* Israel: Soncino Press, 1955.

Esslin, Martin. *The Theater of the Absurd.* New York: Doubleday, 1961.

Ezrahi, Sidra Dekoven. *By Words Alone: The Holocaust in Literature.* Chicago: University of Chicago Press, 1980.

Featherston, Don. "Poetic Representation: Reznikoff's Holocaust and Rothenberg's *Khurbn. Response* (fall/winter, 1998): 129–40.

Fiedler, Leslie. *Death and Love in the American Novel.* New York: Anchor Books, 1992.

Fishman, Charles M. *Blood to Remember: American Poets on the Holocaust.* Lubbock: Texas Tech University Press, 1991.

Forche, Carolyn. *Against Forgetting.* New York: W. W. Norton, 1993.

Franck, Adolphe. *The Kabbalah.* New York: Bell Publishing, 1955.

Freud, Sigmund. *Civilization and its Discontents.* Translated and edited James Strachey. New York: W. W. Norton, 1962.

Friedländer, Albert H., ed. *Out of The Whirlwind: A Reader of Holocaust Literature.* New York: Union of American Hebrew Congregations, 1968.

Friedländer, Saul. *Probing the Limits of Representation.* Cambridge, Harvard University Press, 1992.

Friedman, Philip, ed. *Roads to Extinction: Essays on the Holocaust.* Philadelphia: Jewish Publication Society, 1980.

Friedman, Saul. *Holocaust Literature.* Westport, Conn.: Greenwood Press, 1993.

Fussell, Paul. *The Great War and Modern Memory.* New York: Oxford University Press, 1975.

Garber, Frederick. "Pockets of Secrecy, Places of Occasion." *American Poetry Review* 15 (July/August 1986): 38–48.

Gass, William. *On Being Blue.* Boston: D. R. Godine Press, 1976.

Gilman, Sander. *Freud, Race and Gender.* Princeton: Princeton University Press, 1993.

Ginzberg, Louis. *Legends of the Bible.* One volume version. Philadelphia: Jewish Publication SOciety, 1956.

Gitenstein, R. Barbara. *Apocalyptic Messianism and Contemporary Jewish American Poetry.* Albany: State University of New York Press, 1986.

————. "Coyote Cohen, or the Universal Trickster in Jerome Rothenberg's Evolving Collection *Poland/1931.*" *Studies in American Jewish Literature* 9, no. 2 (1990): 176–85.

Glaser, Elton, ed. "Gerald Stern Speaking." In *Ahros,* an edited compendium extracted from remarks to classes at the University of Akron, November 1982.

Goldberg, Marylin. "The Soul Searching of Norma Rosen." *Studies in American Jewish Literature,* no. 3 (1983): 202–10.

Goldin, Barbara Diamond. *The Family Book of Midrash.* Northvale, N.J.: Jason Aronson, Inc., 1990.

Gomori, George and Newman, Charles, eds. *The New Writing of East Europe.* Chicago: Quadrangle Books, 1968.

Graham, Jorie. "The Terror of their Days." *New York Times Book Review,* February 10, 1985, 30.

Gray, Richard. *American Poetry of the Twentieth Century.* London: Longman Group, 1990.

Greenberg, Moshe, et al, translators, *Tanakh: A New Translation of the Holy Scriptures.* Philadelphia: Jewish Publication Society, 1985.

Ha Levi, Ze'ev ben Shimon. *The Way of Kabbalah.* London: Rider & Co., 1976.

Hallberg, Robert von. "The Swastika Poems, by William Heyen." *Chicago Review* 3, no. 3 (1980): 120–22.

Halperin, Irving. "Holocaust Writers and the Critics." *Jewish Life* (May/June 1967): 19–22.

————. "On the Writing and Reading of Holocaust Literature." *Jewish Heritage* (spring 1968): 41–44.

————. *Messengers from the Dead: Literature of the Holocaust.* Philadelphia: Westminster, 1970.

Hamburger, Michael. *The Truth of Poetry: Tensions in Modern Poetry from Baudelaire to the 1960s.* New York: Harcourt, Brace, Jovanovich, 1969.

———— and Christopher Middleton, eds. *Modern German Poetry, 1910–1960: An Anthology with Verse Translations.* New York: Grove Press, 1962.

Hamilton, David. "An Interview With Gerald Stern," *The Iowa Review* 19, no. 2 (1988): 32–65.

Hampel, Patricia. Review of *Lucky Life. Ironwood.* no. 12 (1978): 103–7.

Hassan, Ihab. *Contemporary American Literature.* New York: Ungar, 1973.

Havel, Vaclav. *Disturbing the Peace.* New York: Vintage Books, 1990.

Hecht, Anthony. *The Hard Hours.* New York: Atheneum, 1967.

Heyen, William. *Depth of Field.* Baton Rouge: Louisiana State University Press, 1970.

——. *My Holocaust Songs*. Concord, N.H.: William B. Ewert, 1980).

——. *Long Island Night: Poems and Memoir.* New York: Vanguard Press, 1979.

——. *Lord Dragonfly*. New York: Vanguard Presss, 1981.

——. *The City Parables*. Athens, Ohio: Croissant, 1980.

——. *The Trains*. Worcester, Mass.: Metacon Press, 1981.

——. *Erika: Poems of the Holocaust*. New York: Vanguard Press, 1984.

——. *The Chestnut Rain*. New York: Ballantine Books, 1989.

——. *The Swastika Poems*. New York: Vanguard Press, 1977.

——. *Erika: Poems of the Holocaust*. St. Louis: Time Being Books, 1991.

——. "What do the Trees Say?" in *American Poets in 1976* edited by William Heyen, 92–105. Indianapolis: Bobbs Merrill, 1976.

——. "Unwilled 'Chaos': In Poem We Trust." In *Writing and the Holocaust,* edited by Berel Lang. New York: Columbia University Presss, 1982.

——, and Louis Daniel Brodsky. *Falling from Heaven: Holocaust Poems of a Jew and a Gentile*. St. Louis: Time Being Books, 1991.

——, and Stanley Rubin. "*The Swastika Poems:* A Conversation," *Manassas Review*, no. 3 (1978): 33–49.

Hill, Donald, ed. *Contemporary American Poetry*. New York: Penguin, 1972.

Hillringhouse, Mark. "An Interview," *American Poetry Review*. 13 (March/April, 1984): 19–31.

Hindus, Milton, ed. *Charles Reznikoff: Man and Poet*. Orono: University of Maine, 1984.

Hirsch, Edward. "A Late Ironic Whitman." *The Nation* 240, no. 2 (19 January 1985): 55–58.

Hochhuth, Rolf. *The Deputy*. American playing version adapted and translated by Jerome Rothenberg. New York: Samuel French, 1965.

——. *The Deputy*. Translated by Richard and Clara Winston, New York: Grove, 1964.

Hoffman, Daniel, ed. "The Poetry of Anguish," *The Reporter* (22 February 1968): 52–54.

——. "Poetry; Dissidents from Schools." In *Harvard Guide to Contemporary American Writing*. Edited by Daniel Hoffman. Cambridge: Harvard University Press, 1979.

Horowitz, Sara R. *Voicing the Void: Muteness and Memory in Holocaust Fiction*. Albany: State University of New York Press, 1997.

Howe, Florence, ed. *No More Masks: An Anthology of Twentieth Century American Women Poets*. New York: Harper Perennial, 1993.

Howe, Irving. "I. B. Singer." *Encounter* 26 (April 1966): 60–70.

——. Letter to the Editor. *Commentary* 58, no. 4 (October 1974): 9, 12.

——. *World of Our Fathers*. New York: Harcourt, Brace Jovanovich, 1976.

Ionesco, Eugene. *The Bald Soprano and Other Plays*. New York: Grove Press, 1958.

————. *Rhinoceros and Other Plays*. New York: Grove Press, 1960.

Katz, Jacob. *The Darker Side of Genius: Richard Wagner's Anti-Semitism*. Hanover, N.H.: University Press of New England, 1986.

Kauver, Elaine. *Cynthia Ozick's Fiction*. New York: The Association of American University Presses, 1993.

Knickerbocker, K. L. H. Willard Reninger, Edward W. Bratton, and B. J. Leggett, eds. *Interpreting Literature*. 7th ed. New York: Holt, Rinehart and Winston, 1985.

Knight, Elizabeth. "A Poet of the Mind: An Interview with Gerald Stern." *Poetry East*, no. 26 (fall 1988): 32–48.

Korwin, Yala. *To Tell the Story: Poems of the Holocaust*. New York: Holocaust Library, 1987.

Kosinski, Jerzy. *The Painted Bird*, 2nd ed. New York: Modern Library, 1983.

Kristeva, Julia. *Powers of Horror: An Essay on Abjection*. New York: Columbia University Press, 1982.

Lang, Berel, ed. *Writing and the Holocaust*. New York: Holmes and Meier, 1988.

Langer, Lawrence. *The Holocaust and the Literary Imagination*. New Haven: Yale University Press, 1975.

————. *The Age of Atrocity: Death in Modern Literature*. Boston: Beacon Press, 1978.

————. *Versions of Survival: The Holocaust and the Human Spirit*. Albany: State University of New York Press, 1982.

————. *Admitting the Holocaust: Collected Essays*. New York: Oxford University Press, 1995.

Lanzmann, Claude. *Shoah*. Paris: Fayard, 1985. Videorecording

Leiter, Robert. "Dante's Hell," *Jewish Exponent* (19 June 1997): 9.

Lenowitz, Harris. "Rothenberg: The Blood," *Vort* 3, no. 1 (1975): 179–84.

Levis, Larry. "Not Life So Proud to be Life: Snodgrass, Rothenberg, Bell and the Counter-Revolution," *American Poetry Review* 18, no. 1 (Jannuary/February 1989): 9–20.

Lieberman, Lawrence. *Unassigned Frequencies: American Poetry in Review*. Chicago: University of Illinois Press, 1977.

Lindbergh, Reeve. *Under a Wing*. New York: Simon and Schuster, 1998.

Malamud, Bernard. *The Fixer*. New York: Farrar, Strauss, & Giraux, 1966.

Malin, Irving, ed. *Contemporary American Jewish Literature: Critical Essays*. Bloomington: Indiana University Press, 1973.

Malkoff, Karl. *Crowell's Handbook of Contemporary American Poetry*. New York: Crowell, 1973.

————. *Escape from Self: A Study in Contemporary Poetry and Poetics*. New York: Columbia University Press, 1977.

Mandel, Eli. "Auschwitz: Poetry of Alienation," *Canadian Literature*, no. 100 (spring 1984): 213–18.

Martin, Margot L. "The Theme of Survival in Cynthia Ozick's *The Shawl*." *Re Artes Liberales* 14, no. 1 (fall/spring 1988): 31–36.

Mazzaro, Jerome. "Sylvia Plath and the Cycles of History," in *Sylvia Plath: New Views on Poetry*, edited by Gary Lane. Baltimore: Johns Hopkins University Press, 1979.

McCorkle, James. "Contemporary Poetics and History: Pinsky, Klepfisz and Rothenberg," *Kenyon Review* (1990): 171–88.

McFee, Michael. "The Harvest of the Quiet Eye," *Parnassas: Poetry in Review* 10, no. 1 (spring/summer 1982): 153–71.

McPherson, Sandra. Review of "The Swastika Poems." *American Poetry Review* 6, no. 6 (1977): 30–33.

Meredith, William. "Poems: Parents and Children,." *New York Times Book Review* (2 October 1977): 26.

Mersmanin, James F. *Out of the Vietnam Vortex: A Study of Poets and Poetry Against the War.* Laurence: University Press of Kansas, 1974.

Metzger, Bruce M. et al. *The HarperCollins Study Bible: New Revised Standard Version.* London: HarperCollins Publishers, 1993.

Miller, Arthur. *Focus.* New York: Reynal and Hitchcock, 1945.

———. *After the Fall.* London: Secker and Warburg, 1964.

———. *Incident at Vichy.* New York: Viking Press, 1965.

———. *Broken Glass.* New York: Penguin, 1994.

Miller, Judith. *One By One, By One, Facing the Holocaust.* New York: Simon and Schuster, 1990.

Milosz, Czeslaw. *Selected Poems.* New York: The Echo Press, 1973.

———. *The Captive Mind.* New York: Ltd. Editions Club, 1983.

———. *The Witness of Poetry.* Cambridge: Harvard University Press, 1983.

Mintz, Alan. *Hurban: Responses to Catastrophe in Hebrew Literature.* New York: Columbia University Press, 1984.

Monroe, Jonathan. "Third Worlds: The Poetry of Gerald Stern." *Northeast Review* 18, no. 2 (1979): 41–47.

Moss, Thylias. *Pyramid of Bone.* Charlottesville: University Press of Virginia, 1989.

Mottram, Eric. "Where the Real Song Begins: the Poetry of Jerome Rothenberg," *Vort* 7 (1975): 113–78.

Moyers, Bill."The Power of the Word." Part 4: "Voices of Memory" (containing a conversation with Gerald Stern). Alexandria, Va.: Public Broadcasting System, 1989. Videorecording.

———. *"The Language of Life: A Festival of Poets."* New York: Doubleday, 1995.

Murdoch, Brian. "Transformations of the Holocaust: Auschwitz in Modern Lyric Poetry." *Comparative Literature Studies* 11, no. 6 (1974): 123–50.

Nelson, Benjamin, ed. *Contemporary Poets.* New York: Meridian Books, 1957.

Novick, Peter. "The Holocaust as an American Jewish Experience," *The Pennsylvania Gazette* 95, no. 8 (June 1997): 29, 32–33.

O'Brien, Geoffrey. "*Gematria* (Runes with a View. Jerome Rothenberg's Wide Wide World)" *Voice Literary Supplement* (December 1994): 28.

Oliver, Mary. *Dream Work*. Boston: Atlantic Monthly Press, 1986.

Orchester, Edward and Peter Oresch, eds. *The Pittsburgh Book of Contemporary American Poetry*. Pittsburgh: University of Pittsburgh Press, 1993.

Orr, Peter, et al. *The Poet Speaks*. London: K. Pairn, 1996.

Osborn, M. Elizabeth, ed. *The Way We Live Now: American Plays and the AIDS Crisis*. New York: Theater Communications Group, 1993.

Ossman, David. "Interview with Jerome Rothenberg." In *The Sullen Art*, edited by David Ossman. New York: Corinth Books, 1963.

Ozick, Cynthia. *The Cannibal Galaxy*. New York: Alfred A. Knopf, 1983.

———. *The Messiah of Stockholm*. New York: Alfred A. Knopf, 1987.

———. *Rosa*. New York: Alfred A. Knopf, 1989.

———. *The Shawl*. New York: Alfred A. Knopf, 1989.

Packard, William. "The Craft of Poetry: Interview With Jerome Rothenberg," *New York Quarterly* 5 (1971): 8–23.

Pamet, Harriet L. "Selected American Poets Respond to the Holocaust: The Terror of Our Days." *Modern Language Studies* 124, no. 4 (fall 1994): 82–86.

Paul, Sherman. *In Search of the Primitive: Rereading David Antin, Jerome Rothenberg, and Gary Snyder*. Baton Rouge: Louisiana State University Press, 1986.

Pawel, Ernest. "Fiction of the Holocaust," *Midstream* 16 (June/July 1970): 11–26.

Perloff, Marjorie. "Soundings: Zaum, Seriality and the Recovery of the Sacred." *American Poetry Review* 3, no. 31 (January/February 1986): 9–20.

Phillips, Robert. *Confessional Poets*. Carbondale: Southern Illinois University Press, 1973.

Pinsker, Sanford. "The Poetry of Constant Celebration: An Afternoon's Chat With Gerald Stern." *Missouri Review* 13. no. 2, (1984): 55–67.

———. Review of *The Red Coal*. *New England Review* 4, no. 3 (spring, 1982): 494–97.

———. "Weeping and Wailing: The Jewish Songs of Gerald Stern." *Studies in American Jewish Literature*, no. 2 (1990): 186–96.

———. "Competing for the Soul of Cynthia Ozick's Art" *Proof-texts* 14, no. 1 (January 1994): 94–102.

Plath, Sylvia. *The Colossus and Other Poems*. New York: Alfred A. Knopf, 1962.

———. *Ariel*. New York: Harper and Row, 1966.

———. *Winter Trees*. New York: Harper and Row, 1972.

———. *The Collected Poems*. Edited by Ted Hughes. New York: Harper and Row, 1981.

Power, Kevin, et al. Review of *Poland/1931*, by Jerome Rothenberg. *Boundary* 3 (1975): 683–705.

———. "Conversation with Jerome Rothenberg," *Vort* 7, no. 3 (1975): 40–53.

Rajagopalachary, M. "Grace Under Pressure: *The Fixer*," *Literary Endeavour* 16 (1985): 120–27.

Rasso, Pamela. "A Winter's Tale," *Modern Poetry Series* 1, no. 2 (1978): 158–60.

Rich, Adrienne. *Your Native Land, Your Life: Poems*. New York: W. W. Norton, 1986,

Richmond, Theo. *Konin: A Quest*. New York: Pantheon, 1995.

Riefenstahl, Leni. *Trumph des Willens (Triumph of the Will)*. Sandy Hook, Conn.: Video Images, 1980. Videocassette German language release of the 1934 film documentary.

Ries, Laurence. *Wolf Masks: Violence in Contemporary Poetry*. Port Washington, N.Y.: Kennekot Press, 1977.

Roche, Judith. "Jerome Rothenberg." *Voice* 2, no. 1 (February 1982): 19–20.

Rodden, John. "Splendor in the Weeds: An Interview With Gerald Stern," *Text and Performance Quarterly* 10 (1996): 270–89.

Rose, Jacqueline. *The Haunting of Sylvia Plath*. Cambridge: Harvard University Press, 1992.

Rosen, Norma. "The Second Life of Holocaust Imagery," *Midstream* (April 1967): 56–59.

Rosenblatt, Jon. *Sylvia Plath: The Poetry of Imitation*. Chapel Hill: University of North Carolina Press, 1979.

Rosenfeld, Alvin H. "The Americanization of the Holocaust." David W. Beilin Lecture in American Jewish Affairs, Lansing: University of Michigan Press, 1995.

———. *A Double Dying*. Bloomington: Indiana University Press, 1980.

———, and Irving Greenberg. *Confronting the Holocaust: The Impact of Elie Wiesel*. Bloomington: Indiana University Press, 1978.

Rosenthal, M. L. *The New Poets: American and British Poetry Since World War II*. New York: Oxford University Press, 1967.

Roskies, David G. *Against the Apocalypse*. Cambridge: Harvard University Press, 1984.

———. *The Literature of Destruction: Jewish Responses to Catastrophe*. Philadelphia: Jewish Publication Society, 1988.

Roth, Philip. *Professor of Desire*. New York: Houghton Mifflin, 1977.

———. *The Ghost Writer*. New York: Farrar, Strauss & Giroux, 1979.

Rothenberg, Jerome. *White Sun, Black Sun*. New York: Hawks Well Press, 1960.

———, trans. The *Deputy*. See Hochhuth, Rolf.

———. *Poland/1931*. New York: New Directions, 1969.

———. "The Craft of Poetry," Interview by William Packard. *New York Quarterly* 5 (1971): 8–23.

———. *A Book of Testimony*. San Francisco: Tree Books, 1971.

———. *A Big Jewish Book* with Harris Lenowitz. New York: Doubleday/ Anchor, 1978.

———. *A Seneca Journal.* New York: New Directions, 1978.

———. *Vienna Blood & Other Poems.* New York: New Directions, 1980.

———. *Prefaces & Other Writings.* New York: New Directions, 1981.

———. *Symposium of the Whole: A Range of Discourse Toward an Ethnopoetics.* Berkeley: University of California Press, 1983.

———.*Technicians of the Sacred.* Berkeley: University of California Press, 1983.

———. *New Selected Poems.* New York: New Directions, 1986.

———. *Khurbn and Other Poems.* New York: New Directions, 1989.

———. *Shaking the Pumpkin.* Albuquerque: University of New Mexico Press, 1991.

———. *Gematria.* Geyersville, California: Sun & Moon Press, 1994.

———. "What is a Jewish Poem?" unpublished lecture, 1994.

———, and Pierre Joris, eds. *Poems for the Millennium,* vol. 1. Berkeley: University of California Press, 1995.

———. "Poetry & Extremity: Articulations of History: Issues in Holocaust Representation." Unpublished lecture, Boston, Photographic Resource Center: May 3, 1995.

———*Seedings.* New York: New Directions, 1996.

———. Letter to Harriet L. Parmet, 13 April 1997. Unpublished.

———. *A Paradise of Poets: New Poems and Translations.* New York: New Directions, 1999.

Różewicz, Tadeusz. *"The Survivor" and Other Poems.* Princeton: Princeton University Press, 1976.

Sachs, June. "Questioning of a Survivor: A Reappraisal of the Role of Mr. Sammler." *UNISA English Studies* 26, no. 2 (1988): 21–26.

Sachs, Nellie. *O the Chimneys.* New York: Farrar, Straus & Giroux, 1967.

Sandy, Stephen. "Experienced Bards," *Poetry* 142 (1982): 301–3.

Santayana, George. *The Life of Reason.* Vol. 1, *Introduction and reason in Common Sense.* New York: C. Scribner Sons, 1905.

Scarry, Elaine. *The Body in Pain.* New York: Oxford University Press, 1985.

Schaeffer, Susan Fromberg. *Anya.* New York: Macmillan, 1974.

Schiff, Hilda, ed. *Holocaust Poetry.* New York: St. Martin's Press, 1995.

Schorsch, Ismar. "What Do Jews Believe?" *Commentary* 102, no. 2 (August 1996): 81–83.

Shapiro, Ann R. *Jewish American Women Writers.* Westport, CT: Greenwood Press, 1994.

Shapiro, Karl. *Poems of a Jew.* New York: Random House, 1958.

Sherman, Joseph. "Guilt as Subtext: I. B. Singer's Memoiristic Fiction." *Studies in American Jewish Literature* 13 (1994): 106–23.

Sherman, Rabbi Nosson. "Kaporos," *The Artscroll Siddur,* edited by Rabbi Meir Slotowitz. Brooklyn, N.Y.: Mesorah Publications, 1996.

Sherwin, Byron L. and Susan G. Ament, *Encountering the Holocaust: An Interdisciplinary Survey.* Chicago: Impact Press, 1979.

Sidney, Sir Philip. "The Defence of Poecy." In *Sir Philip Sidney,* edited by Katherine Duncan-Jones. New York: Oxford University Press, 1989.

Simon, John. Review of "The Deputy," by Rolf Hochhuth. *The Nation* 198 (16 March 1964): 272.

Simpson, Louis. "Facts and Poetry," *Gettysburg Review* 1, no. 1 (1988) 156–65.

Singer, Isaac Beshevis. *The Family Moskat.* New York: Alfred A. Knopf, 1950.

———. *Enemies.* New York: Farrar, Straus & Giroux, 1972.

———. *Shosha.* New York: Farrar, Straus & Giroux, 1978.

Smith, J. R. "Meeting the Work of Martin Buber and Gerald Stern." Master's thesis, Lehigh University, 1993.

Snodgrass, W. D. *Hearts Needle.* New York: Alfred A. Knopf, 1959.

———. *After Experience.* New York: Harper & Row, 1968.

———. *The Fuehrer Bunker Poems: The Complete Cycle.* New York: American Poets Continuum Series, 31. Brockport, N.Y.: BOA Editions, Ltd., 1995.

Sokoloff, Naomi B. "Interpretation: Cynthia Ozick's *Cannibal Galaxy,*" *Proof Texts* (1986): 239–57.

Somerville, Jane. "Gerald Stern Among The Poets: The Speaker as Meaning." *American Poetry Review* 17, no. 6 (1988): 55–67.

———. "Gerald Stern: The Poetry of Nostalgia," *The Literary Review* 28, no. 1 (fall 1984): 99–124.

———. *Making the Light Come.* Detroit: Wayne State University Press, 1990.

Sontag, Susan. *Against Interpretation and Other Essays.* New York: Ferrar, Strauss & Giroux, 1961.

Spolsky, Ellen. *The Uses of Adversity: Failure and Accommodation in Reader Response.* Lewisberg, Pa: Bucknell University Press, 1990.

Steiner, George. "A Kind of Survivor." In *Language and Silence: Essays on Language, Literature and the Inhuman,* by George Steiner. New York: Atheneum, 1967.

———. "To Civilize Our Gentlemen. In *Language and Silence: Essays on Language, Literature and the Inhuman,* by George Steiner. New York: Atheneum, 1967.

———. "Silence and the Poet." In *Language and Silence: Essays on Language and the Inhuman,* by George Steiner. New York: Atheneum, 1967.

———. *Extraterritorial: Papers on Literature and the Language Revolution.* New York: Atheneum, 1971.

———. "The Long Life of Metaphor: An Approach to the Shoah," *Encounter* (February 1987): 55–61.

———. "The Long Life of Metaphor: An Approach to the Shoah." In *Writing and the Holocaust,* by Berel Lang, ed. New York: Holmes & Meier, 1988.

Stern, Gerald. *Lucky Life.* New York: Houghton Mifflin, 1979.

———. "The One Thing No One Else Wanted." *Northeast Review* 18, no. 2 (1979): 29–32.

———. *The Red Coal.* New York: Houghton Mifflin, 1981.

———. "Some Secrets," *In Praise of What Persists,* edited by Stephen Berg. New York: Harper and Row, 1983.

———. *Paradise Poems.* New York: Random House, 1984.

———. "What Is the Sabbath?" *American Poetry Review* 13 (January/February 1984): 17–19.

———. *Rejoicings.* Los Angeles: Metro Book Co., 1984.

———. *Lovesick.* New York: Harper and Row, 1987.

———. "What Is This Poet?" In *Essays from the Eleventh Alabama Symposium on English and American Literature.* Tuscaloosa: University of Alabama Press, 1987.

———. Forward to *Ghosts of the Holocaust,* by Steward J. Florsheim. Detroit: Wayne State University Press, 1989.

———. *Leaving Another Kingdom: Selected Poems.* New York: Harper and Row, 1990.

———. *Bread without Sugar: Poems.* New York: W. W. Norton, 1992.

———. *Odd Mercy.* New York: W. W. Norton, 1995.

———. Interview by Gary Pacernick. April 8, 1996. "Interview with Gerald Stern," unpublished.

———. Interviews by author. August 7, 1996 and August 11, 1996. Untitled, unpublished.

———, et al. "Notes from the River." *The American Poetry Review* 13, no. 1 (1984), 20–21.

Stitt, Peter. "Engagements With Reality," *Georgia Review* 35, no. 4 (1981): 874–82.

———. "The Sincere, the Mythic, the Playful: Forms of Voice in Current Poetry," *Georgia Review* 34 (1980) 205–207.

Stoppard, Tom. *Travesties.* New York: Grove Press, 1975.

Strand, Mark, ed. *Contemporary American Poets.* New York: Mentor, 1971.

Styron, William. *Sophie's Choice.* New York: Random House, 1979.

Tao, Harrison. "Forms of Blue." *Kerem,* no. 4 (winter 1995/96): 57–66.

Thompson, M. Guy. *The Truth About Freud's Technique.* New York: New York University Press, 1994.

Trunk, Isaiah. *Jewish Responses to Nazi Persecution: Collective and Individual Behavior in Extremis.* New York: Stern and Day, 1979.

Wagner, L. W. "The Most Contemporary of Poetics." *The Ontario Review* 7 (fall/winter 1977/78): 88–95.

———. *Sylvia Plath.* London: Rutledge, 1988.

Wakoski, Diane. "20th Century Music." *Parnassus* 1 (winter 1972): 142–47.

Walden, Daniel, ed. *Studies in American Jewish Literature.* Albany: State University of New York Press, 1983.

Whiting, Nathan. "Death and Ikons" *Contact* 2 (1989): 89.

Wiesel, Elie. "On Being a Jew." *Jewish Heritage* (summer, 1967): 46–55.

———. *The Trial of God.* Translated by Marion Wiesel. New York: Random House, 1979.

———.Unpublished lecture, Wynnewood, Pa., Beth-Hillel-Beth-El, April 6, 1997.

Wilbur, Richard, W. D. Snodgrass, and A. C. Mathews. "Writers and Wrongs" *Crane Bag* 7, no. 1. Albany: State University of New York Press, 1986.

Wirth-Nesher, Hana. "The Artist Tales of Philip Roth," *Proof Texts* 3, no. 3 (September 1983): 263–72.

Wojohn, David. "The Red Coal." *Poetry East,* no. 6 (fall 1981): 96–102.

Wolfe-Blank, David. Untitled commentary. *Meta-Parshiot* (21 June 1997): 2.

Yenser, Stephen. "Recent Poetry: Six Poets," *The Yale Review* 68, no. 1 (1978): 83–102.

Young, Gloria L. "The Moral Function of Remembering," *Studies in American Jewish Literature* 9, no. 1 (1990): 61–72.

Young, James E. "'I May be a Bit of a Jew': the Holocaust Confessions of Sylvia Plath." *Philological Quarterly* 66, no. 1 (winter 1987): 127–47.

———. *Writing and Rewriting the Holocaust.* Bloomington: Indiana University Press, 1988.

———. *The Texture of Memory: Holocaust Memorials and Meaning.* New Haven: Yale University Press, 1993.

Index